America's Ailing Cities

America's Ailing Cities

Fiscal Health and the Design of
Urban Policy

Helen F. Ladd
and
John Yinger

The Johns Hopkins University Press
Baltimore and London

The Johns Hopkins University Press, 701 West 40th Street, Baltimore,
Maryland 21211
The Johns Hopkins Press Ltd., London

The paper used in this publication meets the minimum requirements of
American National Standard for Information Sciences--Permanence of Paper for
Printed Library Materials, ANSI Z39.48-1984.

Library of Congress Cataloging-in-Publication Data
Ladd, Helen F.
    America's ailing cities: fiscal health and the design of urban policy / Helen
F. Ladd and John Yinger.
    p.   cm.
Bibliography: p.
Includes index.
ISBN 0–8018–3767–7 (alk. paper)
1. Municipal finance—United States. 2. Intergovernmental fiscal relations—
United States. 3. Municipal services—United States. 4. Urban policy—United
States. I. Yinger, John, 1947-   . II. Title.
HJ9145.L32 1989
336'.014'73—dc19
                                                                88–13653
                                                                   CIP

To our parents

Contents

List of Tables and Figures

Tables

Figures

Preface

Urban decline. Urban fiscal distress. The urban fiscal crisis. Dramatic events, such as New York City's fiscal crisis of 1974, and steady long-term trends, such as suburbanization and the concentration of poverty in cities, have fixed these terms in the nation's public policy lexicon.

The sources of urban fiscal distress are varied and complex. National economic and social trends affect the ability of all cities to deliver public services, but they hurt some cities more than others. In addition, some cities are in fiscal trouble because of mismanagement; because of past decisions, such as poorly built infrastructure or overly generous pensions; because of voters' preferences for high-quality services; or because of severe tax limitations imposed by a state. Given this variety and complexity, it is not surprising that scholars and policy makers with different perspectives and different emphases come to different conclusions about the nature and extent of urban fiscal difficulties.

In this book we provide a foundation for discussions about urban fiscal problems by examining the fiscal effects of economic and social factors that are outside the control of city officials. We do not explore the role of mismanagement or service preferences but focus instead on the underlying or structural causes of cities' fiscal health. To be more specific, we have three key objectives. First, and most important, we want to compare the structural fiscal condition of different cities and of the same city at different points in time. Hence we develop methods for determining which cities are in relatively poor fiscal condition because of economic and social factors outside their control, and we apply these methods to all major central cities in 1972 and in 1982. Second, we want to determine the extent of state governments' assistance to central cities. One form of state assistance, intergovernmental grants, is commonly recognized, but states also assist or hamper their cities by the fiscal rules they establish, such as the taxes they allow their cities to levy. We develop a comprehensive measure of state assistance to each central city. Third, we want to inform the debate on state and federal policy toward cities. Hence we discuss the implications of our results for state and federal aid programs and for the design of our federal system.

We believe that the future of our central cities and of our federal system are topics of concern to all citizens. As a result, we have written this book to be accessible to a wide audience, including public officials and their staffs, journalists, public interest groups, students, and academics. The technical material is confined to a series of appendixes. Moreover, an overview of our approach, of our results, and of the implications for state and federal policy can be obtained by reading the first and last chapters.

All parts of the book are the shared product of the two authors. Although Ladd took the lead on chapters 2, 3, 6, 7, and 8 and Yinger took the lead on chapters 4, 5, 9, 10, and 11, we developed the book's framework together, actively discussed every page (and practically every word), and jointly wrote chapters 1 and 12.

As coauthors we accept full responsibility for all errors in the book. We cannot in good faith, however, claim full credit for the book's contributions. During the first stage of this study, we received significant help from three of our colleagues: Katharine Bradbury, at the Federal Reserve Bank of Boston; Ronald Ferguson, at the Kennedy School of Government of Harvard University; and Avis Vidal, at the New School for Social Research. The five of us collaborated during 1984 and 1985 on a project, which was financed by the U.S. Department of Housing and Urban Development (HUD), to measure the changing economic and fiscal conditions of U.S. cities. The resulting report, coauthored by all five of us, is the source of the data and much of the analysis for this book.

Our largest debt of gratitude is to Katharine Bradbury. We gratefully acknowledge the insights she provided us through her earlier work on U.S. cities, her active involvement as a member of the research team for the HUD report, and her contributions as a coauthor of several of the chapters of that report. All of the book reflects her input, but much of the material in chapters 3 and 6 bears her specific imprint. Indeed, chapter 6 is sufficiently close to the comparable chapter that she wrote with Helen Ladd in the HUD report that she should be viewed as a coauthor of that chapter.

We are also greatly indebted to Ronald Ferguson and Avis Vidal. Ronald Ferguson helped conceptualize and develop the measure of revenue-raising capacity, which is crucial to our approach, and was an active member of the original research team. The material he coauthored for the HUD report appears in revised and restructured form primarily in chapters 3 and 9. Avis Vidal deserves significant credit for developing the measures of city economic activity summarized in chapter 2. Although she bears no responsibility for the way we have presented that material, she did much of the work that made chapter 2 possible.

For their substantive contributions to this book and for their warm collegiality, we thank Kathy, Ron, and Avis.

Many other people contributed to the HUD report. We are grateful to

Peter Fairweather, who served as project manager; Karen Walz, who served as general research assistant and coauthor of one chapter; Alan Plumley, who manipulated tremendous amounts of data with good humor and great expertise; and Andrew Nelson, who assembled the data base on employment and payrolls. We also appreciate the research assistance of Judith Bunnell, Robert Gerber, Anthony O'Brien, Deanne Samuels, and Mark Taylor, and the cheerful demeanor and expert typing of Carol Scanlon. Both H. James Brown and Arnold Howitt of the State, Local and Intergovernmental Center at Harvard provided encouragement and support throughout the project.

Financial support for the original study was provided by HUD Grant HC5655 to Harvard University in 1983, administered through the State, Local and Intergovernmental Center (formerly part of the MIT-Harvard Joint Center for Urban Studies). With the encouragement of our HUD sponsor, John Ross, we, the principal investigators, decided to convert the material in the HUD report into a book that would be accessible to a broad audience. The Ford Foundation generously provided financial support for this project during 1986 and 1987.

Our quest to make this work accessible to a wide readership has been greatly aided by the editorial suggestions of Camille Smith. We thank her for her contributions to every chapter. We thank Anders Richter and Angeline Polites of Johns Hopkins Press for support, encouragement, and editorial advice, and Irma Garlick, our copy editor, for adding clarity to our terminology and tables. We are also grateful to Therese McGuire, who made extensive comments on the entire manuscript.

From early drafts to camera-ready copy, this book was produced by the staff of the Metropolitan Studies Program at the Maxwell School of Syracuse University. We greatly appreciate the skill, dedication, and good humor of Martha Bonney, Eric Heath, Jessica Thomas, and especially Esther Gray and Stephanie Waterman. In addition, we thank Carol Swan for administrative assistance; Kerri Ratcliffe for research assistance; Lynn Kremer for producing the figures; Martha Elbaum and Mary Burcham for helping with the index; Julia Melkers, Bruce Riddle, and the staff at the Syracuse Advanced Graphics Lab for helping produce the final copy; and David Greytak, Director of the Metropolitan Studies Program, for helping assemble this team. We also thank James Capretta at Duke University for research assistance.

Finally, we are grateful for the support we have received from our families over the course of this long project.

Part I

Fiscal Health, Economic Health, and Resident Income

1

National Trends and the Fiscal Health of Cities

O ver the last twenty years, powerful economic, social, and fiscal trends have buffeted the major central cities of the United States. The shift in employment from manufacturing to services, the suburbanization of middle-income households, migration from the Northeast to the Southwest, the urbanization of poverty, the tax revolt, and recent cuts in federal aid all have made it more difficult for many cities to finance out of their own resources such basic public services as police and fire protection, sanitation, and the building and maintenance of streets. These trends hinder some cities more than others, but between 1972 and 1982, they caused a severe deterioration in the fiscal condition of the average city.

Despite widespread agreement that particular cities are in fiscal trouble, scholars have conflicting views about the extent and the causes of the difficulties. Some believe there is a serious urban fiscal crisis; others see the problem as limited to managerial mistakes in a few cities, such as New York and Cleveland. But no one on either side of this debate has systematically traced the impact of broad national trends on the ability of cities to deliver public services.

This lack of understanding about the fiscal condition of cities is troubling, because policy makers are in the midst of a major debate about the future of the federal system in the United States. This system has changed significantly in recent years, and further dramatic changes have been proposed. Since 1967 states have increasingly assumed responsibility for public services, particularly welfare, that were formerly provided by cities. The tax revolt has led to severe property tax and other limitations that place new restrictions on the ability of many cities to raise revenue. Federal aid to state and local governments, especially aid to cities, increased steadily until the late 1970s but has decreased sharply since then. Indeed, current federal policies and proposals portend a major shift of fiscal responsibilities from the federal government back to state and local governments.

Central cities are important players in the U.S. federal system. Changes in their fiscal condition affect a significant share of the nation's population and reverberate through other levels of government. In order to make informed decisions about the best way to reform the federal system, policy makers need to understand the factors that influence the fiscal condition of cities, including the contributions of the state and federal governments.

In this book we present a new approach to urban fiscal health that identifies and measures the impact of broad social, economic, and fiscal trends on the ability of central cities to deliver public services. We measure the current fiscal health of major central cities in the United States; we examine differences in fiscal health across cities in 1982 and changes in the fiscal health of the central city between 1972 and 1982; and we determine the contributions to city fiscal health of state and federal policies. We conclude by offering some recommendations for future state and federal policy toward cities.

Our objective is to measure the impact on city finances of trends that are outside the control of city officials. We make no attempt to study managerial success, and our approach yields a measure of city fiscal health that is independent of a city's actual decisions. This is not to say that management and actual city decisions are unimportant. We determine the fiscal cards each city is dealt; other approaches are needed to see how well each city plays its hand.

The Urban Fiscal Crisis

Studying central cities is like looking through a magnifying glass at many of the most powerful economic and social trends in the United States. The slow but steady shift from manufacturing to service employment appears in the form of idle steel plants in downtown Cleveland and Pittsburgh and in the sprouting of new office buildings in Boston and San Francisco. The growth of office employment combined with the maturation of the baby boom generation are made visible by patches of gentrification in most cities and widespread gentrification in a few, such as Washington, D.C. And the recent urbanization of the poor is evident in sprawling distressed neighborhoods in New York and Newark and many other cities.

Such powerful trends inevitably influence city finances. In complex ways that vary from city to city, these trends alter the ability of cities to raise revenue and the cost of providing public services. A growth in office employment, for example, may bring in more taxable property, but by increasing the number of commuters, it also requires the city to spend more for traffic control and highway maintenance. And the urbanization of poverty lowers cities' taxable resources and increases the amount they must spend for some services, including health, social services, and police.

A large literature on urban distress examines the magnitude, and in some cases the causes, of economic and social trends in cities (see Bahl 1984). Although a few of these studies incorporate fiscal variables, such as tax effort, into their measures of urban distress, none explicitly examines the link between economic and social trends and city fiscal condition. The studies in this literature include Nathan and Adams 1976; Nathan and Fossett 1978; Cuciti 1978; U.S. Treasury 1978; Bunce and Goldberg 1979; Bradbury, Downs, and Small 1982; Clark and Ferguson 1983; and Bunce and Neal 1984. Nathan and Adams, for example, measure urban hardship with an index that reflects unemployment, dependency (people below eighteen or above sixty-four as a share of total population), educational attainment, income level, crowded housing, and poverty. Bradbury, Downs, and Small carefully distinguish between urban distress, namely unfavorable economic and social conditions in a city, and urban decline, which is a deterioration in those conditions, and investigate the extent and causes of these two phenomena in U.S. cities. These three authors explicitly recognize that urban distress and decline are important in part because they influence a city's ability to deliver public services, but their study does not attempt to explain or measure this influence.

Another strand of the literature examines city budgetary deficits and surpluses as indicators of fiscal condition. Studies of this type include Howell and Stamm 1976; Aronson and King 1978; Kramer 1982; and Dearborn 1988. Unfortunately, however, the link between budgetary conditions and fiscal health is widely misunderstood.

A city's budget is its fiscal plan for the coming year. For managerial, political, and often legal reasons, this plan must balance revenue and expenditure. When the plan is realized over the course of the year, a difference between revenue and expenditure, and hence an actual budgetary surplus or deficit, can arise for either or both of two reasons.

First, the city's finances may be affected by events not foreseen by its fiscal planners. An unexpected economic boom, for example, could lead to more revenue than expected from an income or sales tax and hence to a budget surplus. Or an unusually harsh winter could lead to unexpected snow removal costs and hence to a budget deficit.

Second, the budget may involve a systematic bias in the revenue or expenditure forecast. An overly cautious manager, for example, might assume no growth in city revenue and thereby ensure a surplus whenever revenue actually grows. On the other hand, a city that is subject to severe financial pressure may use an "optimistic" forecast of revenue to make its budget plan appear balanced—and thereby end up with a deficit when its optimism proves unwarranted.

In most cases events that place fiscal pressure on a city, such as federal aid cuts or increased demands for city services, are anticipated and therefore are reflected in budget plans. Cities in poor fiscal condition may find it difficult to respond to these events, but many such cities raise the revenues or implement the spending cuts that are necessary to make ends meet. In contrast, a city in good fiscal condition could end up with a budget deficit if it is poorly managed or if it is confronted with unforeseen events.

These issues are carefully examined in a series of articles by Bradbury (1982, 1983, 1984), who distinguishes between "budgetary" fiscal distress and "citizen" or "structural" fiscal distress. Budgetary fiscal distress is an inability to balance the city budget, whereas structural fiscal distress exists when residents cannot "obtain a 'reasonable' level of services at a 'reasonable' level of sacrifice" (1982, 34). Because unforeseen events can cause deficits even in fiscally strong cities and good management can prevent deficits in fiscally weak ones, budgetary measures are inappropriate and often misleading indications of a city's underlying or structural fiscal condition.[1]

Neither strand of the literature, therefore, provides a satisfactory analysis of the extent and causes of unfavorable fiscal conditions in cities. The "urban distress" literature identifies trends in many factors, such as population change, that may be related to a city's fiscal well-being, but it neither measures these links nor tests hypotheses about them. The literature on city budgetary conditions paints an inaccurate picture of structural fiscal distress because a city's budgetary outcome does not reveal its underlying fiscal vitality.

Our Approach

Unlike either strand of the literature, we examine the structural causes of urban fiscal distress and decline, which consist of broad economic, social, and fiscal trends that are outside a city's control. For each of the major U.S. central cities, we measure the impact of these factors on the city's

---

1. Even though they are misleading, budgetary measures are referred to by many policy makers. In a speech to the National Governors' Association on 25 February 1985, President Reagan said, "There's simply no justification, for example, for the Federal Government, which is running a deficit, to be borrowing money to be spent by state and local governments, some of which are now running surpluses."

ability to raise revenue, on the amount it must spend to provide public services of average quality, and on the balance between its revenue-raising capacity and its expenditure requirements. Our objective is to determine a city's underlying or structural ability to deliver public services to its residents, independent of the budgetary decisions made by city officials. Moreover, we focus not on cyclical events but rather on long-term secular changes in cities' fiscal condition.

We build on the work of Bradbury (1983, 1984) and Bradbury et al. (1984), who provide measures of structural fiscal distress in cities.[2] These studies identify economic, social, and institutional factors that are outside a city's control and determine the impact of these factors on its ability to provide, in Bradbury's terms, a reasonable level of services at a reasonable sacrifice. Although we build on this work, our approach is more comprehensive: it incorporates a broader range of economic, social, and institutional factors; it refines the conceptual links between these structural factors and fiscal distress; it separates the role of economic and social factors from that of fiscal institutions; and it examines differences in structural fiscal distress both across cities and, unlike the previous studies, over time.

The level and type of economic activity in a city determine the city's potential for raising revenue through broad-based taxes. The first step in our analysis, therefore, is to document the level of economic activity, as measured by employment and payroll in several key industries, in each city. This step reveals the extent to which overall employment in cities has grown while shifting from manufacturing to service industries.

The second step is to translate information about a city's economic activity into a measure of its revenue-raising capacity. We define a city's *revenue-raising capacity* as the amount of revenue it could raise from broad-based taxes at a selected tax burden on its residents.[3] Because it is tied to a particular tax burden, expressed as a percentage of household income, this approach facilitates comparison of revenue-raising capacity both across cities and in individual cities over time.

Just as private prices vary from one city to another, so does the cost of public services. Some cities must pay more than others to obtain the same level of police or fire protection. The cost of public services is determined

2. A few studies, including that by George Peterson (1976), have discussed the structural determinants of city fiscal distress without attempting to measure them. Inman (1979a) develops an alternative index of structural fiscal condition. Our book indirectly builds on these studies as well.
3. Two of our colleagues have participated in developing this new approach to revenue-raising capacity. See Ferguson and Ladd 1986; and Bradbury and Ladd 1985.

by the cost of hiring public employees and by the environment in which services must be provided. We explore the many factors that determine a city's public service environment. Commuters place demands on city services, for example, so that a city into which many people commute must spend more than one with few commuters to obtain police, highway, and other services of average quality. A city's *standardized expenditure need* is the amount it must spend per capita to provide public services of average quality. The higher a city's costs, the higher its standardized need.

We define *standardized fiscal health* to be the difference between revenue-raising capacity and standardized expenditure need, expressed as a percentage of capacity. A fiscal health index of +20 percent, for example, indicates that a city could provide public services of average quality at the selected tax burden and still have 20 percent of its capacity left over for tax cuts or higher-quality services. An index of -20 percent, on the other hand, indicates that a city would need additional revenue from outside sources equal to 20 percent of its own revenue-raising capacity to be able to provide public services of average quality at the selected tax burden. Without these additional resources, this city must have either a higher-than-average tax burden or a lower-than-average service quality—or both.

State governments determine which taxes a city may employ and the rules under which those taxes must be levied. In addition states give taxing authority to overlying jurisdictions, such as counties, which draw on the income of city residents, and states dispense intergovernmental aid. Thus a city's *restricted revenue-raising capacity* depends on state-determined fiscal institutions and grants as well as on economic factors. We examine fiscal institutions and grants for major central cities and incorporate them into our measure of restricted revenue-raising capacity.

States also decide which public services a city is responsible for providing. We present a measure of a city's service responsibilities that is independent of the city's actual spending on that service. For each public service, it reflects nationwide spending on that service and the state-specific division of responsibilities between cities and other levels of government in the state. A city's service responsibilities, along with its public service costs, affect its *actual expenditure need*. The more services it is responsible for, the more it must spend to obtain average quality services.

To identify the impact of state-imposed fiscal institutions on city fiscal health, we carry out our analysis in two stages. In the first stage, we assume that all cities have the same fiscal institutions. To be specific, we assume that all cities have access to three broad-based taxes (property, earnings, and sales), that overlying jurisdictions impose the same tax rate in all cities, that all cities have average service responsibilities, and that no city

receives intergovernmental aid. On the basis of these assumptions, we calculate each city's standardized fiscal health, which is its fiscal health with
this standardized set of institutions. In the second stage, we calculate each
city's restricted revenue-raising capacity and actual expenditure need,
which depend on its fiscal institutions. A city's *actual fiscal health* is
measured by its restricted capacity minus its actual need, expressed as a percentage of capacity. The difference between a city's actual and standardized
fiscal health measures the impact of state grants and state-imposed fiscal
institutions on the city's fiscal health.

Our approach has several advantages. First, it isolates the contribution
to a city's fiscal health of economic and social factors that are outside the
city's control. Our measures of city fiscal health are not influenced by
managerial skill or by the actual quality of the city's public services; in other
words, they do not reflect a city government's decisions. What they do
reveal is each city's fiscal starting point. Our approach therefore comple-
ments studies of city fiscal management and city decision making.

Second, our method facilitates comparisons across cities. We calculate revenue-raising capacity based on the same tax burden for the residents
of all cities. A city's cost index indicates its public service costs relative to
those of the average city. Indeed, our approach is explicitly designed to place
all cities, in all years, on the same footing.

Third, our method enables us to measure the impact on cities' fiscal
health of many important national trends. For example, we determine the
manner in which and the extent to which changes in the level and composition of employment alter cities' revenue-raising capacity and public service
costs. We also determine the extent to which changes in per capita income
alter revenue-raising capacity and the extent to which the urbanization of
poverty alters public service costs.

Fourth, our method, unlike any previous analysis, allows us to measure
the impact on cities' fiscal health of major state-imposed fiscal institutions.
Our measure of restricted revenue-raising capacity accounts for a city's access to broad-based taxes and for taxes collected by overlying jurisdictions,
as well as for intergovernmental aid. Our measure of actual expenditure
need reflects a city's actual public service responsibilities. And by comparing actual fiscal health with standardized fiscal health, which assumes the
same fiscal institutions in all cities, we discover the combined impact of all
these institutions and grants on a city's fiscal health.

The organization of this book follows the logic of our approach. In Part
I we describe the economic health and economic structure of major central
cities. We do not attempt to explain why these vary across cities or over
time; instead we describe cities' changing economic health and economic

structure and develop categories of city to be used in subsequent chapters. In Part II we calculate cities' standardized fiscal health, that is, fiscal health assuming uniform fiscal institutions. Variation in fiscal institutions comes into the analysis in Part III, where we describe the fiscal institutions in major central cities and incorporate them into our measure of actual fiscal health. Part IV concerns the role of government: we show how city governments respond to changes in city fiscal health; we examine the impact of past state and federal policies on central cities' fiscal health; and we make recommendations for future state and federal policy toward cities.

Major Central Cities

Our objective is to examine the fiscal health of all major central cities in the United States over the period from 1972 to 1982. We count as major central cities both large cities, including those that declined or emerged during the 1970s, and smaller cities that serve as centers for major metropolitan areas. Thus we examine the 86 cities that fall into one or both of the following categories: cities with populations above 300,000 in 1970 or 1980; and central cities in one of the nation's 50 largest metropolitan areas in either 1970 or 1980. This set is not a random sample of large cities; instead, it is the universe of major central cities in the nation.

These 86 major cities range from the giants of New York, Chicago, and Los Angeles down to Troy, New York, and Passaic, New Jersey, which had populations below 60,000 in 1980. Thirty-seven states are represented by at least 1 city, eighteen states are represented by 2 or more, and California is represented by 13. Each of the nine census regions contains at least 4 of these cities. The combined 1980 population of the 86 cities constitutes 21 percent of the 1980 U.S. population and 94 percent of the 1980 U.S. population in central cities containing 50,000 or more people.

The 86 cities (grouped by region), their 1970 and 1980 populations, and their percentage change in population over the period are presented in table 1.1.

Major Findings

Our analysis of the fiscal condition of cities begins with distinctions among three concepts. *City economic health* is the strength of a city's private economy, as measured by private employment per capita. *Resident economic health* is measured by the per capita income of a city's residents.

Table 1.1
Population of Central Cities by Region, 1970 and 1980
(86 Cities)

	Population		Percentage
	1970	1980	Change
New England			
Boston, MA	641,071	562,994	-12.18
Hartford, CT	158,107	136,392	-13.69
Pawtucket, RI	76,984	71,204	- 7.51
Providence, RI	179,213	156,804	-12.50
Warwick, RI	83,694	87,123	4.10
Middle Atlantic			
Albany, NY	115,781	101,727	-12.14
Buffalo, NY	462,768	357,870	-22.67
Clifton, NJ	82,437	74,388	- 9.76
New York, NY	7,894,862	7,071,639	-10.43
Newark, NJ	382,417	329,248	-13.90
Passaic, NJ	55,124	52,463	- 4.83
Paterson, NJ	144,824	137,970	- 4.73
Philadelphia, PA	1,948,609	1,688,210	-13.36
Pittsburgh, PA	520,117	423,938	-18.49
Rochester, NY	296,233	241,741	-18.39
Schenectady, NY	77,859	67,972	-12.70
Troy, NY	62,918	56,638	- 9.98
East North Central			
Akron, OH	275,425	237,177	-13.89
Chicago, IL	3,366,957	3,005,072	-10.75
Cincinnati, OH	452,524	385,457	-14.82
Cleveland, OH	750,903	573,822	-23.58
Columbus, OH	539,677	564,871	4.67
Dayton, OH	243,601	203,371	-16.51
Detroit, MI	1,511,482	1,203,339	-20.39
Indianapolis, IN	744,624	700,807	- 5.88
Milwaukee, WI	717,099	636,212	-11.28
Toledo, OH	383,818	354,635	- 7.60
West North Central			
Kansas City, MO	507,087	448,159	-11.62
Minneapolis, MN	434,400	370,951	-14.61
Omaha, NB	347,328	314,255	- 9.52
St. Louis, MO	*622,236*	*453,085*	*-27.18*
St. Paul, MN	309,880	270,230	-12.80
South Atlantic			
Atlanta, GA	496,973	425,022	-14.48
Baltimore, MD	905,759	786,775	-13.14
Charlotte, NC	241,178	314,447	30.38
Ft. Lauderdale, FL	139,590	153,279	9.81
Greensboro, NC	144,076	155,642	8.03
High Point, NC	63,204	63,380	0.28

Table 1.1 (Cont.)

| | Population | | Percentage |
	1970	1980	Change
Hollywood, FL	106,873	121,323	13.52
Jacksonville, FL	528,865	540,920	2.28
Miami, FL	334,859	346,865	3.59
Norfolk, VA	307,951	266,979	-13.30
Portsmouth, VA	110,963	104,577	- 5.76
Richmond, VA	249,332	219,214	-12.08
St. Petersburg, FL	216,232	238,647	10.37
Tampa, FL	277,767	271,523	- 2.25
Virginia Beach, VA	172,106	262,199	52.35
Washington, DC	756,510	638,333	-15.62
Winston-Salem, NC	132,913	131,885	- 0.77
East South Central			
Birmingham, AL	300,910	284,413	- 5.48
Louisville, KY	361,472	298,451	-17.43
Memphis, TN	623,530	646,356	3.66
Nashville-Davidson, TN	448,003	455,651	1.71
West South Central			
Austin, TX	251,808	345,496	37.21
Dallas, TX	844,401	904,078	7.07
El Paso, TX	322,261	425,259	31.96
Fort Worth, TX	393,476	385,164	- 2.11
Houston, TX	1,231,394	1,595,138	29.54
New Orleans, LA	593,471	557,515	- 6.06
Oklahoma City, OK	366,481	403,213	10.02
San Antonio, TX	654,153	785,880	20.14
Tulsa, OK	331,638	360,919	8.83
Mountain			
Albuquerque, NM	243,751	331,767	36.11
Boulder, CO	66,870	76,685	14.68
Denver, CO	514,678	492,365	- 4.34
Ogden, UT	69,478	64,407	- 7.30
Phoenix, AZ	581,562	789,704	35.79
Salt Lake City, UT	175,885	163,033	- 7.31
Tuscon, AZ	262,933	330,537	25.71
Pacific			
Anaheim, CA	166,701	219,311	31.56
Everett, WA	53,662	54,413	1.40
Garden Grove, CA	121,155	123,307	1.78
Honolulu, HI	324,871	365,048	12.37
Long Beach, CA	358,633	361,334	0.75
Los Angeles, CA	2,816,061	2,966,850	5.35
Oakland, CA	361,561	339,337	- 6.15
Ontario, CA	64,118	88,820	38.53
Portland, OR	382,619	366,383	- 4.24
Riverside, CA	140,089	170,876	21.98

Table 1.1 (Cont.)

	Population		Percentage
	1970	1980	Change
Sacramento, CA	254,413	275,741	8.38
San Bernadino, CA	104,251	117,490	12.70
San Diego, CA	696,769	875,538	25.66
San Francisco, CA	715,674	678,974	- 5.13
San Jose, CA	445,779	629,442	41.20
Santa Ana, CA	156,601	203,713	30.08
Seattle, WA	530,831	493,846	- 6.97

Source: U.S. Department of Commerce, Bureau of the Census, *Census of Population, 1980,* vol. 1, *Characteristics of the Population*, chap. A, pt. 1 (Washington, D.C.: GPO, 1983).

These two types of economic health can differ substantially because a city's economic health, unlike that of its residents, reflects jobs held by commuters into the city. Finally, *city fiscal health* is the ability of a city to deliver public services to its residents. This fiscal health is the balance between a city's ability to raise revenue and the amount it must spend to obtain services of average quality. A city's fiscal health can diverge from the city's economic health or from the economic health of its residents both for economic reasons, such as a high cost of providing public services, and for institutional reasons, such as extensive service responsibilities or an inability to tax commuters' income.

Standardized fiscal health is a city's ability to deliver public services assuming a standard set of fiscal institutions. A city's standardized fiscal health depends on the economic and social factors that determine its ability to raise revenues and its costs for public services. Standardized fiscal health differs widely across cities, and it declined significantly in the average city between 1972 and 1982.

Large cities and those with relatively poor resident economic health have relatively poor standardized fiscal health, both because their revenue-raising capacity tends to be low and because their service costs tend to be high. Indeed, these cities are in critical condition; they must have a large injection of outside resources to achieve the same quality of services at the same tax burden as the average city. Furthermore, these cities fell farther behind other cities between 1972 and 1982.

A city's economic health, as measured by per capita employment, is not clearly linked to its standardized fiscal health. Commuters increase a city's ability to raise revenue but also boost the cost of public services. These two effects roughly offset each other. Between 1972 and 1982 a shift from manufacturing to service employment also had little effect either on a city's ability to raise revenue or on its public service costs and therefore had little effect on its standardized fiscal health.

A city's actual fiscal health depends on the economic and social factors that influence standardized fiscal health and on its state-determined fiscal institutions, including its access to broad-based taxes, the taxes collected by overlying jurisdictions, its service responsibilities, and the intergovernmental grants it receives from its state. Differences in actual fiscal health across cities are less pronounced than differences in standardized fiscal health; fiscal institutions improve the relative fiscal health of the least healthy cities. In addition, average actual fiscal health did not decline as much as did average standardized fiscal health between 1972 and 1982; that is, recent changes in fiscal institutions and in state grants have made it somewhat easier for the average city to provide public services.

Actual fiscal health, like standardized fiscal health, is worse in larger cities than in smaller ones; whether or not one accounts for fiscal institutions, the largest central cities need a massive dose of outside resources to reach the fiscal health of the average city. Cities with relatively poor resident economic health also have relatively poor actual fiscal health; these cities tend to have higher restricted revenue-raising capacity than others but also tend to have higher standardized expenditure need. On the other hand, fiscal institutions provide relatively more assistance to cities with many poor residents and thereby narrow the fiscal gap between those with rich and those with poor residents. Cities with relatively poor economic health do not have poorer actual fiscal health than other cities, just as they do not have poorer standardized fiscal health. After fiscal institutions are accounted for, the impact of city economic health both on revenue-raising capacity and on public service costs still tend roughly to offset each other.

State fiscal institutions and intergovernmental grants boost the fiscal health of the average central city. Moreover, states act to compensate fiscally disadvantaged cities; that is, cities with poorer standardized fiscal health tend to receive more assistance from their state. Between 1972 and 1982, state assistance also offset approximately one-half of the decline in city fiscal health caused by economic and social trends. State officials regard assistance through institutions and through grants as imperfect substitutes for each other, but they do not cut back their assistance to cities that receive relatively high grants from the federal government.

On average, federal grants made almost as large a contribution to city fiscal health in 1982 as did state assistance. Federal categorical aid and federal general revenue sharing both were directed toward cities with the poorest standardized fiscal health, although not to the same extent as is state assistance. Revenue-sharing grants, in particular, were only slightly higher for cities in the poorest fiscal health than for those in the best health. Federal grants increased somewhat over the 1972-82 period, largely because of the introduction of general revenue sharing, which has since been rescinded.

Key Policy Recommendations

Assistance to cities is a key issue in the current debate over the "new federalism." Do cities need more assistance from higher levels of government? If so, what are the roles of the states and of the federal government?

The recent deterioration in the fiscal health of the average major central city and the extremely poor fiscal health of some central cities, including those with relatively large populations or with relatively poor residents, imply that something needs to be done to preserve the quality of city public services. The policy tools available to city governments are not powerful enough to ensure adequate fiscal health; as we measure it, standardized fiscal health reflects national economic and social trends that are largely outside the control of city officials. Moreover, many city residents cannot escape a poor or deteriorating fiscal situation because they cannot afford to move, because they have a handicap that makes moving difficult, or because they face racial or ethnic discrimination in housing or employment.

Because of the constraints on city governments and city residents, three important social objectives cannot be achieved without intervention by higher levels of government.

The first objective is to assist the poor, who are disproportionately represented in central cities. Most government assistance for the poor appropriately comes through income transfer programs, but these programs have little impact on the quality of city public services, even such key services as education and police protection. Thus intergovernmental assistance to city governments is an important complement to income transfer programs.

The second objective is to help people deal with the transitions caused by national trends, such as interregional migration, the suburbanization of employment, and the increase in urban poverty. One way to ease these transitions is to provide intergovernmental assistance to cities whose fiscal health is undermined by these trends.

The third objective is to treat fairly the residents of all jurisdictions in a metropolitan area. Suburban commuters and visitors benefit from central city public services, and cities deserve some form of compensation, such as access to a tax on commuter earnings, for services provided to nonresidents. Moreover, a metropolitan tax system that restricts each jurisdiction to the taxable resources of its own residents can be highly regressive; through no fault of its own, the central city is likely to have a higher tax rate than the suburbs. Assistance from higher levels of government can moderate this regressiveness.

States must play a major role in assisting cities; after all, they control the fiscal institutions, such as access to taxes and the assignment of service responsibilities, that guide city fiscal behavior. Because they make the fiscal rules and because they include representatives from cities and suburbs, states also are in a unique position to tailor policies to each city's particular circumstances. States can provide assistance to cities in many different forms; the most promising are intergovernmental grants directed toward cities in poor fiscal health, the empowerment of cities to use an earnings tax that applies to commuter income, and state takeover of welfare services and courts.

The federal government also has an important role to play. Because their own fiscal health is poor, some states are less able than others to provide assistance to their cities; federal assistance is needed to ensure that city residents, particularly the poor or disadvantaged, are not penalized because they live in states with poor fiscal health. In addition, the federal government is in a better position than are the states to assist the poor and to ease the transitions caused by national trends. Poverty is a national problem, and people throughout the country benefit from assistance provided to the poor, so it is appropriate for taxpayers throughout the country to pay for this assistance. Moreover, federal programs to ease transitions are needed to assure equal treatment of the residents of different states. Expanding current federal aid programs or restoring programs, including general revenue sharing, that have been cut in recent years would not be cost-effective approaches to the federal role. Instead, the federal government should design new aid programs that are more sharply focused on cities in the poorest fiscal health.

2
Economic Health and Economic Structure

The city economy is a natural starting point for any analysis of city fiscal health. The level of economic activity in a city is the primary determinant of the resources available to the city government. Production of goods and services by the city's private and public organizations generates potentially taxable resources: land, buildings, equipment, wages and salaries, and retail sales. In addition, the level and composition of economic activity may affect the cost of providing public services such as public safety, sanitation, and roads. As the taxable resource base changes, a city's ability to provide public services at a given tax burden on its residents may change as well.

Two aspects of the city economy are important here: the overall or total level of economic activity per resident, which we call *economic health*, and the composition of that activity, which we call *economic structure*. We measure a city's total economic activity by the number of people working in the city in the private sector, and we measure its economic health by its private sector employment divided by its resident population. The distribution of private sector jobs between manufacturing and service activities represents a city's economic structure.

A city's economic health, as measured by the number of private jobs per resident, is closely linked to the wages and salaries generated in the city per resident, but it is not the same as the economic health of city residents, which is measured by their per capita income. On the one hand, many jobs in the central city are held by commuters, so the economic health of the city represents job- and income-generating opportunities available to people who live throughout the urban area, not just to those who live in the city itself. Much has been written about the tendency of many people, particularly in middle- and upper-income households, to live in the suburbs and commute to the city to work. This situation implies that a city can be healthy in the sense of generating many jobs per resident at the same time that its residents remain impoverished. On the other hand, some residents work outside the city, and the income of city residents includes income from capital, such as dividends, and from government transfer programs, such as so-cial security, in addition to wages and salaries earned in the city. Thus private sector jobs only partially determine the income of city residents.

Previous studies of cities typically have not distinguished between these two concepts of economic health and have used resident income per capita as one of several measures of the economic health of the city (see Garn and Ledebur 1980; Burchell et al. 1984). These studies argue that resi-dent income indicates local purchasing power and hence is linked to the vitality of the consumer-related sectors of the city economy. This argument contains some truth, but total employment provides a more direct measure of that vitality. Furthermore, a distinction between these two concepts of economic health is illuminating because, as we will show, they have dif-ferent impacts on a city's fiscal condition. In this chapter we focus ex-clusively on the economic health of the city. In chapter 3 we describe the economic health of city residents.

A city's economic health also should be distinguished from its fiscal health, which indicates the ability of the city government to provide public services. As we elaborate in chapter 3, a major component of city fiscal health, namely its revenue-raising capacity, is the income of residents aug-mented by the city's ability to export tax burdens to nonresident taxpayers. A city's economic health affects both the income of its residents and its ability to export tax burdens to nonresidents, but the connections are com-plicated and indirect, so that there need not be a close link between a city's economic health and its revenue-raising capacity. Also, as we discuss in chapter 4, a city that generates many jobs for both residents and commuters may have higher costs of providing public services than a city with fewer jobs. Thus the overall relationship between a city's economic and fiscal health is complex. One of our goals in this book is to examine the nature of this relationship.

The structure of the economies of central cities has changed sig-nificantly in recent decades. Many of the nation's major central cities have experienced substantial economic decline in traditional manufacturing sec-tors at the same time that they have experienced significant growth and vitality in service-related sectors. These structural changes reflect the shift in the national economy away from manufacturing and toward service jobs and the loss to the suburbs of some types of job, such as those in manufac-turing and retailing, faster than other types.

The evolving economic structure of central cities raises two types of concern for policy makers. First, as the composition of city economies shifts, cities provide a changing set of job opportunities to people throughout the metropolitan area. Many service jobs in central cities, for example, may be lower paying than the manufacturing jobs they replace or, if higher paying, may not be suited to the job skills of city residents. Typically, large numbers of city residents do not have the education required for many of the knowledge-based jobs that are becoming increasingly common (see Paul Peterson 1985).

Second, and of direct concern here, a shift away from manufacturing and toward service activity may weaken a city's ability to provide public services. Some observers worry, for example, that such a change will shrink the local property tax base, because manufacturing activity tends to be more property intensive than service activity.[1] In addition, the changing structure of city employment may affect the costs to the city of providing public services. For example, office buildings might place higher demands than manufacturing structures on local public safety services. In subsequent chapters we illuminate this policy issue by examining the links between changes in a city's employment structure and its fiscal health.

In this chapter we provide an overview of the economic health and structure of central cities in the United States in 1982 and of changes in them between 1972 and 1982. We do not attempt to explain variation across cities or changes over time; the model of economic development required for such a task is well beyond the scope of this book. Instead our goals are to describe broad trends and to group cities into categories defined by the level of and change in their economic health and economic structure. We employ these categories in subsequent chapters to determine the extent to which changes in cities' fiscal health are related to changes in their economic health and economic structure.

---

1. In fact, the capital intensity of manufacturing relative to service activity is not clear. Ganz and O'Brien 1973, for example, assert that "the average amount of taxable capital per worker is much lower in services than in manufacturing." They cite data from Kendrick 1973 indicating that the real net stock of capital per worker in finance and service activities was 60 percent of that in manufacturing in 1966. Bahl and Greytak 1976, in contrast, find that the market value of taxable property per employee in 1969 was lower for manufacturing than for the nine other business sectors they studied in New York City, but they point out that the conclusion might have been different had business personalty been included in the New York City tax base. In a recent study using the same data on property tax bases that is used in this book, Bradbury and Ladd 1987 conclude that the manufacturing activity that remains in cities appears to be less capital-intensive than many forms of commercial and service activity.

Measures of Economic Health and Economic Structure

Previous studies of U.S. cities have used a variety of measures of city economic health or performance, including, for example, employment, payroll, establishments, value added of manufacturing firms, the local unemployment rate, and the income of residents (see Garn and Ledebur 1980; Burchell et al. 1984). The limitations of resident income as a measure of city economic health have already been mentioned. The unemployment rate of residents is subject to the same criticism; although justifiable as a measure of residents' welfare, it does not measure the economic health and vibrancy of the city itself.

We measure a city's economic activity by its private sector employment, a comprehensive measure that is available for all sectors of the local economy. This measure is easy to comprehend and has the additional advantage of being part of the language of local public officials. Local economic development, for example, typically is discussed in terms of jobs. Although employment is a somewhat less complete measure than value added in the city (a concept that is comparable to gross national product at the national level), such a measure is not available for cities.

Because of tremendous differences in the population of major central cities, cross-sectional comparisons of economic activity are best made on the basis of employment per resident. The comparable measure of change in economic activity is change in employment per resident. This per capita approach makes city economic health directly comparable to our measures of city fiscal health, discussed in subsequent chapters, which we also measure on a per capita basis. The focus on economic activity per capita reflects our ultimate concern with city residents, and specifically with the ability of each city to meet the public service needs of its current residents.

This per capita definition of economic health implies that a city undergoing identical percentage decreases in employment and population is deemed to experience no change in its economic health. What matters is the level of economic activity relative to the number of people living in the city. A more common approach in the analysis of cities focuses on changes in the size of the city, as measured by population or employment: those losing population or employment or both are typically described as declining cities, and those gaining population or employment are growing cities.[2]

---

2. For a discussion of the forces affecting city size and of the interaction between population and employment, see Bradbury, Downs, and Small 1982, 179-90 and chap. 5.

To be sure, changes in population and employment may be indicative of the relative attractiveness of the city to firms and households and may well be correlated with changes in the components of a city's economic vitality such as the strength of the local housing market and the income of city residents. For example, population loss typically reduces the demand for housing, may lead to abandoned dwellings, and, if middle- and upper-income households are overrepresented among the people leaving, reduces the average income of remaining residents. Population loss is not necessarily undesirable, however, and population growth need not be advantageous. A decrease in the population of an extremely overcrowded city, for example, can improve the quality of life of the remaining city residents and other users of the city. Similarly, population growth attributable, for example, to a large influx of refugees may temporarily decrease the economic strength of a city (examples from Bradbury, Downs, and Small 1982, 19). Hence we measure changes in economic health by changes in employment relative to changes in city population.

Changes in city population and in economic activity interact in complex ways to determine changes in the level of employment per resident. A recent study of urban decline finds both that jobs follow people and that people follow jobs among metropolitan areas. Within metropolitan areas, however, households are more likely to be the leaders; they make their decisions about whether to live in the city or the suburbs on the basis of a variety of factors, including their demand for space and the levels of public amenities and taxes, and then the jobs follow the people (ibid., chap. 5). Without attempting to untangle the causes, we focus on the resulting balance between the overall employment and population in each city and changes in that balance over time.

The Data: Sources and Aggregate Trends

Before analyzing the economic health and economic structure of the specific cities, we briefly describe the data on employment and payroll and present some aggregate trends.

We collected or estimated employment and payroll data for the eight private sector industrial categories and four public sector categories reported in table 2.1. Some of the payroll and employment data were directly available for cities; the rest were available only for counties. For city-counties, that is cities that are also counties, the county data could be used

Table 2.1
Employment Trends in Central Cities, 1972-1982
(86 Cities)

Sector	Employment (in thousands)			Employment Change, 1972-1982	
	1972	1977	1982	Thousands	Percentage
Private					
Manufacturing	4,849	4,490	4,385	-464	-9.6
Retail	2,947	3,014	3,606	659	22.4
Services	4,393	4,667	6,264	1,871	42.6
Wholesale	1,509	1,460	1,685	176	11.7
TCPU[a]	1,714	1,573	1,601	-13	-0.8
FIRE[b]	1,982	2,089	2,344	362	18.3
Construction	1,107	1,023	1,017	-90	-8.1
Minerals	85	102	178	93	109.4
Total Private	18,585	18,418	21,179	2,594	14.0
Public					
City	1,170	1,128	1,089	-81	-6.0
Noncity local	874	977	986	112	12.8
State	653	756	798	145	22.2
Federal	1,055	1,034	1,035	-20	-1.9
Total public	3,751	3,895	3,908	156	4.2
Total	22,336	22,313	25,089	2,752	12.3

Source: Data are from the following publications of the U.S. Department of Commerce, Bureau of the Census: Data for manufacturing, retail trade, selected services, and wholesale trade for 1972 and 1977 are from the *County and City Data Book, 1977* (Washington, D.C.: GPO, 1978); *1983* (Washington, D.C.: GPO, 1983). All data for TCPU, FIRE, construction, minerals, and excluded services, as well as 1982 data for manufacturing, retail trade, selected services, and wholesale trade, are estimates of city economic activity based on figures from *County Business Patterns, 1972* (Washington, D.C.: GPO, 1973); *1977* (Washington, D.C.: GPO, 1979); *1982* (Washington, D.C.: GPO, 1984). City government data are from the *Census of Governments, 1972*, vol. 3, *Public Employment* (Washington, D.C.: GPO, 1974); *1977* (Washington, D.C.: GPO, 1979); *1982*, vol. 3, *Government Employment* (Washington, D.C.: GPO, 1984). All other public sector data are estimates derived from county data as described in the appendix to chap. 2.
[a]Transportation, communications, and public utilities.
[b]Finance, insurance, and real estate.

directly. For all other cities, we utilized the city share of total county employ-ment to estimate city employment in the relevant categories.[3]

The addition of the public sector categories distinguishes this data set from many others that focus on the private sector alone. In 1982 public sec-tor employment accounted for over 15 percent of total employment in the 86 cities. In addition, our services category is significantly more com-prehensive than the selected services category reported by the U.S. Census and typically used in other studies. We supplemented the selected services figures from the Census with estimates of employment and payroll in the categories of medical and health services, museums, nonprofit membership organizations, and miscellaneous services such as noncommercial research and accounting and bookkeeping. Careful collection of data on jobs in the service sector is important because of their large contribution to the employ-ment base of central cities.

Table 2.1 summarizes employment data aggregated over all 86 cities for the years 1972, 1977, and 1982. Overall, city employment increased by 12.3 percent during the ten-year period 1972-82, with the private sector ex-hibiting more vibrancy than the public sector. Despite declines of 464,000 jobs in manufacturing, 13,000 in transportation, communications, and utilities, and 90,000 in construction, the number of private sector jobs in-creased by almost 2.6 million during this period. Almost three-quarters of the net growth occurred in the service sector.

Although the 14 percent growth rate of private employment in central cities was only half the growth rate of private employment in the economy as a whole, the performance of city economies during this period was stronger than many observers in the late 1970s predicted (see, for example, Black 1980; Garn and Ledebur 1980). At least two factors account for this outcome. First, earlier analysis of secular trends in cities was hampered by the 1974-75 recession, the effects of which lingered in the 1977 data. Table 2.1 shows that private sector employment in the 86 cities declined some-what between 1972 and 1977, for the growth in service sector jobs was too small to offset the decline in manufacturing jobs. This relatively small growth in the service sector led some observers to be pessimistic about the future employment prospects in central cities in the United States.

Second, limitations on available data led to underestimates of the growth in service employment in many cities. The most widely available data source for cities describes four major sectors: manufacturing, retail,

---

3. See the appendix to this chapter for details of the estimation process and for a more complete description of data sources.

wholesale, and selected services. These four sectors accounted for only about two-thirds of private sector employment in central cities in the 1970s; they do not include some fast-growing services, such as health, education, and financial services. Our more comprehensive coverage of services and the inclusion of data for 1982, itself a recession year, provide convincing evidence that U.S. cities, in the aggregate, need not lose employment simply because of the decline in manufacturing employment. Like the nation, cities are experiencing a significant restructuring of their economies away from manufacturing and toward services, but many cities are also experiencing growth in total private employment per capita.

Table 2.1 indicates that public sector employment increased by only 4.2 percent during the ten-year period. This represents a substantial slowdown in the rate of growth in public sector employment in U.S. cities compared to the previous five-year period, when it grew at a 12 percent rate. The two largest categories of public sector employees, city and federal government employees, declined during the ten-year period, while the smaller categories of noncity local and state government employees both grew quite rapidly.

Economic Health of Individual Cities: Levels and Changes

The typical major central city had slightly more than one-half of a job per resident in 1982, but the figure varies substantially across cities, from 0.25 in Virginia Beach, Virginia, to 1.06 in Salt Lake City. Cities such as Hartford, Connecticut, with its concentration of insurance and financial institutions, and Boston, with its concentration of financial and business services, rank high. Residential cities such as Garden Grove, California, or low-income cities such as Paterson, New Jersey, rank low. Differences in government employment per resident account for only a small portion of this variation. The level of government employment stands out in only a few specific cities, such as Washington, D.C., and Portsmouth, Virginia, where federal government employment is particularly large, or in state capitals such as Albany, New York, where state government employment is large.

We measure a city's economic health by its private sector employment alone. In contrast to public sector activity, most private sector activity is subject to the major revenue producer of local governments, the property tax. Moreover, private sector activity exerts a larger impact on the costs of providing public services than does public sector activity. We focus on the private sector, therefore, because it is more closely linked to a city's fiscal health. Among major central cities in 1982, private sector jobs per resident averaged just under 0.5 and ranged from 0.20 to 0.92.

We divide the 86 sample cities into fifths, also called quintiles, based on their 1982 private employment per resident, ranked from low to high. We use these quintiles throughout the book to represent categories of city grouped by economic health. Cities in the higher quintiles are predicted to have greater capacity to finance public services, the magnitude of the advantage depending on the specific tax vehicles available to each city. Working in the other direction is the possibility that the cost of providing city services may be greater in cites with higher employment per resident. How these forces balance out is an empirical question examined in subsequent chapters.

Not surprisingly, private sector jobs per city resident vary directly with the amount of nonresident commuting into the city. This link is seen most clearly in payroll data, which enable us to estimate the shares of city payroll accruing to residents and nonresidents.[4] Figure 2.1 indicates private sector payroll per city resident averaged across all cities in each employment quintile. Thus, for example, payroll per resident averages $4,500 in the lowest quintile and about $12,600 in the highest. The lower line of each bar indicates the payroll generated in the city that is paid to city residents. This average amount is lowest in the first quintile, rises from the first through the fourth, but falls somewhat from the fourth to the fifth quintile. The figure indicates that, on average, the increasingly higher levels of economic activity per city resident in the top three quintiles is attributable almost entirely to larger amounts of wages and salaries paid to commuters rather than to higher earnings for residents.

Figure 2.1 also illustrates that the share of city payroll paid to nonresidents in U.S. cities is large; indeed, in 48 of our 86 cities, more than one-half of the earnings generated in the city accrue to nonresidents. As is discussed in chapter 3, this fact has significant implications for the ability of city residents to shift tax burdens onto nonresidents when a local income or earnings tax is used.

Figure 2.2 clearly illustrates that city economic health, as measured by private employment per resident, bears little relationship to the economic health of city residents, as measured by Census money income. One might hypothesize that this outcome reflects in part differing wages for different types of job, but a comparable graph with per capita payroll on the horizon-

---

4. See chap. 3 for details of the estimation.

Figure 2.1
Average Payroll Per Capita, 1982
(86 cities)

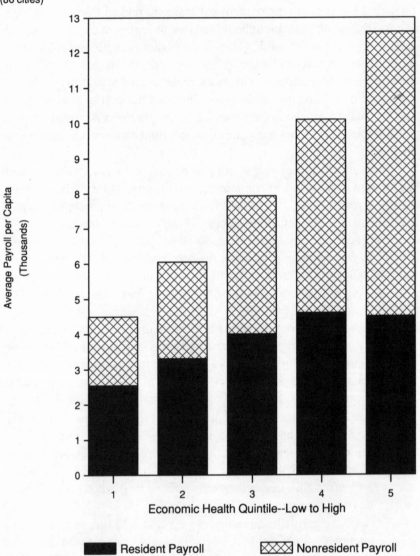

Economic Health Quintile--Low to High

■ Resident Payroll   ▨ Nonresident Payroll

Figure 2.2
Private Employment and Resident Income Per Capita, 1982
(86 cities)

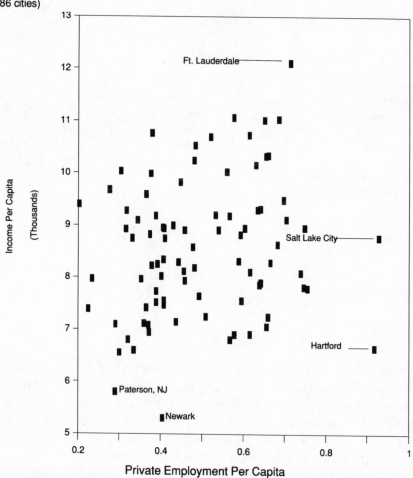

Private Employment Per Capita

Table 2.2
Categories of City Economic Health
(71 cities)

	Number of Cities	Average Private Employment per Resident, 1972	Average Change in Private Employment per Resident, 1972-82 (percent)
Below-average economic health, 1972			
Low growth	11	.36	-0.4
Medium growth	9	.33	18.2
High growth	15	.27	52.0
Above-average economic health, 1972			
Low growth	15	.51	5.1
Medium growth	14	.53	27.6
High growth	7	.50	39.6

Note: City economic health is defined to be private employment in the city divided by city population. The 1972 average value (based on all 86 cities) that serves as the cutoff for below- and above-
average health in 1972 is 0.41 workers per resident.

tal axis looks almost identical. Two explanations for the absence of a
relationship have just been mentioned: the large public sector employment
or payroll per resident in a few cities and, more importantly, variations
across cities in the role of commuters. Additional explanations include
variation across cities in the amount of income per capita received in the
form of public transfer payments, such as social security or Aid to Families
with Dependent Children; variation in the amount of property income, such
as rents, dividends, interest, and capital gains; and variation in the reverse
commuting of city residents to the suburbs. The economic health of city
residents is discussed in chapter 3.

We also group central cities into a second set of categories based on
changes in economic health between 1972 and 1982. To construct these
categories, we first divide the 86 cities into those with below-average and
those with above-average private sector employment per capita in 1972.
Within each of these groupings, we further divide cities into three equal
groups characterized by low, medium, and high growth in economic health.

Cities in the low-growth category experienced changes in private employment per capita that range from -22 percent to +14 percent. Thirteen of these cities experienced a decline in jobs relative to the size of their population during the period, and 5 cities, namely Detroit, Chicago, Baltimore, Philadelphia, and Newark, New Jersey, suffered absolute declines in employment. The only surprise in this group of cities with declining economic health is Ontario, California, whose rapid employment growth was accompanied by even greater growth in population. Medium-growth cities experienced growth in employment per capita of between 14 and 30 percent; and high-growth cities experienced growth of between 30 and 120 percent. Most of the cities in this last group are in the South and West. Heading the list are, Boulder, Fort Lauderdale, and Garden Grove, California.

Combining level and change categories produces the six categories shown in table 2.2. We use these categories throughout the book to examine the extent to which changes in fiscal outcomes are associated with changes in city economic health. The entries in the table indicate average per capita employment and growth for the cities in each category. These entries are based on the 71 cities for which the complete set of data required for subsequent chapters is available.[5]

Economic Structure of Individual Cities: Levels and Changes

Table 2.3 indicates that the average economic structure of major central cities differs substantially from that of the nation as a whole. This contrast exists whether economic activity is measured by employment or by payroll. The 1982 pattern is inconsistent with the historically based image of cities as the center of manufacturing and retail activity. Only 21 percent of private sector city employment is in manufacturing in contrast to almost 27 percent for the nation as a whole. Similarly, retail trade accounts for only 17 percent of employment in cities in contrast to 20 percent nationwide. Services account for the largest proportion of city employment, almost 30 percent in 1982. This share is well above the 25 percent share for the national economy. Table 2.3 also indicates that other information- and communication-based sectors (TCPU and FIRE), as well as wholesale trade, are relatively concentrated in central cities.

The patterns based on payroll are similar to those based on jobs. The

---

5. See the table A5.1 for a list of the 71 cities.

Table 2.3
Private Sector Employment and Payrolls, 1982
(86 Cities)

	Private Sector Employment		Private Sector Payrolls	
	Cities (%)	U.S. (%)	Cities (%)	U.S. (%)
Manufacturing	20.7	26.5	24.3	32.1
Retail	17.0	20.7	9.6	11.8
Services	29.6	25.2	25.6	21.3
Wholesale	8.0	7.1	9.8	8.7
TCPU[a]	8.0	6.3	11.0	8.7
FIRE[b]	11.1	7.4	12.5	8.0
Construction	4.8	5.3	5.9	6.6
Minerals	0.8	1.6	1.3	2.4
Total	100.0	100.0	100.0	100.0

Source: U.S. Department of Commerce, Bureau of the Census, *County Business Patterns, 1982* (Washington, D.C.: GPO, 1984).
[a]Transportation, communications, and public utilities.
[b]Finance, insurance, and real estate.

major difference is the smaller contributions of retail trade and services to the total in both cities and the economy as a whole. These smaller contributions reflect the disproportionately high reliance on part-time workers and the relatively low wages in these sectors.

As is shown in table 2.4, the relative importance of service and manufacturing employment varies by city type. This table reports average employment mixes for cities grouped by functional categories developed initially by Noyelle and Stanback (1983) for metropolitan areas. The initial three categories are diversified service centers. Cities in these categories provide a varied and specialized set of services to consumers, retailers, and manufacturers in national, regional, or subregional market areas. Cities such as New York and Los Angeles provide a wide array of services to a national, and even international, market. A larger group of smaller cities, including Boston, Houston, and Denver, serve the needs of medium-sized regions of the country. Subregional centers such as Omaha, Salt Lake City, and Richmond, Virginia have even smaller markets.

The fourth group, functional and manufacturing centers, includes cities, such as Detroit, Akron, Pittsburgh, and Hartford, Connecticut, that

Table 2.4
Employment Mix, 1982
(86 Cities)

Functional Type	Number of Cities	Percentage of Private Employment in:					Public Employment as a Percentage of Total Employment
		Manufacturing	Retail	Services	FIRE[a]	TCPU[b]	
Diversified service centers							
National	6	20.8	15.8	30.3	12.2	8.7	16.0
Regional	23	21.5	17.6	28.5	9.8	8.6	14.3
Subregional	10	18.5	19.5	26.1	9.7	9.4	16.1
Functional and manufacturing	22	32.7	16.0	25.5	8.5	6.0	12.3
Government and education	6	17.4	20.5	38.1	8.0	5.9	27.7
Industrial, mining, and military	7	17.4	25.7	29.0	7.1	6.6	23.5
Residential, resort, and retirement	12	17.7	24.5	29.8	8.0	6.4	14.4

Source: All data for private sector employment are estimates of city economic activity based on figures from the U.S. Department of Commerce, Bureau of the Census, *County Business Patterns, 1982* (Washington, D.C.: GPO, 1984). City government data are from the U.S. Department of Commerce, Bureau of the Census, *Census of Governments, 1982*, vol. 3, *Public Employment* (Washington, D.C.: GPO, 1984). All other public sector data are estimates derived from county data as described in the appendix to chap. 2.
[a]Finance, insurance, and real estate.
[b]Transportation, communications, and public utilities.

are the headquarters for major corporations. Many of these developed initially as major manufacturing centers, specializing in particular products such as automobiles or steel. In these cities, nearly one in three private sector jobs is in manufacturing compared to one in four jobs in services. Manufacturing jobs exceed service jobs on average only for cities in this category.

Government and education centers include Washington, D.C., and the larger state capitals. A low share of manufacturing employment and substantial concentrations of jobs in services and in the public sector distinguish this group of cities. Industrial, mining, and military centers are the sites of major military installations. These cities, which include Norfolk,

Virginia, and San Antonio, Texas, depend heavily on the public sector, which typically accounts for almost one-quarter of all city employment. Finally, residential, resort, and retirement centers have in common strong consumer-oriented economies based on both retailing and consumer services. A typical city of this type has almost one-quarter of its employment in retailing.

This variation in employment structure across cities is relevant for subsequent analyses. By affecting the share of the property tax base that is taxable, for example, the share of public sector employment may affect a city's revenue-raising capacity. Similarly, to the extent that manufacturing activity is more property-intensive than service activity, the property tax base in cities with high concentrations of manufacturing employment may be greater than in those cities more concentrated in services. And heavy concentration in retailing may provide above-average potential to export sales taxes to tourists or commuters. The composition of city employment might also affect the costs of providing public services. For example, to achieve a certain level of public safety, higher spending on police services might be required per unit of retail property than per unit of manufacturing property. If so, cities with high proportions of retail activity would have higher police costs, all else equal, than cities with high proportions of manufacturing activity.

Three broad national trends influence changes in the composition of city employment over time. The first trend is the well-known shift from manufacturing to service employment. Between 1972 and 1982 national manufacturing employment increased by only 5 percent compared to a 67 percent increase in service employment. This difference led to a decrease of 6 percentage points in manufacturing's share of total private employment nationwide and an increase of 6 percentage points in service's share. Presumably this national trend is a key determinant of the even greater decline—9 percentage points—in manufacturing's average share of city employment.

Supplementing this national industrial trend is continuing suburbanization of employment. Incentives for firms to move out of the central city to the suburbs vary by type of firm. Hence suburbanization of employment proceeds at different rates for major industrial categories and thereby changes the employment mix of the central city. Although this process of decentralization affected all central cities between 1972 and 1982, its impact on individual cities varies with the city's previous history of decentralization and its current relationship to its suburbs.

The third trend is the continuing interregional disparity in the rates of business investment, with more investment in the sunbelt states than in the frostbelt states. The relative attractiveness of regions varies by type of firm. The location decisions of manufacturing firms, for example, may be more responsive than those of other types of firm to variations across regions in production costs. Similarly, firms directly serving people may be more likely than other types of firm to follow the movement of households to the South and West. Thus variation by region in the rates of business investment, like the other trends, is likely to change the mix of employment in the various regions and in the cities within those regions.

These three trends interact in complicated ways to influence changes in the mix of employment over time in particular cities. A key question for us is whether the resulting structural changes in city economies affect the ability of U.S. cities to provide public services. To examine this question, we group cities into categories by the amount of structural change they experienced in the 1970s. We then look across categories for patterns of change in fiscal health or its components. In creating the categories, we control for changes in the economic health of cities to avoid confounding the effects of structural change with those of changes in economic health.

We define structural change as the shift away from jobs in the manufacturing sector to jobs in the services and finance, insurance, and real estate (FIRE) sectors. Specifically, we measure the extent of structural change in each city as the absolute value of the change in manufacturing's share of total private employment plus the absolute value of the change in service and FIRE's share of total private employment between 1972 and 1982. Thus, for example, if manufacturing's share falls from 18 to 12 percent of total private employment and the share of services and FIRE employment increases from 25 to 34 percent, the city's structural change index would be 15 percent.

This approach is similar to that used by Noyelle and Stanback (1983) to analyze patterns of structural change across metropolitan areas. Their measure differs from ours in that it is based on changes in employment shares for all categories of employment whereas ours is based on manufacturing and services (plus FIRE) alone. Their measure indicates overall economic disruption; the higher their index, the greater total shifts among all types of production activity. Our index, in contrast, is designed to focus on those structural changes that are likely to have the clearest implications for city fiscal health, namely the shift away from manufacturing jobs to service jobs.

On the basis of the index, we divide the 86 cities into three categories of structural change: low, medium, and high. This index combines a great deal of information about employment shifts into one summary measure. Like all summary measures, however, it must be interpreted carefully. Various combinations can lead to the same value of the index. Thus, for example, an index value of 15 could represent a 5 percent decline in manufacturing's share combined with a 10 percent increase in service's share, a 2 percent increase in manufacturing's share combined with a 13 percent increase in service's share, or any other combination that adds up to 15 percent. Strictly speaking, therefore, the measure represents changes in sector shares without necessarily implying a shift away from manufacturing and toward services and FIRE.

The data show, however, that most cities experienced declines in the manufacturing share and increases in the service share during the 1972-82 period. This result is illustrated in table 2.5, which shows the average changes in the shares of manufacturing with FIRE and service employment for

Table 2.5
Categories of Structural Change
(71 Cities)

	Number of Cities	Average Change in Manufacturing Share (percentage points)	Average Change in Service and FIRE[a] Share (percentage points)	Average Structural Change Index
Low growth in economic health				
Low structural change	5	-2.3	2.0	4.7
Medium structural change	6	-3.8	6.3	10.6
High structural change	15	-0.5	10.2	19.6
Medium growth in economic health				
Low structural change	9	-1.1	1.9	4.7
Medium structural change	8	-2.7	7.6	10.3
High structural change	6	-7.3	9.9	17.2
High growth in economic health				
Low structural change	8	0.1	2.5	4.5
Medium structural change	11	-3.7	6.6	11.1
High structural change	3	-3.8	12.3	17.9

Note: City economic health is defined to be private employment in the city divided by city population. The growth categories are defined in table 2.2. Structural change is defined as the absolute value of the change in manufacturing's share of total private employment plus the absolute value of the change in the share of services and FIRE.
[a]Finance, insurance, and real estate.

cities in each of the nine employment growth and structural change categories. The entries in this table, like those in table 2.2, are based on data for the 71 cities with complete data. The number of cities in each category is indicated in the first column.

The entries in table 2.5 reveal some key characteristics of the cities in each structural change category. A typical city experiencing medium employment growth and medium structural change, for example, had a 2.7 percentage point decline in the share of manufacturing employment and a 7.6 percentage point increase in the share of service and FIRE employment. In general the growth in the services share exceeds the decline in the manufacturing share. This finding means that our structural change index measures both the shift away from manufacturing and toward services and the relative growth of the service sector.

Summary

In this chapter we provide a foundation for later chapters by describing the economies of major central cities in the United States and by developing categories of city based on their economic health and economic structure.

We measure the economic health of a city by its private sector employment per city resident. On the basis of this measure, we sort cities into quintiles from low to high defined by their economic health in 1982. The second set of economic health categories summarized in table 2.2 divides cities into groups based on the 1972 levels and 1972-82 rates of change in their economic health. Our expectation is that stronger city economic health and greater improvement in economic health over time lead to stronger and more rapidly improving city fiscal health. This outcome is not assured, however. As we discuss in subsequent chapters, the links between city economic and fiscal health are complicated, even when we ignore variation across cities in fiscal and political institutions. Taking account of those institutions complicates the relationship further.

Widespread concern that the changing structure of city economies away from manufacturing and toward service activities might adversely affect the fiscal health of central cities motivated the construction of the categories presented in table 2.5. We use these categories in later chapters to examine the extent to which changes in fiscal health or its components are related to changes in city economic structure, when changes in city economic health are controlled for.

Appendix: Sources of Employment and Payroll Data

This appendix describes the sources of our employment and payroll data for both the private and the public sectors of major central cities.

Private Sector Employment and Payrolls

Table A2.1 summarizes the sources of published data on private sector employment and payrolls. The information in the *County and City Data Book* comes from one of the four economic U.S. censuses: *Manufactures, Retail Trade, Wholesale Trade*, and *Selected Services*. We transformed this data in three ways: we estimated city data from county data, we constructed a category of other services to supplement the selected services category reported by the Census, and we converted quarterly to annual data.

Estimating City Data from County Data

We used county data to estimate employment and payrolls in each city for those time periods and industrial sectors for which city-specific data were not available. Using the city and county data for 1972 and 1977 for the four basic sectors (the first four in table A2.1), we calculated the proportion of county employment located within city boundaries. For each of the other industrial sectors, we assumed that the proportion of county employment in the city is equal to the proportion for one of the four basic industrial sectors.

We matched the basic industrial sectors with the sectors for which we had no city information on the basis of the degree of employment centralization in each sector. This centralization is measured by employment in the central county relative to employment in the standard metropolitan statistical area (SMSA) in the 50 largest SMSAs (See Brown, Phillips, and Vidal 1983). This analysis led us to use the city-to-county proportion for selected services to determine city employment in FIRE and in "other services," the proportion for wholesale trade to determine city employment in transportation, communications, and public utilities TCPU, the proportion for retail trade to determine city employment in construction, and the proportion for manufacturing to determine city employment in minerals.

We estimated 1982 city employment in each sector by multiplying county employment in that sector by the city-to-county employment ratio. This ratio was obtained from 1980 *Place of Work* data from the *Census of Housing and Population*. Minor adjustments were made in specific cities when this approach produced 1982 employment levels that were out of line with those for earlier years.

Table A2.1

Private Sector Employment and Payrolls:
Sectors and Availability of Data

Sectors	Availability[a]	
	City and County	County Only
Manufacturing	1972, 1977	1982
Retail trade	1972, 1977	1982
Wholesale trade	1972, 1977	1982
Total services Selected services	1972, 1977	1982
Other services (2-4 digit)		all 3 years
Contract construction		all 3 years
TCPU[b]		all 3 years
FIRE[c]		all 3 years
Minerals		all 3 years

Source: Data are from the following publications of the U.S. Department of Commerce, Bureau of the Census: Data for manufacturing, retail trade, wholesale trade, and selected services for 1972 and 1977 are from the *County and City Data Book, 1977* (Washington, D.C.: GPO, 1978); *1983* (Washington, D.C.: GPO, 1983). Data for 1972 and 1977 for other services, contract construction, TCPU, FIRE, and minerals are from *County Business Patterns, 1972* (Washington, D.C.: GPO, 1973); *1977* (Washington, D.C.: GPO, 1979). All 1982 data are from *County Business Patterns, 1982* (Washington, D.C.: GPO, 1984).

[a]Availability at the time the data were collected.

[b]Transportation, communications, and public utilities.

[c]Finance, insurance, and real estate.

Expanding Selected Services to Total Services

We supplemented the selected services figures from the Census with estimates of city employment and payrolls in other services. These other services include the 2-4 digit categories of medical and health services, museums, nonprofit membership organizations, and miscellaneous services such as noncommercial research and bookkeeping. We converted this county data to city data using the method described above.

Converting Quarterly or Mid-March Data to Annual Data

The reported employment figures for manufacturing are annual averages. For all other industrial sectors, the reported figures represent employment in mid-March or for the week including 12 March. Using national aggregates to analyze the seasonality of activity in each sector, we concluded that for all sectors except construction, the March employment figures quite closely represent the average level of employment during the year. We adjusted the March employment figures for construction for each city using national ratios of annual to mid-March employment.

City payroll data for 1972 are available only for the first quarter of the year. We used year-specific national ratios of annual to first quarter payrolls for each sector to convert this quarterly payroll data to annual data.

Government Employment and Payrolls

Public sector employment in central cities includes three components: employees of local governments (both city and noncity), state governments, and the federal government. Data on noncity local, state, and federal government employment are available only at the county level.

Federal Government Employment and Payrolls

The U.S. Office of Personnel Management publishes information on federal employment by county in their *Report of Employment by Geographic Area* (annual before 1980, biennial thereafter). We used the ratio of federal employees in each city to those in overlying counties, as reported in the 1980 *Place of Work* volume of the *Census of Housing and Population*, to transform county figures to city figures for all four years. The use of the 1980 patterns for all sample years appears reasonable because the location of federal employment within a county is likely to be relatively stable over time.

Payrolls for federal employees were estimated with average federal salary figures for each city in 1977 and 1982, as provided by the U.S. Office of Personnel Management. For 1972 only national average salaries were available. For each city we extrapolated the ratios of the city's average salary to the national average salary backward from 1982 to 1972. We then multiplied these estimated ratios by the appropriate national average to obtain salary levels by city for the earlier year.

State Government Employment and Payrolls

We obtained information on state government employment by county for all three years from the U.S. Bureau of Economic Analysis. We allocated county employment to each central city in proportion to the ratio of local government employment in the city (including both city and noncity governments) to total local government employment in the county.

We estimated payrolls for state government employees in each city by multiplying the number of employees by a state-specific average salary for state government employees, calculated from the annual Government Employment series of the *Census of Governments*.

Local Government Employment and Payrolls

Employment and payrolls for municipal governments are available in the *Census of Governments*, vol. 3. For the other local governments that overlie the central city, we determined the total amount of noncity local public employment at the county level in 1977 from the U.S. Census publication, *Local Governments in Metropolitan Areas*, and then allocated a share of this employment to the city in line with the city's share of county population. Comparable information on noncity local employment within counties was not available for 1982, so we used the 1977 ratio of noncity to total local employment to estimate the noncity share of local government employment in each county in 1982. We used comparable procedures for payrolls.

Table A2.2 lists our estimates of total private and total public sector employment.

Table A2.2
Private and Government Employment by City, 1972 and 1982
(86 Cities)

	1972		1982	
	Private Employment	Government Employment	Private Employment	Government Employment
Akron, OH	109,814	13,804	105,110	15,106
Albany, NY	46,517	31,612	58,634	29,264
Albuquerque, NM	85,206	25,276	127,102	30,276
Anaheim, CA	77,080	9,365	142,124	13,052
Atlanta, GA	312,876	46,401	318,541	54,323
Austin, TX	72,951	45,823	148,282	66,377
Baltimore, MD	335,945	83,149	285,009	90,297
Birmingham, AL	143,378	22,740	163,053	24,138
Boston, MA	403,187	81,786	422,066	75,507
Boulder, CO	18,521	6,222	37,413	7,857
Buffalo, NY	167,249	34,204	151,551	29,681
Charlotte, NC	139,097	16,647	204,830	22,553
Chicago, IL	1,338,929	198,764	1,211,751	186,768
Cincinnati, OH	212,807	35,875	233,502	31,921
Cleveland, OH	352,360	50,163	315,923	40,604
Clifton, NJ	36,001	2,619	35,829	3,201
Columbus, OH	216,438	46,346	260,282	51,975
Dallas, TX	448,691	54,867	621,315	73,210
Dayton, OH	136,133	29,287	115,579	15,495
Denver, CO	257,535	52,485	329,790	61,096
Detroit, MI	505,687	86,974	328,855	78,785
El Paso, TX	89,014	21,830	132,543	28,355
Everett, WA	26,594	3,081	39,674	3,639
Ft. Lauderdale, FL	61,696	8,395	109,229	9,756
Fort Worth, TX	138,914	21,111	215,636	26,393
Garden Grove, CA	14,702	5,047	34,588	5,914
Greensboro, NC	81,325	9,636	94,664	13,287
Hartford, CT	114,372	12,541	124,688	13,664
High Point, NC	42,027	3,495	40,583	4,631
Hollywood, FL	28,129	5,005	45,960	6,314
Honolulu, HI	188,402	62,783	245,810	71,020
Houston, TX	542,060	70,371	1,055,691	113,372
Indianapolis, IN	307,004	56,196	320,250	60,312
Jacksonville, FL	168,201	32,647	209,199	36,719
Kansas City, MO	253,634	40,586	262,704	44,473
Long Beach, CA	105,299	25,871	138,959	27,860
Los Angeles, CA	1,060,018	192,507	1,346,075	204,703
Louisville, KY	165,665	25,422	174,016	24,669
Memphis, TN	217,535	47,744	261,811	52,042
Miami, FL	162,577	22,442	193,985	28,387
Milwaukee, WI	277,691	41,529	278,431	43,885

Table A2.2 (Cont.)

	1972		1982	
	Private Employment	Government Employment	Private Employment	Government Employment
Minneapolis, MN	224,148	29,976	256,495	29,260
Nashville-Davidson, TN	178,739	37,247	216,520	38,916
Newark, NJ	168,149	26,895	128,993	29,027
New Orleans, LA	218,652	48,486	225,400	51,356
New York, NY	3,043,950	573,109	2,889,397	514,270
Norfolk, VA	88,956	33,421	96,913	32,625
Oakland, CA	126,670	40,462	132,973	40,205
Ogden, UT	18,126	7,386	25,609	7,218
Oklahoma City, OK	161,087	50,730	238,497	51,781
Omaha, NB	144,540	24,947	174,042	28,345
Ontario, CA	17,043	3,954	22,413	4,809
Passaic, NJ	22,863	1,197	17,781	1,453
Paterson, NJ	46,359	6,418	40,038	7,693
Pawtucket, RI	31,763	7,614	29,119	3,971
Philadelphia, PA	671,970	151,354	595,179	135,832
Phoenix, AZ	217,894	40,414	334,548	54,384
Pittsburgh, PA	240,305	34,496	275,080	27,133
Portland, OR	199,737	32,427	234,860	36,183
Portsmouth, VA	24,559	16,515	23,579	21,044
Providence, RI	99,335	22,539	102,486	24,290
Richmond, VA	127,034	43,158	148,465	47,361
Riverside, CA	31,187	9,821	54,491	11,857
Rochester, NY	175,664	16,444	179,544	13,606
Sacramento, CA	79,539	40,051	123,463	48,391
St. Louis, MO	310,422	56,459	286,236	48,003
St. Paul, MN	144,034	27,686	155,060	26,988
St. Petersburg, FL	62,656	9,633	79,246	12,371
Salt Lake City, UT	104,322	18,264	151,503	22,481
San Antonio, TX	178,654	65,415	302,839	73,370
San Bernardino, CA	31,354	9,083	48,095	9,822
San Diego, CA	198,018	57,330	332,120	68,422
San Francisco, CA	362,386	86,962	472,521	79,236
San Jose, CA	107,785	25,178	198,492	32,460
Santa Ana, CA	58,280	8,478	106,593	11,207
Schenectady, NY	46,575	4,386	32,458	4,377
Seattle, WA	231,700	53,030	317,882	54,299
Tampa, FL	126,056	20,416	176,075	24,649
Toledo, OH	145,120	19,690	136,753	19,865
Troy, NY	16,932	3,172	17,764	3,137
Tucson, AZ	80,484	24,924	123,487	28,982
Tulsa, OK	135,900	15,941	215,630	19,655

Table A2.2 (Cont.)

	1972		1982	
	Private Employment	Government Employment	Private Employment	Government Employment
Virginia Beach, VA	23,756	7,932	56,680	13,048
Warwick, RI	21,430	6,416	29,700	3,442
Winston-Salem, NC	78,613	8,892	105,104	10,525
Washington, DC	300,725	243,354	328,011	260,577

Part II

Fiscal Health Assuming Uniform Fiscal Institutions

3
Revenue-Raising Capacity

A ctual revenue collected is a poor measure of a city's capacity to raise revenue. Some central cities place heavy tax burdens on their residents because they must spend more than other cities to obtain public services of the same quality. Others impose heavy tax burdens because their citizens want high-quality services. In neither case does high revenue mean that the city is blessed with extensive taxable resources.

Any measure of the underlying ability of a city to raise revenue requires some form of standardization across cities. Our approach standardizes by specifying a uniform tax burden on city residents, defined as a certain percentage of resident income. Thus our measure of revenue-raising capacity indicates how much revenue a city could raise at a given tax burden on its residents. A city with a relatively high revenue-raising capacity can raise more money at a given burden on residents (or the same money at a lower burden) than the average city.

In this chapter we define and implement this measure of revenue-raising capacity for major central cities, on the basis of the assumption that all cities have access to the same set of taxes and face the same division of responsibilities between city and noncity governments in a state. Because this measure does not depend on the particular fiscal institutions within which a city must operate, it measures the full, in contrast to the restricted, revenue-raising capacity of each city. Similarly, in chapter 4 we assume that cities provide a uniform package of public services, and we develop a measure of standardized expenditure need that is independent of the actual package of services that a city provides. In chapter 5 we combine revenue-raising capacity with standardized expenditure need to measure a city's standardized fiscal health.

The use of standardized fiscal institutions in these initial chapters allows us to highlight the fiscal effects of the broad economic and social changes occurring in U.S. cities, changes over which city and state officials have little control. In subsequent chapters, we bring in state grants and fiscal institutions such as restrictions on a city's use of certain taxes, the role of overlying tax districts, and the package of public services a city is expected to provide. This approach allows us, in chapters 9 and 11, to determine the extent to which fiscal institutions and grants reinforce or counteract the effects on city fiscal health of economic and social trends.

Measuring Revenue-Raising Capacity

Our approach to measuring revenue-raising capacity starts with the principal source of tax revenue: resident income. If all city workers, property owners, and consumers lived in the city, all taxes levied by the city would ultimately be paid from the income of the city residents, regardless of the mix of taxes actually used. In this closed economy, the aggregation of individual taxpayers' ability to pay, typically measured by income, would represent the basic constraint on the ability of the jurisdiction to raise revenue for public spending, and income could serve as a reasonable index of a city's revenue-raising capacity.[1]

The situation is more complex in an open economy because some tax burdens may fall on nonresidents. The precise mix of taxes available to a jurisdiction affects the revenue-raising capacity of the jurisdiction through the contribution of each tax base to the exportability of tax burdens. In this more realistic open economy situation, the income of city residents is augmented by the income of nonresidents to the degree that city tax instruments are able to tap it.

We use the term revenue-raising capacity to measure how much revenue the city could raise with a standard tax burden on city residents from three uniformly defined broad-based taxes: a property tax, a general sales tax, and an earnings tax. The potential or standard base for each tax is defined identically across cities and can be calculated for each city whether or not it is allowed to levy that tax. The specified burden is most naturally expressed as a percentage of resident income and can be interpreted as a standard level of resident tax effort. This standard tax burden is the same for all cities and makes the measure comparable across cities and over time.

---

1. Revenue-raising capacity is often referred to in the literature as fiscal capacity. For various approaches to the measurement of fiscal capacity, see Reeves 1986 and ACIR 1986. The appropriate income measure for our approach would be income defined comprehensively to include imputed as well as realized returns from wealth. When so defined, income would represent the flow from all types of wealth including financial assets, real property, and human capital, and hence it would not need to be supplemented with a measure of wealth to represent fully the ability to pay. Barro 1986 discusses the difficulties involved in measuring income for this purpose.

Thus we define the per capita revenue-raising capacity of a city, RRC, as

$$RRC = K^* Y(1 + e),$$

where K^* is the standard burden on residents, Y is per capita income of residents, and e is the tax burden on nonresidents per dollar of burden on residents, assuming that the city has access to the three standard tax bases. If K^* were set at 3 percent, for example, the tax revenue collected from city residents would equal 3 percent of their income (K^*Y). This revenue would then be augmented by revenues from nonresidents equal to eK^*Y. Underlying this formulation is the assumption that cities cannot arbitrarily raise the export ratio, e, by applying higher tax rates to those portions of each tax base ultimately borne by nonresidents. Importantly, this measure bears no simple relationship to the tax revenue a city actually collects. Nor does it vary with a city's choice about the composition of taxes.[2]

In this approach, revenue-raising capacity varies across cities for two reasons: variation in the per capita income of residents and variation in the ability of cities to export part of the city tax burden to nonresidents. Consider the following example. Assume that two cities have the same per capita resident income, that a city retail sales tax is the only tax for which a portion of the burden can be shifted to nonresident taxpayers, and that a higher

---

2. In a recent study, Barro 1985 proposed a comparable measure of capacity for states. His approach is similar to ours in that fiscal capacity is based on resident income adjusted for exporting of tax burdens. Unlike our measure, however, his incorporates a standardized behavioral response; according to his approach, fiscal capacity is the amount of revenue voters in the jurisdiction would choose to raise given their income and ability to export taxes, if average preferences are assumed. Thus, to implement his measure, estimates are needed of price and income elasticities of demand. Importing of burdens from other jurisdictions can be ignored because of its relatively small impact on a city's revenue-raising capacity. Consider an increase in the local earnings tax rate, say from 0 to 1 percent. If 50 percent of the tax is borne by commuters, then exporting augments the amount raised from residents by 100 percent. If 30 percent of the earnings of city residents are earned outside the city, a corresponding rise in earnings taxes in nearby jurisdictions lowers the net-of-tax income of these "reverse commuters" by 1.0 percent, a reduction that amounts to only 0.3 percent of all earnings in the city. Exports and imports are asymmetrical because exported taxes directly augment city revenues whereas imported taxes reduce residents' incomes, only a fraction of which is available to the city government.

proportion of the sales tax is paid by nonresidents in city A than in city B. Then, regardless of how much revenue each city actually raises, potential revenue-raising capacity is greater in city A than in city B. Similarly, if the cities have the same income and the same potential to export sales taxes, their measured capacities to raise revenues would be the same, regardless of whether they choose (or are allowed) to use the sales tax as a source of revenue.

To implement this approach, we must first estimate how much of the burden of each standard tax can be exported to nonresidents per dollar of burden on residents. In the following section we describe how we accomplish this task. We then calculate the overall export ratio, e, for each city as a weighted average of the export ratios for each of the three standard taxes. Economic theory suggests that the weights should depend on the relative responsiveness of the nonresident and resident portions of each tax base to changes in tax rates (as discussed more fully in Ferguson and Ladd 1986). Unfortunately, existing studies provide almost no information about these responses.[3] In addition, these responses presumably vary from one metropolitan area to another depending on the relationship between the central city, its suburbs, and nearby urban areas. Hence all the capacity measures presented below use the arbitrary weights of 50 percent for the standard property tax, and 25 percent each for the local sales and earnings taxes. Experimentation with more refined measures does not change any of our substantive conclusions (see ibid.).

Existing formulas for distributing federal aid to cities typically use per capita income as the measure of city revenue-raising capacity. Because it ignores tax exporting, per capita income provides a misleading picture of the capacity of cities with very high or very low ability to export tax burdens. In addition, data presented below show that variation in per capita income understates the extent to which revenue-raising capacity varies across U.S. central cities.

The conclusion that per capita income is a flawed measure of a jurisdiction's revenue-raising capacity is not new. Indeed, recognition of the importance of tax exporting led the U.S. Advisory Commission on Intergovernmental Relations (ACIR) to develop its representative tax system

---

3. One of the authors has recently used some of the data from this study to estimate the response of city tax bases to local tax rates, but we know of no studies that estimate the differential response to taxes of the nonresident and resident portions of the tax base. See Bradbury and Ladd 1987.

(RTS) approach for states in 1971.[4] The RTS measure indicates how much tax revenue each state could raise if it applied national average tax rates to each of its potential, or uniformly defined, tax bases, independently of whether the state chooses to use that tax base. The ACIR has replicated this approach many times for states and also has applied it to metropolitan areas. Later in this chapter, we present the first application of this approach to U.S. cities.

Though straightforward and now relatively well known, the RTS measure of fiscal capacity is not suitable for this study of cities. Implicit in the RTS approach is the view that each jurisdiction could reasonably be expected to impose average tax rates on each of its tax bases, because no jurisdiction's tax rates would then be out of line with those of other jurisdictions. By standardizing in terms of tax rates, however, the RTS approach essentially ignores the resulting tax burdens on city residents. As is documented below for major central cities, the RTS approach leads to tremendous variation across cities in the burden of taxes on residents as a fraction of their income. In contrast, we focus explicitly on the well-being of city residents. This perspective makes it more natural to achieve comparability across cities by imposing a standard tax burden on residents than by imposing average tax rates, as in the RTS approach.

Compared to the RTS approach, our measure of revenue-raising capacity has the additional advantage of being easy to adjust for restrictions on tax usage and for other fiscal rules under which cities operate. Consider, for example, a city, such as Boston, that has access only to the local property tax. Presumably the residents of Boston are willing to impose a heavier property tax burden than they would if they were also taxing themselves through income and sales taxation. Because the RTS measure is based on national average tax rates, this increased willingness of city residents to tax themselves through the property tax is difficult to introduce into the RTS framework.[5]

---

4. See ACIR 1981, for the ACIR's approach and philosophy. The ACIR currently publishes estimates of the fiscal capacity of states on a regular basis in *Significant Features of Fiscal Federalism*.
5. According to the RTS approach a city's unrestricted revenue-raising capacity would be measured as the weighted average of the three standard tax bases. The most straightforward way to incorporate the restrictions prohibiting the use of income and sales taxes would be to give zero weight to the bases the city is not authorized to use. But this would understate the city's capacity to raise tax revenue; not paying sales or income taxes, residents would undoubtedly be willing to tax themselves more heavily through the property tax. Any attempt to adjust for this in the RTS measure would be ad hoc and arbitrary.

Our measure, in contrast, readily accommodates the restrictions on tax use because it starts with the ultimate source of tax revenue, resident income. Restrictions on the use of certain taxes simply mean that more resident income is available for the permitted taxes (see chapter 6 for further discussion). This advantage over the RTS approach is particularly important for cities, which are often subject to prohibitions and restrictions imposed by state law. Because cities have less control than states over the fiscal rules under which they operate, the concept of restricted revenue-raising capacity is more relevant for cities than for states.

The Ability to Export Tax Burdens to Nonresidents

Exporting of city tax burdens to nonresidents is a distinctive component of our measure of revenue-raising capacity and one that varies substantially across cities. A small city that attracts many suburban commuters can export a larger portion of the burden of a city earnings tax, for example, than can a city that has few commuters. Because the literature contains no estimates of tax exporting for cities, we estimate export ratios for the three broad-based taxes for each major central city in several different years. (See McLure 1967 for estimates of exporting by states.) In the following discussion we summarize these calculations. (See the appendix to this chapter and Bradbury and Ladd 1985, app. A, for a more complete description of our data sources and methodology.)

The fraction of a city tax borne by nonresidents depends first on how we define standard tax bases. A property tax base that exempts part of the residential tax base, for example, leads to more exporting per dollar of burden on residents than a base without that exemption. Second, exporting depends on who ultimately bears the burden of the tax. This issue, which is known as tax incidence, is particularly controversial for the property tax. Third, the degree of tax exporting depends on whether the ultimate payers of the tax live in the city or elsewhere. This issue is conceptually straightforward but sometimes hard to calculate with precision.

Who ultimately bears the burden of any tax change depends on the extent to which people and firms are able to alter their behavior in response to that change. Local wage earners, for example, may be able to avoid the burden of a local tax on earnings by shifting their workplace to a nontaxed locality. Similarly, local retailers may be able to avoid the burden of a local retail sales tax by moving their business to a jurisdiction without the tax. The potential for these types of response depends in part on the nature of the change being considered.

We base our analysis of the shifting of tax burdens on a tax change that applies to an entire metropolitan area. This approach means that taxpayers can avoid the burden of taxes only by moving outside the metropolitan area or by curtailing the taxed activity, not by changing the location of the taxed activity to another community within the metropolitan area. We prefer this metropolitan approach to the alternative of assuming that taxes in nearby communities are not related to the tax burdens in the central city because we want to focus on tax structure, which is defined by state law and typically is similar within a metropolitan area, and not on city-suburban tax differences.[6]

Property Taxes

All U.S. cities rely on local property taxes, but the definition of the tax base varies across cities. Some, for example, do not tax business machinery, and others exempt substantial portions of residential real estate. For our standard property tax base, we ignore these differences and define the base comprehensively as the estimated total market value of both real and personal property within the city, excluding only those types of property such as churches, schools, and government buildings that are almost always exempt from local property taxation.

A simple approach to the estimation of export ratios for the standard property tax would be to classify each of the classes of property such as owner-occupied housing, rental housing, or commercial real estate as either resident or nonresident, so that the portion of taxes borne by nonresidents in each class would be either 0 or 100 percent. Instead, we use a more sophisticated approach. We first determine the incidence of the taxes associated with each class on the basis of reasonable assumptions about mobility. Because we assume that owners of capital can escape the burden of local property taxes by shifting their investments from one metropolitan area to another, the tax burden ends up being shared by consumers of housing services in the city, consumers of goods and services produced in the city, workers in the city, and city landowners. We then allocate the resulting burdens to residents and nonresidents using city-specific data such as the share

---

6. The simplifying assumption that taxes move together in a metropolitan area puts us midway between the approach used in a 1958 study of Michigan taxes and that used in a 1959 study of Wisconsin taxes. Michigan's tax structure was examined assuming no change in the tax structure of other states. The Wisconsin study argued that state taxes tend to move together and hence that a change in one state's taxes would be accompanied by a change in those of other states. For reference to the two approaches see McLure 1967, p. 51.

of commuters into the city or the size of the city relative to the metropolitan area.

The estimated export ratios vary considerably across cities. This variation reflects two major differences among cities—the fraction of the base that is housing and the importance of the city in its metropolitan area. The more housing there is relative to business property or the greater a city's population is relative to that of its metropolitan area, the lower in general is the city's ability to export the burden of the property tax to nonresidents.

General Sales Taxes

A broadly defined local sales tax base would include services such as entertainment and dry cleaning as well as retail sales of goods. We have limited the standard base to retail sales, however, to be consistent with normal practice. Our estimates of export ratios assume that retail sales taxes are borne fully by consumers in the form of higher prices. The relatively small size of the retail sector in most city economies (10 to 20 percent of total city employment) means that even though the total amount of land or labor in an urban area may be limited and immobile, the amount available for the provision of retail goods is adjustable. Hence owners of factors of production are able to avoid paying the tax by using these factors in other activities. The tax, therefore, is shifted to consumers, who have less opportunity to adjust their behavior in favor of untaxed alternatives.

Hence the proportion of the tax exported to nonresidents is simply the proportion of retail sales in the city not made to residents. We estimated purchases of city residents by multiplying their per capita income by an estimate of their average propensity to consume disaggregated into three categories—purchases at food and drug stores, purchases of food and drink at restaurants, and purchases of other taxable items. Our procedure produces reasonable results but underestimates tax exporting to the extent that city residents shop outside the city.

Estimated export ratios for sales taxes exhibit substantial variation across cities. In general the export ratios are relatively high where tourism is important and low for the cities with the largest populations.

Earnings Tax

We assume that local earnings taxes are borne fully by workers in the form of lower wages. Nontax considerations, such as the location of family and friends, are likely to play a bigger role than tax-related wage differentials in a worker's choice of an urban area. This observation implies that workers might accept lower wages than they could earn elsewhere in order to remain in their preferred metropolitan area.[7]

With workers bearing the burden, a typical city earnings tax allows a city to export some of its tax burden directly onto commuters. The export ratio for a city earnings tax depends, however, on the definition of the tax base. At one extreme, the export ratio is zero if nonresident earnings are excluded from the tax base. With nonresident earnings taxable, the export ratio is smaller if resident earnings outside the city or resident unearned income are included in the base than if they are not.

We define our standard earnings tax base as all earnings received in the city by both residents and nonresidents. This definition excludes from the base residents' earnings outside the city. Taxes on those earnings would probably accrue to other jurisdictions, given the assumption that all local governments in the metropolitan area use an earnings tax. The standard base also excludes the unearned income of residents, such as dividends and interest, because only a few of our sample cities include such income in their tax bases.

The export ratio for this standard tax base is simply nonresident earnings in the city divided by resident earnings in the city. We calculate this ratio with 1970 and 1980 census data on the earnings of people in various residence and work site categories. The calculated export ratios tend to be higher in cities with populations that constitute relatively small fractions of the population in their metropolitan area.

Average Export Ratios in 1982

Table 3.1 reports average 1982 export ratios for the 78 cities having complete 1982 data.[8] Averages are reported for cities grouped by city economic health, resident income, and city size. The relatively large magnitudes of the average export ratios, especially those for property and earnings taxes, indicate the substantial contribution that tax exporting can make to the potential fiscal capacity of U.S. central cities. With a standard property tax, for example, cities on average can raise 52 cents from nonresidents for each dollar raised from residents. (Put in terms of the division of the total property tax burden, of each dollar of property taxes raised, 34 cents

---

7. Note that if the form of the tax change involved a tax on earnings in the central city alone, workers would be able to avoid more of the burden of the tax because they could more easily shift their place of work to a nontaxed jurisdiction without changing where they lived.

8. The 8 excluded cities are Birmingham, Ala.; Boulder; Hartford, Conn.; Passaic, N.J.; Paterson, N.J.; Schenectady, N.Y.; Seattle; and Troy, N.Y. Most are excluded because of incomplete information on property tax bases.

Table 3.1
Export Ratios by Type of Tax, 1982
(78 Cities)

	Number of Cities	Standard Property Tax[a]	Standard Sales Tax	Standard Earnings Tax
Average	78	0.52	0.21	1.27
City economic health[b]				
Quintile 1	14	0.30	0.16	0.88
Quintile 2	17	0.46	0.24	0.99
Quintile 3	15	0.45	0.15	1.17
Quintile 4	16	0.61	0.20	1.42
Quintile 5	16	0.78	0.30	1.87
Resident income per capita				
Quintile 1	12	0.60	0.08	1.70
Quintile 2	17	0.60	0.34	1.44
Quintile 3	16	0.52	0.13	1.09
Quintile 4	17	0.48	0.29	1.11
Quintile 5	16	0.44	0.17	1.15
City population in thousands				
Less than 100	7	0.62	0.49	1.60
100-200	18	0.63	0.32	1.69
250-500	29	0.50	0.16	1.26
500-1,000	18	0.46	0.13	0.95
Greater than 1,000	6	0.39	0.06	0.71

Note: Each entry is the average export ratio for the indicated category of city. Export ratios are defined as the estimated burden on nonresidents per dollar of burden on residents.

[a]Variable is based on 1981 property value data.

[b]City economic health is defined as private employment in the city divided by city population. See chapter 2.

[= 0.52/(1+0.52)] is collected from nonresidents and 66 cents from residents.)

This average export ratio for property taxes substantially exceeds the 0.21 average for the sales tax but falls well below the 1.27 average for the standard earnings tax.[9] The greater-than-one average export ratio for the

---

9. Recall, however, that the export ratios for the general sales tax are somewhat too low because of our inability to account for consumer spending by city residents outside the city.

earnings tax implies that on average more than one-half of the earnings tax base belongs to nonresidents, a conclusion that directly reflects the large proportion of city payrolls accruing to nonresidents, which was shown earlier in figure 2.1. Remember, however, that these export ratios indicate a city's potential to export, rather than its actual exporting. In fact, only 18 of the 86 cities actually used an earnings or an income tax in 1982 and thereby were able to take advantage of this high exporting potential.[10]

A city's ability to export tax burdens to nonresidents generally increases with its economic health, as measured by employment per resident. The averages by employment quintiles indicate clear patterns for property and earnings taxes, with average export ratios for cities in the top quintile being more than twice for those in the bottom quintile. The pattern for sales taxes is less clear in that export ratios increase only as one goes from the middle to the top quintile.

The explanation for these patterns of export ratios is most transparent for the earnings tax. Recall figure 2.1, which shows that payrolls accruing to nonresidents per dollar accruing to residents are larger in the cities with greater economic activity than in the other cities. Combining this finding with our incidence assumption—that the burden of the earnings tax falls on workers—leads directly to the pattern of export ratios by employment quintiles shown in table 3.1. The story for the property tax is more complex, given the multiplicity of assumptions that enter into the analysis of tax incidence. Although tracing through the various effects is difficult, the observed outcome is reasonable: higher economic activity per resident brings with it more opportunities to export property tax burdens to nonresidents in the form of higher prices of exported goods, lower land rents accruing to nonresident landlords, and lower wages for city workers, many of whom live in the suburbs.

Although export ratios for property taxes rise with the economic health of the city, they decline with the economic health of city residents, as measured by resident income. We have already shown in figure 2.2 that city economic health and resident economic health are essentially uncorrelated, so the above-average export ratios in low-income cities are not attributable to above-average economic health in these cities.[11] The explanation appears

---

10. Actually, not all of the 18 cities were able to take advantage of the high potential export ratios because of the way their specific earnings or income taxes were defined. See chap. 6.
11. Moreover, a regression analysis of property tax export ratios on resident income that controls for employment and city size continues to indicate a negative association between property tax export ratios and resident income.

to be that low resident income leads to low housing values in the city and, typically, to a below-average residential share of the property tax base. Combining this with our incidence assumptions that less of the property tax on residential property than on business property is exported leads to the observed pattern, which is that lower-income cities can export more of the property tax burden per dollar of burden on residents than can higher-income cities.

Similar reasoning accounts for the pattern of export ratios for the earnings tax across cities grouped by resident income. Low income among residents is associated with low earnings for residents and typically with a low resident share of total earnings in the city and consequently with a high export ratio. The absence of a pattern for the sales tax is not surprising; the possibility of exporting sales tax burdens has more to do with how the city relates to its surrounding metropolitan area and whether it is a tourist center than with the income of city residents.

Finally, strong patterns emerge for all three taxes across cities of different size. Starting with cities with a population over 100,000, greater population appears to be associated with a lower ability to export tax burdens to nonresidents. Presumably, the more people who live in the city, the greater the probability that economic transactions involving taxes will take place among residents rather than with nonresidents, and hence the smaller the amount of tax exporting. [12]

Revenue-Raising Capacity: Variation across Cities

Table 3.2 illustrates how residential income and the potential to export tax burdens to nonresidents interact to determine a central city's ability to raise revenues from the three standard tax bases. This table reports results for 7 illustrative cities and summary measures for the 78 cities for which we have complete 1982 data. The 7 cities were chosen to provide variation along several dimensions, including geography, tax exporting, resident income, and, of relevance for later chapters, use of particular taxes and service responsibilities.

Column 1 is simply per capita money income of city residents in 1981

---

12. This negative relationship between ability to export tax burdens and city size continues to hold even when we use regression analysis to control for the effects of employment per capita and resident income.

Table 3.2

Alternative Measures of a City's Capacity to Raise Revenue, 1982
(Illustrative Cities)

	(1)	(2)	(3)	(4)	(5)
	Per Capita Money Income 1981	Aggregate Export Ratio[a]	Revenue-Raising Capacity[b]	Representative Tax System[c]	Representative Tax System as Fraction of Resident Income[d]
Illustrative cities					
Atlanta, GA	7,809 (0.92)	1.12	497 (1.19)	481 (1.16)	0.032
Baltimore, MD	7,076 (0.83)	0.54	327 (0.78)	238 (0.57)	0.024
Boston, MA	7,783 (0.91)	1.12	495 (1.18)	418 (1.00)	0.029
Denver, CO	10,319 (1.21)	0.69	524 (1.25)	556 (1.34)	0.034
Detroit, MI	7,090 (0.83)	0.58	336 (0.80)	184 (0.44)	0.018
Oakland, CA	9,171 (1.08)	0.76	483 (1.15)	386 (0.93)	0.028
San Antonio, TX	6,936 (0.81)	0.30	270 (0.65)	330 (0.79)	0.037
All cities in study[e]					
Average	8,609 (1.00)	0.63	419 (1.00)	415 (1.00)	0.032
Median	8,629 (1.01)	0.58	498 (0.98)	395 (0.95)	0.031
Minimum	5,292 (0.62)	0.11	218 (0.52)	184 (0.44)	0.018
Maximum	12,099 (1.42)	1.65	724 (1.73)	1,177 (2.83)	0.068
10th percentile	7,090 (0.83)	0.25	319 (0.76)	258 (0.62)	0.024
90th percentile	10,330 (1.21)	1.12	524 (1.25)	568 (1.37)	0.038
Standard deviation	1,232 (0.14)	0.33	91 (0.22)	143 (0.34)	0.007

Source: Per capita money income for 1981 comes from the U.S. Department of Commerce, Bureau of the Census, *Current Population Reports*, P-26/82 (Washington, D.C.: GPO, 1982).

Note: In all except the last row, numbers in parentheses represent index values, calculated by dividing each dollar or decimal figure by the average for all cities. For the standard deviation, this entry is equivalent to the coefficient of variation, that is, the standard deviation divided by the mean.

[a]Variable is calculated as a weighted sum of export ratios with the weights of 0.5 for the property tax and 0.25 each for the sales and earnings taxes.

[b]See definition in text. Variable is calculated as 0.03 times the product of column 1 and (1 + column 2).

[c]Variable is calculated as a weighted average of the three broad-based taxes with the weights equal to average tax rates for cities in the sample.

[d]Variable is the resident portion of the tax burden divided by resident income.

[e]Entries are based on the 78 cities for which complete information is available for 1982.

as reported by the U.S. Census. The numbers in parentheses represent index values relative to the average for all cities in the sample and are useful for identifying a city's relative position. Column 2 reports weighted averages of city-specific export ratios for the three standard taxes with the weights of 50 percent for the property tax and 25 percent each for the sales and earnings taxes. Column 3 combines income and exporting to produce our measure of revenue-raising capacity, with the standard burden, K^*, set at 3 percent of resident income. The 3 percent figure approximates the average burden of city taxes on residents in 1982.[13] This approximation suffices for the analysis of relative capacity; changing the percentage simply scales all the absolute figures in column 3 proportionately, leaving unchanged the indexes, which are expressed in relation to the average burden.

In 2 of the illustrative cities, Atlanta and Boston, well above-average exportability of tax burdens more than offsets below-average income of city residents to produce above-average revenue-raising capacity. In the other 5 illustrative cities, however, relative positions with respect to income and export potential tend to reinforce each other. Thus, for example, the above-average revenue-raising capacity of Denver reflects above-average values of both income and exporting, and the below-average capacity of San Antonio, Texas, reflects below-average values of both components.

Revenue-raising capacity varies by more than 3.3:1 across cities, from 48 percent below the average in El Paso, Texas, to 73 percent above the average in Everett, Washington. This range exceeds the 2.3:1 range for resident income, which varies from 38 percent below the average in Newark, New Jersey, to 42 percent above the average in Fort Lauderdale. Another indicator of variation, the standard deviation relative to the average, illustrates the same point. For a typical variable, more than one-half of the observations will fall within one standard deviation of the average. Dividing this standard deviation by the variable's average value makes the degree of variation comparable across variables with different averages. The standard deviation of revenue-raising capacity across cities is about 22 percent of the average (shown in parentheses in the last row of table 3.2), substantially higher than the 14 percent for income. These patterns indicate that per capita income provides a misleading picture of the revenue-raising capacity of those cities with very high or very low export ratios and understates the extent to which revenue-raising capacity varies across cities.

---

13. The median burden on city residents of state and local taxes combined is about 12 percent of resident income, with about 3 percent representing the burden of city government taxes alone.

Column 4 of table 3.2 applies the RTS approach for the first time to central cities. Following the ACIR's methodology for states, each of the three potential tax bases in each city was weighted by its average tax rate, calculated as the total tax revenue collected in all 78 cities divided by the sum of all the tax bases. Clearly, the results differ in significant ways from our measure of potential capacity. As was already noted, the RTS approach is flawed because its standard tax structure imposes differential burdens on residents in different cities. Column 5 of table 3.2 shows that this problem is severe. These figures are calculated by multiplying the average tax rates by the resident portion of each potential tax base to determine the amount that would be borne by residents, summing across the three taxes, and expressing this amount as a fraction of resident income. The figures show that the smallest burden represents less than 2 percent and the largest burden almost 7 percent of resident income.

To what extent is a city's revenue-raising capacity related to the economic health of the city or its residents? Clear patterns emerge in the first column of table 3.3: Capacity increases both with the economic health of the city, as measured by employment per capita, and with the economic health of residents, as measured by resident income per capita. This similarity occurs despite the contrasting patterns of aggregate export ratios across cities grouped by economic health and by income. Export ratios rise from 0.41 to 0.93 across the employment categories but fall from 0.75 to 0.55 across the income categories. In effect, variation in average export ratios plays the dominant role across the employment categories whereas variation in average income, not surprisingly, dominates across income categories.

Revenue-raising capacity also is related to city size. Larger cities have lower per capita capacity on average than smaller ones. This pattern is attributable almost exclusively to variation in average export ratios. These ratios decline by more than 50 percent from the smallest to the largest cities, whereas average income is essentially constant across city size categories.

Changes in Revenue-Raising Capacity, 1972-1982

The income of city residents plays a crucial role in our analysis. Not only is per capita income the key building block for our measure of revenue-raising capacity, but it also represents the average economic health of city residents. It is natural to ask, therefore, how changes over time in revenue-

Table 3.3
Revenue-Raising Capacity, 1982
(78 Cities)

	Number of Cities	Revenue-Raising Capacity	Per Capita Money Income	Aggregate Export Ratio
Average	78	$419 (1.00)	$ 8,609 (1.00)	0.63 (1.00)
City economic health[a]				
Quintile 1	14	359 (0.86)	8,480 (0.99)	0.41 (0.65)
Quintile 2	17	369 (0.88)	8,083 (0.95)	0.54 (0.86)
Quintile 3	15	403 (0.96)	8,710 (1.02)	0.56 (0.88)
Quintile 4	16	448 (1.07)	8,866 (1.04)	0.71 (1.13)
Quintile 5	16	512 (1.22)	8,927 (1.05)	0.83 (1.48)
Resident income per capita				
Quintile 1	12	359 (0.86)	6,870 (0.81)	0.75 (1.19)
Quintile 2	17	405 (0.97)	7,733 (0.91)	0.74 (1.17)
Quintile 3	16	397 (0.95)	8,489 (1.00)	0.56 (0.88)
Quintile 4	17	435 (1.04)	9,117 (1.07)	0.59 (0.93)
Quintile 5	16	455 (1.16)	10,422 (1.22)	0.55 (0.87)
City population in thousands				
Less than 100	7	468 (1.12)	8,525 (1.00)	0.83 (1.32)
100-250	18	472 (1.13)	8,708 (1.02)	0.82 (1.30)
250-500	29	403 (0.96)	8,467 (0.99)	0.61 (0.97)
500-1,000	18	393 (0.94)	8,757 (1.03)	0.60 (0.79)
Greater than 1,000	6	357 (0.85)	8,635 (1.01)	0.39 (0.62)

Source: Per capita money income for 1981 comes from U.S. Department of Commerce, Bureau of the Census, *Current Population Reports*, P-26/82 (Washington, D.C.: GPO, 1982).

Note: Each entry is the average value of the specified variable for the indicated category of city. Numbers in parentheses represent index values, calculated by dividing each dollar or decimal figure by the average for all cities reported in the first row.

[a]City economic health is defined as private employment in the city divided by city population. See chapter 2.

raising capacity are related to changes in the economic health of residents. A city where the average income of residents is declining is likely to have more difficulty in maintaining public service levels than one where the income of residents is increasing. In the absence of other changes, falling real income requires that tax burdens increase relative to income simply to maintain constant spending out of own sources in real terms. As is shown in chapter 4, falling real income also may bring with it higher costs for providing a given quality of public services. From a policy perspective a decline in the income of city residents is likely to create more cause for concern in cities with low initial income levels than in those with high initial income levels.

In light of these considerations, table 3.4 reports information for cities grouped into six categories defined by the level and growth of resident income. Entries in the table are based only on the 71 cities for which we have complete property tax data, but the categories themselves are based on all 86 cities.[14] The cities in categories 1, 2, and 3 all had 1971 per capita resident income below the average for the 86 cities. Those in categories 4, 5, and 6 had above-average income. Cities also are grouped by their 1971-81 growth in real per capita income, with income deflated by the price deflator for state and local government purchases.[15] The growth categories low, medium, and high refer to thirds of the 86-city distribution of growth rates. Ten-year growth rates ranged from -15.8 percent to +3.0 percent in the low growth categories, 14 cities (11 in the 71-city subset) experiencing falling real income during the period. Growth rates ranged from 3.8 to 8.5 percent in the medium-growth category, and from 8.7 to 27.5 percent in the high-growth category. At one extreme are the category 1 cities such as Cleveland, Boston, and Philadelphia with below-average income and low income growth. At the other extreme are the category 6 cities for which income was above average in 1971 and grew rapidly during the decade. Included in this category are Houston, Denver, and San Diego. Overall, the cities in categories 1, 2, and 4 are most limited by the level or growth of the real income of city residents. If they were closed economies, these cities would have the weakest revenue-raising ability over time.

Because cities are not closed economies, however, changes in the exportability of tax burdens also need to be considered. Striking patterns emerge by type of tax. First, property tax export ratios declined in almost one-half of the cities, but they remained constant or increased in a substantial number, including some with low growth in or declining real income. Decreasing export ratios in more than one-half of the cities in categories 1, 2, and 4 exacerbated the fiscal difficulties associated with declining or slowly growing real income.

---

14. The missing cities are Albuquerque, N.M.; Austin; Birmingham, Ala.; Boulder; Dallas; El Paso, Tex.; Everett, Wash.; Fort Worth, Tex.; Houston, Tex.; Newark, N.J.; Passaic, N.J.; San Antonio, Tex.; Schenectady, N.Y.; Seattle; and Troy, N.Y.
15. The choice of the 1971-81 data decade was dictated by the fact that 1981 is the most recent year for which city income data were available. The 1971 city income data were estimated by interpolating data from 1969 and 1972.

Table 3.4

Changes in Revenue-Raising Capacity by Resident Income, 1972-1982
(71 Cities)

	(1)	(2)	(3)	(4)	(5)	(6)	(7)
						Change in	
	Number	Change	Export Ratios[b]			Revenue-Raising Capacity	
	of	in Real per	(Declines/Increases)			3 Bases	Property
	Cities	Capita Income[a]	Property	Sales	Income	(50-25-25)	Tax Only
		(%)				(%)	(%)
Below-average income in 1971							
Low growth	18	-2.3	10/8	12/2	0/18	2.1	-3.0
Medium growth	10	5.2	6/3	7/3	0/10	6.4	2.5
High growth	6	11.7	1/4	7/1	0/6	20.0	20.8
Above average income in 1971							
Low growth	7	-0.3	5/2	5/2	3/3	-1.3	-2.1
Medium growth	17	6.0	8/8	10/6	1/16	9.9	6.7
High growth	13	14.2	5/7	4/4	3/10	18.2	14.6
Average (or total)	71	5.2	35/32	45/18	7/63	8.6	5.4

Note: Each entry in columns 2, 6, and 7 is the average value of the specified variable for the indicated category of city.

[a]The percentage change in income is for the period 1971-81.

[b]Number of cities in each category with increases or decreases in the specific export ratio greater than 0.02.

Second, export ratios for sales taxes typically declined during the decade. Table 3.4 shows that within the 71-city subset, the ability to export sales taxes declined in 45, increased in only 18, and was essentially constant in the others. The declining sales tax export ratios probably reflect the growth of suburban shopping centers and the general decentralization of retail facilities. A declining ability to export sales tax burdens was common in cities in all the income categories, but the average magnitude of the decline was larger in categories 1 and 2 than in others. Thus, if one focuses on the two most commonly used tax bases, property and sales taxes, one finds that the economic changes experienced by central cities in the United States during the 1970s frequently reduced the ability of a city, especially those with low and declining real income, to reap fiscal benefits from non-residents.

A different picture emerges for earnings taxes. Most cities in all income categories experienced an increase in their ability to export the burden of earnings taxes, in sharp contrast to property and sales taxes. The ratio of nonresidents' to residents' earnings in the city increased in 63 of the 71 cities during the decade. The increase presumably reflects faster movements of households than of jobs out of the central city to the suburbs during the 1970s, combined with faster growth of wages for suburban commuters than for city residents. This striking finding suggests that, legal or political limitations aside, an earnings tax base that included commuter earnings would probably have been advantageous to most cities during the 1970s. Few cities actually made use of this tax, however.

The change in each city's revenue-raising capacity reflects the combined effects of change in the money income of residents and in their ability to export tax burdens to nonresidents. Using the 50, 25, and 25 percent weights for the property, sales, and earnings taxes respectively, table 3.4 shows that on average, revenue-raising capacity grew faster than resident income in all cities (8.6 percent compared to 5.2 percent) and in each of the income categories except the high income-low growth category. The relatively rapid growth in capacity primarily reflects the rising export ratios for the earnings tax.

To see this result more clearly, consider the final column of table 3.4. It reports changes in a narrower measure of revenue-raising capacity, namely how much revenue a city could raise from property taxes alone given the standard burden on residents. This narrower measure is calculated in the same way as the full capacity measure, except that it is based on each city's property tax export ratio rather than a weighted average of export ratios. Overall, the average percentage change in this narrower measure is quite similar to that for the percentage change in money income. In categories 1, 2, and 4, in which cities are most constrained by the level and growth of resident income, however, average percentage changes in this property-tax-only measure of capacity are smaller than average changes in resident income. In other words, if cities in these categories had been constrained to use only the property tax, their revenue-raising capacity would have declined more or improved less than is indicated by the change in resident income. Thus, table 3.4 hints at the potential role for tax diversification, particularly through the earnings tax.

The key finding to emerge from table 3.4 is that changes in the revenue-raising capacity of U.S. cities are closely linked to changes in the economic health of city residents. The table shows, for example, that for both lower- and higher-income cities, the average change in capacity in cities with high income growth exceeds that in low-growth cities by more than 17 percentage points. This outcome is not surprising given the key role of resident income in our measure of capacity. Significantly, however, part of the variation in growth rates of capacity is caused by the more rapidly rising export ratios in cities with rapidly rising income than in those with slowly growing income.

Table 3.5 shows that changes in revenue-raising capacity also are closely linked to changes in the health of the city economy. On the basis of employment categories discussed in chapter 2, this table shows a clear pattern of greater improvement in capacity in cities with high employment growth per capita than in those with low growth. The importance of the rising export ratio for the earnings tax is once again highlighted by a comparison of the full capacity measure with the property-tax-only measure. The average export ratio for the property tax declined in all groupings characterized by low or medium growth in economic health. This outcome contrasts with small average increases in the weighted export ratio. Since the sales tax export ratio declined in many cities, the rising weighted export ratio generally reflects the rising ability of cities to export burdens through the earnings tax.

The Role of Structural Change

Finally, consider the impact of the structural change in a city's economy, namely the shift away from manufacturing and toward service activity, on the city's revenue-raising potential. In the following discussion, we focus first on the impact of structural change on a city's property tax base, for which the predictions are the clearest. We then turn to the impact of structural change on revenue-raising capacity, represented first by the narrow measure that includes only property taxes and then by the broader measure that includes all three taxes. The clearest finding is that the shift of city employment away from manufacturing and toward services adversely affects the growth of city property tax bases. Despite this finding, employment shifts appear to have had little systematic impact on the overall revenue-raising capacity of cities.

The major mechanism through which structural change might adversely affect a city's property tax base is relatively straightforward. To the extent that the amount of land, buildings, and machines per manufacturing employee exceeds the amount needed per service employee, it follows that the size of the taxable base per manufacturing employee will exceed that

Table 3.5

Changes in Revenue-Raising Capacity by City Economic Health, 1972-1982
(71 Cities)

	Number of Cities	Change in Revenue-raising Capacity		Change in Components		
		Potential (50-25-25) (%)	Property Tax Only (%)	Per Capita Income (%)	(1+e) (50-25-25) (%)	(1+e) Property Tax Only (%)
Below-average economic health in 1972						
Low growth	11	2.8	-1.8	2.3	0.4	-4.2
Medium growth	9	5.8	3.9	5.4	0.4	-1.4
High growth	15	16.0	11.7	10.1	5.5	1.5
Above-average economic health in 1972						
Low growth	15	3.9	-0.6	1.1	2.8	-0.5
Medium growth	14	6.7	-2.9	5.2	1.6	-2.2
High growth	7	19.5	20.7	7.4	11.4	12.45
Average (or total)	71	8.6	5.4	5.2	3.3	0.2

Note: Each entry is the average value of the specified variable for the indicated category of city. See the text for detailed definitions of column heads. The economic health categories are defined in table 2.2.

per service employee. Testing this relationship directly is not possible with our data because we cannot identify the components of the property tax base associated with manufacturing or service employment.

Following from this relationship, however, is the hypothesis that those cities experiencing large structural change should experience lower rates of growth of the property tax base than those experiencing less structural change, controlling for overall employment growth. Column 2 of table 3.6 provides clear support for this hypothesis. In each employment growth category, the rate of growth of the per capita property base declines with the amount of structural change. Moreover, the effects are large. Consider cities with medium rates of overall employment growth. The per capita property tax base grew only 21 percent during the ten-year period in a typical city with high structural change in contrast to 60 percent in a typical city with low structural change.[16]

16. These patterns are statistically significant for cities with medium and high employment growth, but not for those with low growth.

Table 3.6
Impact of Structural Change, 1972-1982
(71 Cities; in Percentages)

	(1)	(2)	(3)	(4)	(5)	(6)	(7)	(8)	(9)
	Number of Cities	Change in per Capita Property Tax Base			Change in Revenue-raising Capacity		Change in Components		
		Total	Business	Housing	Property Only	3 Bases (50-25-25)	Per Capita Income	(1+e) Property Only	(1+e) 3 Bases (50-25-25)
Low employment growth									
Low structural change	5	14.8	7.0	20.2	3.7	5.4	4.5	-0.8	0.8
Medium structural change	6	12.5	17.9	18.6	-1.8	1.6	-2.4	0.8	4.3
High structural change	15	0.8	-8.7	13.4	-1.3	3.5	2.2	-3.6	1.1
Medium employment growth									
Low structural change	9	59.6	74.3	58.1	5.4	6.5	5.5	-0.2	1.0
Medium structural change	8	27.2	20.4	36.4	7.3	10.1	5.0	2.3	5.0
High structural change	6	20.8	-5.6	50.0	-5.2	1.1	5.4	-10.0	-4.0
High employment growth									
Low structural change	8	85.8	105.6	79.2	12.1	16.6	9.3	2.5	6.8
Medium structural change	11	56.4	77.1	51.3	15.4	17.1	9.5	5.5	7.1
High structural change	3	30.3	67.5	16.8	18.0	18.9	8.0	9.4	10.1

Note: Structural change is defined as the shift of city employment away from manufacturing in favor of services. See chap. 2. All dollar figures are deflated by the state and local deflator for government purchases.

These results are based on the entire property tax base, which includes residential as well as business property. An additional process could be at work here, namely that lower-paying service jobs lead to lower income and consequently lower housing values than would be the case in a manufacturing based economy. Or alternatively, if residents capture a higher proportion of service jobs than of manufacturing jobs, their income could increase with the shift to services. Column 3, which represents the percentage change in the business (that is, nonhousing) component of the property tax base, and column 4, which refers to the growth in the housing component, help sort out the direct and indirect effects on the property tax base of the shift to a service economy. The pattern of effects of structural change on the business component is generally consistent with the prediction that structural change dampens the growth of this base. Particularly striking are the findings for the medium-growth cities, in which high structural change reduces the growth of the business base 80 percentage points below the rate in cities with low structural change. The growth rate of the housing component also exhibits a negative relationship with structural change. Except in the high-growth cities, the effects on the housing base are smaller than those for business property. Once again the differences are statistically significant for the medium- and high-growth categories but not for the low-growth categories.[17]

The fact that structural change typically reduces the growth rate of a city's property tax base need not imply that such change will reduce its revenue-raising capacity, even its capacity to raise revenue through the property tax alone. One needs to look in more detail at the effects of structural change on the income of residents and on the exportability of tax burdens. The previous results are suggestive. Since export ratios for business property are typically higher than those for residential property, to the extent that structural change reduces the business base more than the residential base, structural change is likely to reduce a city's ability to export tax burdens.

The results for the property-tax-only measure of capacity are mixed. For cities with low or medium employment growth, those undergoing high structural change experienced lower average rates of growth of revenue-raising capacity than those undergoing low structural change. The differences are about 5 percentage points in the low-growth category and about 10 percentage points in the medium-growth category. These results are sug-

---

17. These conclusions, based on ten-year changes, are less strong for five-year changes. For a more complete discussion of the effects of changing economic structure on the property tax base of central cities, see Bradbury and Ladd 1987.

gestive but not definitive. In neither case is there a consistent pattern as one moves from low to medium to high structural change. In the high-growth category a pattern emerges, but not the predicted one. Relative growth of services in these high-growth cities is associated with rising revenue-raising capacity, which reflects the rising export ratios across the structural change categories. This result, though somewhat surprising, is consistent with the large decline in the growth of the residential base relative to the business base in these cities, a growth pattern that shifts the property tax burden onto the more exportable component of the tax base. Thus the results provide only limited support for the hypothesis that structural change adversely affects the fiscal capacity of U.S. cities, even when fiscal capacity is defined in terms of the property tax alone.

The patterns for full revenue-raising capacity mirror the patterns found for the property-tax-only measure. This result is not surprising given the assumption that 50 percent of revenue for this broader measure is from the property tax. The differences across categories are smaller, however. The addition of sales and earnings bases to the capacity measure weakens the relationship between structural change and capacity. Moreover, most of the differences are not statistically significant.

In summary, the changing employment mix of U.S. central cities between 1972 and 1982 has clear adverse impacts on the property tax base but much less clear impacts on revenue-raising capacity, even when the latter is defined in terms of the property tax alone. Some evidence of adverse effects on capacity emerges, but we cannot rule out the possibility that these observed effects reflect chance outcomes rather than true causal relationships.

Conclusions

Several conclusions emerge about the capacity of U.S. cities to raise tax revenue from local broad-based taxes. First, exporting of burdens to nonresidents turns out to be an important component of revenue-raising capacity. Our calculations show that in 1982 central cities could raise substantial amounts of revenue from nonresidents per $1.00 from residents for each of the three uniformly defined broad-based taxes: on average, $0.52 for the property tax, $1.27 for the earnings tax, and $0.21 for the general sales tax. Remember, however, that these are measures of potential, rather than actual, exporting. In fact, very few central cities are permitted by state law to take advantage of the high export potential of the standard earnings tax. Second, per capita revenue-raising capacity varies substantially across cities, because of variation both in the basic source of city tax payments, income of residents, and in the ability to export tax burdens to nonresidents. That both components contribute to variation means that per capita income, the measure of revenue-raising capacity most commonly used in federal aid distribution programs, understates the variation in revenue-raising capacity across cities.

Over the 1972-82 period the average city experienced an 8.6 percent increase in its revenue-raising capacity, with substantially higher increases in cities with the greatest improvement in their economic health than in those with declines or small improvements. Fifteen of the 71 cities for which complete data are available, or more than 1 in 5, experienced an absolute decline in inflation-adjusted revenue-raising capacity during the ten-year period. The situation looks bleaker when one focuses on city capacity to raise revenue from the property tax alone; 25 cities, or more than 1 in 3 experienced a decline in this narrower measure of revenue-raising capacity between 1972 and 1982. In short, changes in the overall economic health of U.S. central cities have led to a significant deterioration in the ability of many to finance public services out of their own resources.

Contrary to our expectations, however, changes in the mix of city employment away from manufacturing and toward services have had little discernible impact on revenue-raising capacity, despite the dampening of the growth of the property tax bases as a result of this structural change in city economies.

Appendix: Measuring Revenue-Raising Capacity and Tax Exporting

This appendix provides the theoretical underpinning for our measure of revenue-raising capacity and summarizes the theory and calculations underlying our estimates of tax exporting. For more detail on exporting, see Bradbury and Ladd 1985.

Revenue-Raising Capacity

Our measure of revenue-raising capacity can be derived formally as follows. Let r_i be the tax rate applied to the ith tax base, B_i, so that $r_i B_i$ represents the revenue raised from the ith base. In addition, let B_i^R denote the portion of the ith tax base belonging to residents and B_i^N the portion belonging to nonresidents, so that $B_i = B_i^R + B_i^N$ for each of the three standard tax bases, $i = 1, 2, 3$. Then the city's revenue-raising capacity is defined as the revenue that the city would raise if it chose tax rates so as to

$$\text{maximize } \sum_{i=1}^{3} r_i B_i$$

$$\text{subject to } \sum_{i=1}^{3} r_i B_i^R = K^* Y .$$

where $K^* Y$ is the benchmark tax burden on residents. Implicit in this formulation is the assumption that for each tax base the tax rate applied to non-residents is the same as that applied to residents.

If a city has only one tax base and its size is unresponsive to the rate at which it is taxed, the revenue-maximizing tax rate is determined by the constraint in this maximization problem, and the maximum revenue obtainable is given by the expression in the text, namely $K^* Y (1+e)$, where e is the export ratio for the specified tax base.

More realistically, a city will have more than one potential tax base, and each base may be a decreasing function of the rate at which it is taxed. To find revenue-maximizing tax rates (and hence revenue-raising capacity) in this case, we rewrite the maximization problem in terms of a Lagrangian function:

$$\text{Max } \pounds = \sum_{i=1}^{3} r_i B_i + \lambda (K^* Y - \sum_{i=1}^{3} r_i B_i^R) ,$$

where the Lagrangian multiplier, λ, is the amount by which revenue-raising capacity would increase if the resident burden constraint were increased by one dollar. The first-order conditions of this problem indicate that revenue will be maximized if the tax rate r_i on each base B_i is set so that

$$\frac{B_i [1 + E(r_i, B_i)]}{B_i^R [1 + E(r_i, B_i^R)]} = \lambda ,$$

where $E(r_i, B_i)$ is the elasticity of the ith tax base with respect to the ith tax rate and $E(r_i, B_i^R)$ is the elasticity of the residential component of the base, again with respect to a change in the ith tax rate. The numerator of the fraction is simply the total marginal revenue from the tax source (from both residents and nonresidents) associated with a small increase in the tax rate. The denominator is the marginal revenue from (or marginal burden on) residents. Thus, to maximize the additional revenue generated with a given additional burden on residents, the city should increase taxes that, at the margin, raise the most revenue from nonresidents per dollar raised from residents.

Thus revenue-raising capacity, which is the revenue a city can raise at revenue-maximizing tax rates, depends both on the fraction of each tax that can be exported and the responsiveness of each base to tax rates. As we noted in the text, existing studies provide almost no information about typical values for the relevant response elasticities. In addition, these elasticities presumably vary from one metropolitan area to another depending on the relationships among the central city, its suburbs, and nearby urban areas.

Despite these limitations the revenue-raising measure that we present in the text captures the essential components of the theoretical model, namely the standard burden on resident incomes and the exportability of tax burdens to nonresidents. Moreover, our measure of restricted, in contrast to full, revenue-raising capacity (discussed in chaps. 6 and 9) approximates the theoretical ideal to the extent that cities behave as if they were maximizing revenue from nonresidents per dollar of revenue from residents. (See Inman 1981 for evidence of this type of behavior.)

Tax Exporting

The fraction of a city's tax burden ultimately borne by nonresidents depends on how much of the tax is borne by various types of taxpayer and the proportion of each type of taxpayer that lives outside the city. In this section we describe our approach to these issues for the three standard tax bases. As was noted in the text, the property tax poses the most challenging conceptual problems; the sales and earnings taxes are more straightforward.

Property Taxes

We used data from the *Census of Governments* on assessed values, assessment-sales ratios, and land use types, supplemented by data from individual cities where necessary, to calculate the market value of property by city for the eight land use categories shown in table A3.1.

The first step in estimating export ratios is to determine which groups ultimately bear the burden of local property taxes for each of the eight land-use classes. Because we assume that owners of capital can escape the burden of local property taxes by shifting their investments from one metropolitan area to another, local property tax burdens end up being shared by consumers, workers, and landowners. For example, we allocate 100 percent of the tax burden on owner-occupied housing to the consumers (and

Table A3.1
Shares of the Tax Base and Export Ratios
by Type of Property, 1976

Property Class	Percentage of Total Market Value	Export Ratio
Owner-occupied housing	33	0.00
Rental housing, single family	7	0.06
Rental housing, 2-4 unit structures	4	0.07
Rental housing, 5 or more unit structures	6	0.17
Commercial, real and personal	31	1.80
Industrial, real and personal	13	1.78
Vacant, acreage, and other	3	6.67
State-assessed[a]	3	10.61

Source: Composition of market value is based on data from U.S. Department of Commerce, Bureau of the Census, *Census of Governments, 1977*, vol. 2, *Taxable Property Values and Assessment-Sales Ratios* (Washington, D.C: GPO, 1978). Some missing values were replaced with data obtained from cities.

Note:Averages over all cities for which data were available. Export ratio is dollars of city tax burdens borne by nonresidents per dollar of city tax burdens borne by residents.

[a]State-assessed property generally consists of public utilities and railroads.

owners) of that housing, but we allocate only 80 percent of the tax on rental residential property with five or more units to renters and the rest to landowners. For commercial property, both real and personal, we allocate 42 percent of the burden to consumers, 38 percent to workers, and 20 percent to landowners. The corresponding percentages for industrial property are 14 percent to consumers, 75 percent to workers, and 11 percent to landowners. The different percentages for commercial and industrial property reflect different degrees of market power, different factor shares, and differential responses of workers to taxes. (For the underlying theory see McLure 1970 and 1977 and Mieszkowski 1972.)

The second step is to determine whether the ultimate taxpayers live inside or outside the city. Owner-occupants and renters of residential property, by definition, live in the city. We assume that the proportions of other groups of taxpayers (for example, consumers of commercial and industrial products and workers) who live in the city vary across cities in line with factors such as the size of the city relative to its metropolitan area and the proportion of city payrolls accruing to commuters. For landowners we use national estimates of corporate ownership by type of property and then assume that corporate owners are nationally dispersed whereas noncorporate owners live within the metropolitan area.

Combining our assumptions about tax incidence, which vary by property type but not by city, with our city-specific estimates of where people live produces the 1976 average export ratios by property type shown in table A3.1. These ratios vary from one city to another because of differences in the proportions of final taxpayers who live in the city. On average, residential property has considerably lower export ratios than business property because most of the residential tax burden is passed forward to consumers who live in the city. State-assessed and vacant property have the highest average export ratios.

Each city's overall ability to export property taxes is calculated as the sum across classes of the exported tax base divided by the resident tax base. Stated differently, the overall export ratio is a weighted average of the export ratios for each class of property in a city, the weights reflecting the contribution of each class to the city's standard property tax base. The average export ratio in 1976 was 0.54. Large variation across cities comes from two major sources: the fraction of the tax base that is housing and the size of the city relative to its metropolitan area.

Sales Taxes

We derived estimates of potential sales tax bases from the *Census of Retail Trade, 1972* and *1977*. Because the 1982 Census was not available at the time the data were collected, the 1982 bases are derived from *Survey of Buying Power*, special issue of *Sales and Marketing Management*, 1982. Though less reliable than the figures for the earlier years, these 1982 estimates were the best available and are consistent with observed trends.

As we discuss in the text, we assume that local sales tax burdens are fully shifted to consumers in the form of higher prices. Hence the proportion of sales tax burdens that are exported to nonresidents is simply the proportion of retail sales in the city not made to residents.

Estimates of retail spending by residents are obtained by multiplying a city's per capita income by an estimate of residents' average propensity to consume (APC) disaggregated into three categories: purchases at food and drug stores, purchases of food and drink at restaurants, and purchases of other taxable items. The APCs are based on ratios of SMSA retail sales to SMSA income, adjusted (using coefficients estimated from a multivariate regression equation) for differences between city and SMSA income and purchases by tourists.

Our method yields reasonable results as judged by patterns of export ratios across spending categories, across cities, and over time. The estimates, however, seem low. One explanation for the low estimates is that our approach ignores the possibility that city residents might shop outside the city. Such behavior would produce overestimates of spending by residents and underestimates of export ratios. We have no data to allow us to adjust for this possibility.

Another possible explanation is that our approach ignores the effects on resident consumption of the distribution of income across households within the city. We tried estimating APCs from data on the variation in APCs across income levels. On average the estimates of tax exporting in 1972 from this alternative approach are higher than those reported in the text, but the patterns of change over time are similar. We rejected this approach, however, because of a lack of data on 1982 spending patterns; we believed it was inappropriate to extrapolate 1972 household spending patterns by income class to 1982.

Earnings Taxes

As is discussed in the text, we define the standard earnings tax base as all earnings received in the city by both residents and nonresidents. With this standard base and the assumption that earnings taxes are borne by workers, the export ratio is simply the ratio of nonresident earnings to total earning in the city. This ratio is available for central cities in the 1970 and 1980 censuses. We used the 1970 ratio for 1967, the 1980 ratio for 1982, and interpolated estimates for 1972 and 1977.

A major problem that arises in carrying out these calculations is that central cities as defined by the Census often consist of more than one city. Data on the number of people who live and work in each of a metropolitan area's central cities from the U.S. Census volume, *Journey to Work*, were used to sort out commuting patterns for multiple-city SMSAs and to calculate export ratios for each of the 86 central cities.

Revenue-Raising Capacity by City

Table A3.2 presents 1972 and 1982 per capita revenue-raising capacity in the 71 cities for which complete data are available for both years. As is discussed in the text, capacity is calculated as 3 percent of per capita income, multiplied by 1 plus the aggregate export ratio. The aggregate export ratio is a weighted sum of export ratios for the three standardized broad-based taxes with the weights of 0.5 for the property tax and 0.25 each for the sales and earnings taxes. The property-tax-only measure of revenue-raising capacity is calculated in a similar manner, except that the export ratio is that for the standardized property tax base alone.

Table A3.2
Alternative Measures of Revenue-Raising Capacity, 1972 and 1982
(71 Cities)

	1972		1982	
	3 Bases (50-25-25)	Property Only	3 Bases (50-25-25)	Property Only
Akron, OH	372	379	409	415
Albany, NY	530	499	565	538
Anaheim, CA	530	468	590	532
Atlanta, GA	479	439	497	442
Baltimore, MD	344	358	327	302
Boston, MA	482	492	494	494
Buffalo, NY	353	343	350	311
Charlotte, NC	355	365	367	381
Chicago, IL	365	391	360	371
Cincinnati, OH	442	463	448	434
Cleveland, OH	433	463	409	377
Clifton, NJ	472	381	436	371
Columbus, OH	343	353	353	356
Dayton, OH	475	468	433	379
Denver, CO	422	419	524	497
Detroit, MI	368	357	336	304
Ft. Lauderdale, FL	521	406	639	492
Garden Grove, CA	392	309	516	406
Greensboro, NC	387	373	440	423
Hartford, CT	516	490	508	442
High Point, NC	340	319	429	416
Hollywood, FL	414	365	501	406
Honolulu, HI	323	293	364	304
Indianapolis, IN	330	336	361	364
Jacksonville, FL	256	264	283	293
Kansas City, MO	404	402	383	344
Long Beach, CA	455	449	437	409
Los Angeles, CA	401	419	384	385
Louisville, KY	383	371	393	337
Memphis, TN	259	269	282	281

Table A3.2 (Cont.)

	1972		1982	
	3 Bases (50-25-25)	Property Only	3 Bases (50-25-25)	Property Only
Miami, FL	444	358	490	409
Milwaukee, WI	329	326	344	314
Minneapolis, MN	458	425	466	382
Nashville-Davidson, TN	294	300	349	349
Newark, NJ	373	380	346	352
New Orleans, LA	282	293	344	357
New York, NY	336	358	309	332
Norfolk, VA	307	293	333	319
Oakland, CA	458	422	483	410
Ogden, UT	382	344	455	384
Oklahoma City, OK	334	326	434	430
Omaha, NB	313	308	370	353
Ontario, CA	360	326	409	356
Pawtucket, RI	351	326	362	331
Philadelphia, PA	309	312	292	289
Phoenix, AZ	298	295	342	358
Pittsburgh, PA	420	396	508	489
Portland, OR	452	420	479	453
Portsmouth, VA	288	282	306	293
Providence, RI	402	388	392	346
Richmond, VA	415	391	446	387
Riverside, CA	358	364	395	384
Rochester, NY	456	416	527	486
Sacramento, CA	416	382	448	400
St. Louis, MO	429	357	439	376
St. Paul, MN	411	384	473	405
St. Petersburg, FL	321	311	327	317
Salt Lake City, UT	486	444	591	526
San Bernardino,CA	440	398	458	392
San Diego, CA	330	330	366	362
San Francisco,CA	516	534	517	517
San Jose, CA	325	326	372	363
Santa Ana, CA	453	399	484	405
Tampa, FL	327	260	427	372
Toledo, OH	332	355	354	376
Tucson, AZ	298	305	332	299
Tulsa, OK	329	331	451	445
Virginia Beach, VA	297	309	328	337
Warwick, RI	402	330	459	370

Table A3.2 (Cont.)

	1972		1982	
	3 Bases (50-25-25)	Property Only	3 Bases (50-25-25)	Property Only
Winston-Salem, NC	397	391	482	467
Washington, DC	564	538	615	536
Average	389	372	421	389

Note:"3 Bases" stands for a revenue-raising capacity measure in which a city relies on property, income, and sales taxes, with weights of 50 percent, 25 percent and 25 percent, respectively. "Property Only" refers to a revenue-raising capacity measure in which a city relies exclusively on the property tax. All entries are in 1981 dollars.

4

Public Service Costs and Standardized Expenditure Need

J ust as cities differ in their revenue-raising capacity, so also do they differ in the amount of money they must spend to achieve a given quality
of public services—that is, in their expenditure need. For example, cities
with a harsh environment in which to provide police and fire services, such
as Newark, New Jersey, and Cleveland, must spend much more to obtain a
given level of police and fire protection than cities with a favorable environment, such as Albuquerque, New Mexico. In this chapter we describe the
impact of environmental factors on the cost of public services, estimate differences in public service costs across cities and over time, show how service costs influence a city's expenditure need, and develop the concept of
standardized expenditure need to complement the concept of revenue-raising capacity developed in chapter 3.

The impact of public service costs on a city's fiscal situation has been
recognized since the work of Bradford, Malt, and Oates (1969). Nevertheless, few studies of city finances have actually estimated service cost variation across cities. Brazer and Anderson (1975), Chambers (1978), and
Wendling (1981), incorporate selected cost factors into an analysis of
education spending; Bradbury et al. (1984) estimate service costs and expenditure need in Massachusetts cities and towns. But to our knowledge no
previous study has attempted to measure service costs and expenditure need
across cities in different states.

Overview

Actual per capita public expenditure in a city is the product of three
components: the extent of the service responsibilities assigned to that city
by its state government, the quality of the public services selected by the
city government, and the per capita cost of public services in that city (per
unit of service quality).

Our objective in part II (chapters 3-5) is to measure the fiscal health of cities with *uniform* fiscal institutions, including service responsibilities. In the calculations in this chapter, therefore, we assume that service responsibilities are the same in all cities. Our objective in part III (chapters 6-9) is to measure the fiscal health of cities with their actual fiscal institutions. As we document in chapter 8, the division of responsibility for public services among cities, other local governments, and state governments varies widely from one state to another. Our calculations in part III consider the impact of this variation on cities' actual expenditure need.

The quality of the public services a city actually provides reflects that city's response to its fiscal circumstances and therefore cannot be used as a measure of those circumstances. Some cities spend more than others with the same resources, for example, simply because their residents are willing to pay for higher-quality services. In this chapter, therefore, we hold service quality constant across cities, using a methodology that is described below.

The third component of public expenditure is the cost of public services. Cities with relatively high costs must spend more than other cities to obtain the same quality of services. These service costs are determined by the cost of labor and other inputs and by the social and economic environment in which the services must be provided. Higher input costs or a harsher environment imply higher costs for public services. Even with uniform service responsibilities and the same service quality, therefore, cities that face different costs must spend different amounts per capita for public services because they face different costs.

Our objective is to measure costs that are outside a city's control. To some extent, of course, a city's actual costs may reflect decisions by city officials; for example, a city may decide to offer generous wages to its employees, or it may be slow to implement managerial reforms. As a result, we employ cost variables that are beyond the direct influence of city officials. We measure the cost of labor by the wage that must be paid to attract employees away from the private sector, and we measure the harshness of the environment with broad indicators of a city's social and economic condition. Thus our cost indexes are not influenced by managerial inefficiency, corruption, or generous settlements with public employee unions.

In short, our cost measures, like our measure of revenue-raising capacity, describe external constraints on a city government's ability to provide public services. The cost-side constraints can be summarized with the notion of a city's *standardized expenditure need*, which is the amount it must spend to obtain a standardized service quality for a standardized package of service responsibilities.

In this chapter we explain the links between the cost of city services and both input prices and environmental factors, and we identify the environmental factors that influence the cost of general, police, and fire services. We summarize our results with cost indexes for each of these services in each of the 86 major central cities. On the basis of these cost indexes, we then calculate an index of standardized expenditure need. A technical description of our cost indexes and expenditure need calculations is provided in the appendix to this chapter.

To identify the environmental factors that influence public service costs, we use a statistical analysis based on data from the 86 central cities between 1967 and 1982, which is presented in the appendix to chapter 10. As we noted above, public expenditure is the product of service responsibility, service quality, and service cost. Thus we estimate the impact on public expenditure of input prices and of a variety of environmental cost factors, controlling for service responsibilities and the variables that determine service quality.

Input Prices, Environmental Factors, and the Cost of City Services

Input prices have a straightforward impact on the cost of city services. In order to provide public services, cities must purchase employees, police cars, fire trucks, and other inputs. The higher the price of these inputs, the more a city must pay to provide a given level of services.

Input prices are influenced by wages and prices in the private sector. Cities in high-wage regions, for example, must pay more than other cities to entice private workers into city jobs. As we noted earlier, however, input prices also may be influenced by the decisions of city officials. To ensure that a city's costs reflect only that component of input prices that is external to city actions, we measure the price of labor facing a city by the manufacturing wage rate in that city's state and we measure the overall price of inputs by a metropolitan consumer price index that excludes taxes.

Most public discussions of city services focus on the activities of city employees, such as police patrols and geometry lessons. The cost of these activities clearly depends on the prices of inputs, such as policemen, police cars, teachers, and chalk. These activities are only intermediate outputs, however. The services actually valued by voters, that is, the final outputs, are protection from crime, children's learning, and the analogous services for other government activities. The cost of these final outputs depends on the cost of the relevant intermediate outputs and hence on the prices of inputs. In addition, however, the cost of these final outputs depends on the environment in which they are produced.

Consider the case of fire services, for which the final output is protection from fire. A given number of firemen and fire trucks yields more protection from fire in a city with brick ranch houses on one-acre lots than in one with old, poorly constructed apartment buildings. To obtain a given level of protection from fire, therefore, a city with old apartments must spend more on fire services per capita than a city with brick ranches. Similarly, cities with social and economic conditions that breed crime will have to pay more per capita to obtain a given level of crime protection than will those facing more favorable conditions. In short, the per capita cost of any final output depends both on the cost of inputs and on the harshness of the environment in which that output must be provided.

A city's expenditure need is the amount it must spend to obtain a standardized level of final outputs. Cities with harsher environments therefore have higher expenditure need. This notion of expenditure need is simply a statement about the cost of inputs and the technology of public production, not a value judgment about what is good or just. It does not imply that cities with a harsher environment are more deserving, only that they must spend more to achieve the same level of final outputs than cities with a favorable environment.

Note that the amount a city actually spends is not a measure of the quality of its final outputs. As we explained earlier, actual spending reflects service responsibilities, service quality, and service costs. Cities with high costs may decide to spend more than other cities to maintain service quality, or they may decide to spend the same amount as others and thereby accept lower service quality. One cannot tell which choice a city has made simply by looking at its expenditure.

Although environmental factors are particularly important in the public sector, it may prove helpful to point out that they also influence the cost of private goods. Consider the cost of heating a home. The price of the input, gas or oil, varies from one region of the country to another, as does the environment, namely the weather. Not only must some households pay more per unit of fuel, but some must buy more fuel to bring their home up to a given temperature. Thus the cost of the final output, comfort, depends on the price of the intermediate output, units of fuel, and on the environment. It follows that the amount a household needs to spend to achieve a certain comfort level varies from one region to another. Furthermore, one cannot measure the comfort level in a house by the amount the household spends on fuel, just as one cannot measure the quality of a city's services by its expenditure.

The final outputs of city services, such as learning and protection from crime and fire, are difficult if not impossible to measure. Therefore we cannot directly measure the impact of environmental factors on the level of final outputs. Nevertheless, we can indirectly measure these impacts by analyzing city expenditure. To be specific, by carefully controlling for service responsibilities and service quality, we isolate the relationship between environmental factors and city expenditure and translate this relationship into a measure of service costs. As we noted earlier, our method for identifying important environmental cost factors is presented in the appendix to chapter 10.

The Input and Environmental Costs of General, Police, and Fire Services

Different environmental factors influence the cost of different city services. In this section, therefore, we examine three broad types of service: general, police, and fire. General services include airports, health, highways, housing and urban renewal, corrections, libraries, parking, parks and recreation, sanitation, sewers, and water transportation. In some cities they also include elementary and secondary education, higher education, and hospitals.

Environmental factors fall into four broad categories: a city's population and population density, its concentration of disadvantaged residents, its relationship with its suburbs, and the composition of a its property. We explain which factors in each category have a statistically significant effect on the cost of each type of city service, which means that their observed impact on service costs is very unlikely to have arisen by chance.

The cost of city services varies across cities because input prices and environmental factors vary across cities. For a particular environmental factor, say, poverty, one might want to know how much more a city with a relatively high poverty rate must pay for, say, police services than a city with an average (or mean) poverty rate. The most straightforward answer to this type of question is to compare police costs for a city with a poverty rate one standard deviation above the average and for a city with an average poverty rate. A standard deviation is a measure of variation; for a typical variable, a majority of cities will fall within one standard deviation of the mean. Hence a comparison of a city one standard deviation above or below the mean with a city at the mean indicates the impact of a "typical" variation in that cost factor on the cost of services. All costs are expressed in per capita terms.

Input Prices

Public employees are the primary input for general and police services. Not surprisingly, therefore, the cost of these services increases with the cost of labor, as measured by the state manufacturing wage. A 1 percent difference in this private sector wage between two cities leads to a 1.03 percent difference in the cost of general services and a 1.09 percent difference in the cost of police services. As is shown in table 4.1, a city in a state with a private wage rate one standard deviation above the 1982 mean faces costs for general and police services about 10 percent above those of a city with average wages.

Both public employees and fire equipment are key inputs into the provision of fire protection. In the private sector, product prices reflect both wage rates and the prices of materials and intermediate goods. A metropolitan consumer price index minus taxes and housing, which is external to a city's actions, therefore approximates the wage and equipment prices that a city faces in providing fire services. This consumer price index has a strong impact on fire costs.[1] The magnitude of this impact is similar to that of wages on the cost of other services; a city with a consumer price index one standard deviation above the mean must pay fire protection costs about 12 percent above a city at the mean.

Population and Population Density

General and police services exhibit diseconomies to population scale; the larger a city's population, the more difficult it is to organize and coordinate these services. These diseconomies are much stronger for police services than for general services. A 10 percent difference in population between two cities leads to a 1.4 percent difference in the per capita cost of general services and to a 2.1 percent difference in the per capita cost of police services. Suppose city A and city B have the same characteristics, except that city A has a population equal to the 86-city mean and city B has

---

1. The well-known consumer price index is not available for central cities. Our measure of consumer prices is based on city-specific budgets for a moderate-income family that were estimated by the Bureau of Labor Statistics through 1981. (See U.S. Department of Labor, 1982.) We obtain a consumer price index by restating these budgets, minus taxes and housing, in index form.

Table 4.1
Impact of Input Prices and Environmental
Factors on Public Service Costs

Cost Factor	Marginal Impact[a]	Impact Relative to Average	
		Plus One Standard Deviation	Minus One Standard Deviation
General Service Costs			
Wage rate[b]	1.034	1.103	0.906
Population[b]	0.136	1.137	0.880
Population density[c]	(b)	0.931	1.111
Old housing	0.006	1.112	0.899
Share of metropolitan population	-0.005	0.904	1.107
Employment per capita[b]	0.292	1.102	0.908
Police Costs			
Wage rate[b]	1.090	1.109	0.902
Population[b]	0.207	1.214	0.824
Single-family houses	-0.007	0.874	1.144
Poverty	0.055	1.364	0.733
Share of metropolitan population	-0.006	0.872	1.147
Employment per capita[b]	0.392	1.139	0.878
Government employment[d]	0.022	1.006	0.994
Rental housing[e]	0.096	1.102	0.924
Fire Costs			
Consumer prices[b]	3.397	1.119	0.893
Old housing	0.007	1.134	0.882
Poverty	0.042	1.270	0.787
Employment per capita[b]	0.399	1.141	0.876
Rental housing[e]	0.131	1.141	0.898
Trade property[e]	0.177	1.144	0.907
Service property[e]	-0.205	0.770	1.188
Industrial property[e]	-0.195	0.888	1.112

[a]The marginal impact indicates the percentage impact on costs of a one unit difference in the variable.

[b]Variable is expressed as a logarithm; the marginal impact is the percentage impact of a 1 percent difference in the variable.

[c]Variable is in quadratic form; marginal impact of density is -0.310^{-4}, and coefficient of density squared is $0.1 \cdot 10^{-8}$.

[d]Variable is defined relative to private employment.

[e]Variable is defined relative to owner-occupied housing.

a population one standard deviation above this mean. Then according to these estimates, city B would face per capita costs for general services that were 13.7 percent above the costs of city A and per capita costs for police services that were 21.4 percent above the costs in city A. Fire services exhibit neither diseconomies nor economies to population scale.[2]

The cost of general services, but not of police and fire, is also influenced by population density; a relatively high or a relatively low population density raises a city's costs. Cities with low densities face high transportation and coordination costs, whereas cities with high densities face severe congestion. The minimum cost is at a density of about 15,800 people per square mile, well above the 1982 average of 5,468 people and well below the 1982 maximum of 23,550 people, which is found in New York City. The cost at a density of 15,800 is about 11 percent below the cost at the average density and about 6 percent below the cost at the maximum density. All else equal, therefore, both New York with its relatively high density and cities with very low densities, such as New Orleans (2,870 people per square mile) or Nashville (950), face relatively high costs for general services.

Disadvantaged Residents and Old Housing

A concentration of disadvantaged residents affects the cost of all three types of city service, but the nature of this link varies from one type to another.

The most direct measure of disadvantage is the poverty rate. Poor people are more likely than other people to be victims of crime, and some people in impoverished circumstances resort to crime. Not surprisingly, therefore, cities with more poverty face higher costs for achieving a given level of crime protection.[3] Indeed, table 4.1 reveals that variation in poverty has a larger impact on variation in police costs than does any other environmental factor. A city with a poverty rate 1 percentage point higher than another city's will have police costs that are 5.5 percent higher. Furthermore, a city with a poverty rate one standard deviation above the 1982 mean must pay 36.4 percent more for police services than a city with average

---

2. Strictly speaking, we find small economies to population scale, also known as "publicness," for fire services, but our result is not statistically significant. Some other studies have found a high degree of publicness in fire protection. See, for example, Brueckner 1981.

3. For a detailed discussion of the links between poverty and both criminal victimization and the commission of crimes, see Estrich 1984. Craig 1987 also examines the link between poverty and the cost of police services, and Hamilton 1983 explores the general relationship between income and public service costs.

poverty. This factor hits Newark particularly hard because its estimated 1982 poverty rate is more than twice as high as the 86-city average.

Some general services, such as health and housing, are provided to disadvantaged residents, so cities with more disadvantaged residents must spend more than other cities to provide the same level of these services. Although the poverty rate does not have a statistically significant effect on the cost of general services, a related measure does, namely the extent of housing more than twenty years old. Old housing tends to be deteriorated, so this measure approximates the share of a city's population living in deteriorated housing. In addition, the extent of old housing is an indication of the age of a city's infrastructure. Other general services, such as street and sewer maintenance, are directly linked to a city's infrastructure, and the older the infrastructure, the more expensive it is to use and to maintain.[4] Thus a 10 percentage point difference between two cities in the extent of old housing leads to a 6 percent difference in the cost of general services. Cities with a concentration of old housing that is one standard deviation above the 1982 mean face costs 11 percent above those of cities with an average concentration.

Both the extent of old housing and the poverty rate affect the cost of fire services. In general, poor people can afford only low-quality housing units. Old and other low-quality housing units are more likely than others to have defective or combustible materials and are therefore more expensive than other units to protect from fire. Furthermore, extensive old housing, and hence an old infrastructure, may be associated with low water pressure, narrow streets, or other problems that increase the difficulty of fighting fires. The effect of old housing is larger for fire than for general services. A 10 percentage point difference between two cities in the share of old housing leads to a 6.9 percent difference in the cost of fire protection. A city with old housing one standard deviation above the 1982 mean faces fire costs that are 13 percent above a city at the mean. The effect of poverty is smaller for fire than for police services. A 1 percentage point difference between two cities in the poverty rate leads to a 4 percent difference in fire costs. A city with poverty one standard deviation above the 1982 mean faces fire costs 27 percent above a city at the mean.

---

4. Of course, the capital cost of old infrastructure may be relatively low because the bonds that financed it may be paid off. We focus exclusively on operating spending.

Relations with Suburbs

City population relative to metropolitan population and city employment per capita both measure a city's relationship with its suburbs and both affect the cost of public services.

Consider first a city's share of metropolitan population. In 1982 this share varied from 3.5 percent in Everett, Washington, to 90.7 percent in El Paso, Texas. All else equal, a central city with a small population relative to its suburbs must spend more per capita on crime protection, traffic control, parking, parks, and other general services to keep up with the flow of people into and through the central city. A 10 percentage point difference between two cities in this share leads to a 4.6 percent higher cost for general services and to a 6.2 percent higher cost for police services in the city with the smaller share. Subtracting one standard deviation from the mean share raises the cost of general services by 10.7 percent and of police services by 14.7 percent. A city's share of metropolitan population does not affect its cost for fire services.

In addition, the greater the employment in the city, when city population is controlled for, the greater the burden of commuters on general and police services and the greater the number of buildings that must be protected from fire. All else equal, cities with many commuters, such as Salt Lake City with 0.92 private jobs per capita, have higher costs than those with few commuters, such as Ontario, California, with 0.21 private jobs per capita. A 10 percent difference between two cities in private employment per capita leads to a 2.9 percent higher cost for general services and to a 3.9 percent higher cost for both police and fire services in the city with the higher employment. A city with private employment per capita one standard deviation above the mean must pay about 10 percent more for general services and over 14 percent more for police and fire services than a city with an average value for this variable. In addition, police costs increase slightly with government employment per capita; a city with government employment per capita one standard deviation above the 1982 sample mean faces police costs 0.6 percent above the cost for cities at this mean.

Property Composition

The cost of police and fire services, but not of general services, also depends on the type of property in a city. Multifamily buildings are more expensive to protect from crime than are single-family houses, and rental property is more expensive to protect from both crime and fire than is owner-occupied property. Note that these two environmental factors are related but not identical; some single-family houses are rented and some owner-occupied units, such as condominiums, are in multifamily buildings.

A 10 percentage point difference between two cities in the share of housing units in single-family houses leads to a 7.5 percent difference in the cost of police services. Cities with shares one standard deviation below the 1982 mean face costs that are 14.4 percent above cities at the mean. Similarly, a 10 percentage point difference in the ratio of the value of rental to owner-occupied housing leads to a 10 percent difference in the cost of police services and to a 13 percent difference in the cost of fire services. Cities with ratios one standard deviation above the 1982 mean face police costs about 10 percent above and fire costs about 14 percent above cities at the mean.

Finally, the composition of nonresidential property has a significant impact on fire protection costs. Relative to owner-occupied housing, property used for wholesale and retail trade is expensive to protect from fire, and property used for services (such as finance, insurance and real estate) or for manufacturing is inexpensive to protect from fire. Variation in the shares of trade and service property (which are expressed relative to the share of owner-occupied property) account for a relatively large share of the variation in fire costs across cities. Cities with a share of trade property one standard deviation above the 1982 mean face fire costs that are about 14 percent above those of a city at the mean, and cities with shares of service property that are one standard deviation below the 1982 mean face costs almost 19 percent above those of a city at the mean. The effect of manufacturing property is somewhat weaker; cities one standard deviation above the mean face costs 11 percent higher than those of a city at the mean.

Cost Indexes for General, Police, and Fire Services

In this section we combine the effects of input and environmental factors into a service cost index. The first step in this process is illustrated in table 4.2, which shows how 1982 police costs deviate from the 1982 sample average in 10 cities.[5] Albuquerque faces police costs that are 51.8 percent below those in a city with 1982 average characteristics, largely because it has a lower-than-average poverty rate (column 4) and a higher-than-average share of metropolitan population (column 5). In other words, Albuquerque's police costs equal police costs in a city with an average value for every cost

---

5. An algebraic description of our cost indexes is provided in the appendix to this chapter.

Table 4.2
Calculating a Cost Index for Police Services, 1982
(Illustrative Cities)

	(1) Private Wage Rate	(2) Population	(3) Single-Family Houses	(4) Poverty Rate	(5) Share of Metropolitan Population	(6) Private Employment per Capita
Albuquerque, NM	3.3	2.3	- 7.3	-23.3	-26.6	-9.8
Cleveland, OH	14.0	11.9	6.5	60.1	1.6	8.7
Houston, TX	- 0.6	44.3	0.7	-21.8	-16.8	7.6
Kansas City, MO	1.9	7.2	- 7.9	-18.0	- 9.8	9.7
Miami, FL	-16.3	6.2	11.6	87.3	4.4	-0.8
Newark, NJ	5.5	- 0.2	38.1	261.4	9.7	-4.8
New Orleans, LA	- 9.2	13.0	0.7	101.6	- 7.5	-6.5
Richmond, VA	-10.2	- 7.4	- 3.0	20.9	- 1.1	15.9
Salt Lake City, UT	3.3	-12.6	0.6	-12.8	9.5	30.3
Tampa, FL	-16.3	- 2.3	- 9.3	19.1	9.9	12.0
1982 vs. 1972	0.7	0.5	2.2	38.7	1.3	7.3

	(7) Government Employment Per Capita	(8) Percent of Housing for Rent	(9) Total	(10) City with Average Traits	(11) Average City in 1982	(12) Average City in 1972
				Index Relative to:		
Albuquerque, NM	1.2	-4.3	**-51.8**	48.2	40.4	64.1
Cleveland, OH	-1.2	-4.2	**127.4**	227.4	190.5	302.5
Houston, TX	-1.4	-1.2	**- 1.4**	98.6	82.6	131.2
Kansas City, MO	-0.2	-1.2	**-19.5**	80.5	67.4	107.1
Miami, FL	-0.8	11.3	**112.4**	212.4	178.0	282.6
Newark, NJ	-1.0	-0.8	**438.4**	538.4	451.2	716.4
New Orleans, LA	0.6	92.9	**249.7**	349.7	293.1	465.3
Richmond, VA	2.2	-1.3	**12.6**	112.6	94.4	149.9
Salt Lake City, UT	-0.5	-2.0	**10.2**	110.2	92.4	146.7
Tampa, FL	-0.9	-0.9	**6.8**	106.8	89.5	142.1
1982 vs. 1972	-2.8	-0.6	**50.7**	150.7	158.8	N.A.

factor multiplied by (1 - 0.518) = 0.482. This number, expressed in percentage form, appears in column 10. Cleveland, in contrast, faces police costs that are 127.4 percent above a city with an average environment; that is, its police costs equal the costs in a city with an average environment multiplied by (1 + 1.274) = 2.274. These high costs primarily reflect Cleveland's high poverty rate, although its relatively high wages, population, and per capita employment also contribute. Finally, Salt Lake City faces police costs that are only 10.2 percent above those in a city with an average environment. The negative impact on police costs of its relatively low population and poverty rate are offset by its relatively small share of metropolitan population and its relatively high employment per capita.

Two further steps are necessary to define a cost index. First, the most natural base for an index is the average cost in the 86-city sample; however, average cost in the sample is not equal to the cost in a city with an average environment, that is, with an average value for every cost factor. In fact, the average police cost is 19.3 percent higher than police cost for a city with average cost factors. To switch to the more natural base, therefore, the entries in column 11 equal the entries in column 10 divided by 1.193. Albuquerque's police cost, for example, is 40.4 percent of the cost for the average city in 1982.

Second, input and environmental cost factors change over time. To reflect changes in these factors between 1972 and 1982, cost indexes can be expressed in a 1972 base. As is shown in the last row of table 4.2, changes in the average values of the cost factors boosted police costs by 50.7 percent between 1972 and 1982, which corresponds to a growth rate of 4.2 percent per year, largely because of increases in the poverty rate and in private employment per capita in central cities. Note that this is a real cost increase, that is, it is an increase over and above inflation. The impact of the average change in every cost factor slightly understates the increase in police cost in the average city; in fact, average police cost was 58.8 percent greater in 1982 than in 1972.[6] A cost index with a 1972 base is simply the entry in column 11 adjusted for this increase in average police cost. As is shown in column 12, the index with a 1972 base is (40)(1.588) = 64 in Albuquerque, (191)(1.588) = 303 in Cleveland, and (96)(1.588) = 147 in Salt Lake City.

From this point onward, all cost indexes express real per capita costs

---

6. Because of the algebraic form we employ, the average cost index for major central cities is not the same as the cost index in a city with average values for every cost factor. See the appendix to this chapter.

relative to a 1972 base. These indexes can be interpreted as the relative cost of public serices per unit of service quality, given a standardized set of service responsibilities.

Table 4.3 describes the variation in general, police, and fire costs across the sample cities in 1982. This table also presents cost indexes for 10 selected cities. For general services the 1982 cost indexes range from 69.6 to 163.4, with an average of 112 and a standard deviation of 22. The cost of these services was over twice as high in the city with the harshest environment as in the one with the most favorable environment, but the standard deviation, which indicates how close to the average most cities are likely to be, is only about 20 percent of the average.

The variation across cities is much greater for the cost of police services than for general services. The cost of police services was over twenty times as high in the city with the harshest environment as in the one with the most favorable environment, and the standard deviation is about 70 percent of the average. The variation in fire costs falls between the cost variation for the other two services. The highest-cost city had to pay almost four times as much as the lowest-cost city for the same fire services, and the standard deviation was more than 25 percent of the mean.

Table 4.3
Indexes of Public Service Costs and Standardized Expenditure Need, 1982
(Illustrative Cities)

	Cost Index for:			Index of Standardized Expenditure Need
	General Services	Police Services	Fire Services	
86 Cities				
Average	112.0	158.8	133.4	115.0
Standard deviation	22.0	110.9	51.7	29.5
Maximum	163.4	709.9	343.9	214.5
Minimum	69.6	35.0	43.1	58.3
Selected Cities				
Albuquerque, NM	76.9	63.6	83.2	71.0
Cleveland. OH	150.8	299.8	217.8	172.0
Houston, TX	118.3	130.0	95.4	111.5
Kansas City, MO	144.4	106.1	99.2	126.2
Miami, FL	75.2	280.1	193.9	114.0
Newark, NJ	102.1	709.9	343.9	214.5
New Orleans, LA	113.4	461.2	110.1	162.2
Richmond, VA	112.3	148.5	187.6	118.3
Salt Lake City, UT	163.4	145.4	141.2	149.4
Tampa, FL	111.5	140.8	137.9	112.2

The cost indexes for specific cities illustrate the range of possible cost patterns both across and within cities. Some cities, such as Albuquerque, have relatively low costs for all three services. Others, such as Cleveland, have relatively high costs for all three services. Relative costs for the three services need not be the same, however. Miami has relatively low costs for general services and relatively high costs for police and fire; New Orleans has average costs for general services, relatively high costs for police, and relatively low costs for fire; Salt Lake City has relatively high costs for general services and about average costs for police and fire; and Richmond, Virginia, has average costs for general and police services, but relatively high costs for fire.

The explanation for this variation lies in the cost factors discussed earlier. As was shown in table 4.2, Albuquerque has relatively low police costs because its poverty rate is somewhat below average and its share of metropolitan population is relatively large, and Cleveland has relatively high police costs primarily because of its high concentration of poverty. High poverty is also the main cause of high fire costs in Cleveland, high police costs in New Orleans, and high police and fire costs in Newark and Miami. Population density does not affect police and fire costs, but high or low densities boost the cost of general services. Miami has relatively low general service costs despite its high other costs because it has relatively low wages and because its population density, about 12,300, is near the lowest-cost density. Salt Lake City and Richmond have relatively high general service costs because their population densities, below 2,500, are extremely low. Finally, New Orleans has low fire costs despite its high poverty because it has a high value of service and manufacturing property (relative to owner-occupied housing), which are relatively inexpensive to protect from fire.

Expenditure Need with Uniform Service Responsibilities

We define *standardized expenditure need* as the amount a city must spend to provide a standardized service quality with a standardized package of service responsibilities. Because it is calculated with service quality and service responsibility standardized at the sample average, this expenditure need depends solely on costs. By definition, cities with higher per capita costs must spend more to obtain the same quality services. Because costs vary by broad type of service, a separate standardized expenditure need must be calculated for general, police, and fire services. For each service a city's standardized need is the average spending on that service multiplied by that city's cost index.[7] Overall standardized expenditure need is the sum across services of standardized needs and is therefore simply a weighted average of the needs for the three types of service. General service costs have the strongest effect on overall need because general services consume over one-half of the average city's budget. This standardized expenditure need is expressed in index form, with the 1972 average set equal to 100.

Standardized expenditure need in 1982 is presented in the last column of table 4.3. The average value for this expenditure need index is 115, which indicates that the average city needed to spend 15 percent more in 1982, over and above inflation, to achieve the 1972 average service quality. Standardized expenditure need varies widely across cities. The standard deviation in need is about 25 percent of the mean, and the highest-cost city would have to spend over three times as much as the lowest-cost city to achieve the same service quality. By definition, cities with relatively high costs for all types of service, such as Cleveland, have relatively high standardized need, and those with relatively low costs for all services, including Albuquerque, have relatively low standardized need. Salt Lake City has relatively high standardized need despite average police and fire costs because of its high general service costs and the high weight these costs receive in calculating expenditure need. Similarly, Miami has an average standardized need despite its high police and fire costs because of its low general service costs.

Public Service Costs and Standardized Expenditure Need by Type of City

Table 4.4 presents public service cost and standardized expenditure need indexes in 1982 for cities in various population, income, and employment classes. Several patterns emerge from this table.

First, there is a strong relationship between costs and city size for all three types of service: per capita costs rise with population. This link is particularly strong for police services; costs for the largest cities are two and one-half times greater than those for the smallest cities. Consequently, standardized expenditure need per capita also increases with population. In the case of general and police services, the principal reason for this link is

---

7. To be precise, a city's standardized expenditure need for a given service equals the average responsibility index for that service across all cities multiplied by the city's cost index for that service. See the appendix to this chapter.

Table 4.4
Public Service Costs and Standardized Expenditure Need, 1982
(86 Cities)

	Number of Cities	General Service Costs	Police Service Costs	Fire Service Costs	Standardized Expenditure Need
All cities	86	112.0	158.8	133.4	115.0
City population in thousands					
Less than 100	11	103.1	108.5	123.3	99.9
100-250	20	106.3	136.0	133.0	107.4
250-500	32	114.5	158.8	139.9	117.3
500-1,000	17	114.2	176.1	125.8	118.7
Greater than 1,000	6	128.3	277.9	139.5	146.0
Resident income per capita					
Quintile 1	17	110.7	259.9	198.7	135.9
Quintile 2	17	105.6	163.0	130.0	110.9
Quintile 3	17	120.2	155.4	128.9	119.8
Quintile 4	17	112.6	98.9	105.6	103.5
Quintile 5	18	111.2	119.1	105.4	105.6
City economic health[a]					
Quintile 1	17	94.5	120.9	116.6	95.3
Quintile 2	17	100.2	182.0	136.4	110.8
Quintile 3	17	114.1	163.3	125.3	116.5
Quintile 4	17	126.1	139.2	134.0	121.8
Quintile 5	18	124.5	187.0	153.5	130.0

Note: Each entry is the average index for the indicated category of city. The average index for all cities is set equal to 100.0 in 1972.
[a]City economic health is private employment in the city divided by city population.

that population itself is a cost factor; a larger population makes it more difficult to provide and coordinate these services. But the association between costs and population is stronger than the effect of population as a cost factor alone, and population is not a cost factor for fire services. Apparently other cost factors, such as wage rates and old housing, are correlated with population.

A strong association also exists between per capita income and the costs of police and fire services; these costs decrease as income increases. Remember that per capita income is a measure of resident economic health.

Thus cities with residents in the poorest economic health must pay the most to obtain a given quality of police and fire services. This result reflects the strong impact on costs of the concentration of disadvantaged citizens in a city. On the other hand, there is no apparent link between income and the cost of general services. The cost factors for general services, which do not include the poverty rate, do not appear to be correlated with income. When these links are averaged into standardized expenditure need, a weak association between income and need remains, with by far the highest need in the lowest income quintile.

Finally, the costs of all types of service tend to increase with city economic health, as measured by per capita employment. This relationship is not smooth, however; police and fire costs in the second employment quintile are almost as high as costs in the highest quintile. Nevertheless, standardized expenditure need increases steadily with employment. The link reflects the role of per capita employment as a cost variable. A large flow of commuters into a city enhances its ability to export tax burdens and therefore raises its revenue-raising capacity, but this flow also boosts the cost of all city services and raises a city's standardized need. In fiscal terms, the presence of commuters is a mixed blessing.

Changes in Public Service Costs and Standardized Expenditure Need, 1972-1982

The average 1982 cost indexes for general, police, and fire services are all above 100. Because these indexes use 1972 as a base, this result means that the costs of general, police, and fire services all rose in real terms between 1972 and 1982. The average percentage increase in costs was 12 percent for general services, 59 percent for police, and 33 percent for fire. On average, standardized expenditure need increased by 15 percent.

These cost increases reflect changes in average real input prices and in the average values of environmental cost factors. The primary causes of the increase in the cost of general services were increases in old housing, which boosted costs by 4 percent, and increases in per capita employment and decreases in density, which both boosted costs by about 2 percent. Large increases in city poverty rates between 1972 and 1982 contributed the most to the increase in police costs. Increases in employment per capita made a smaller but still substantial contribution. Finally, the increase in the cost of fire services was due primarily to increases in poverty and in per capita employment, with a small contribution from the increase in old housing.

As is shown in table 4.5, changes in costs and standardized need are not closely linked to city size. The smallest cities experienced the smallest percentage increase in all costs, and the largest cities faced the largest police cost increases, but otherwise no pattern is discernible.

For general services cost increases were greatest for the cities with the highest income growth. Thus an increase in per capita income adds to fiscal capacity but also is associated with an increase in general service costs. The opposite is true for police and fire costs; among cities with below-average income in 1971, the lower the growth in income, the higher the growth in the cost of these services.

Employment growth and income growth have similar links to changes in costs, at least for general and police services. Employment growth tends to raise the cost of general services and to lower the cost of police services. Table 4.5 reveals no clear link between employment growth and changes in fire costs.

Finally, structural change in a city's economy, which was defined in chapter 2 to be a shift from manufacturing to services, appears to have no connection with changes in a city's costs or in its standardized need. This finding reflects the role of economic structure as a cost factor. As was shown earlier, the structure of a city's economy is not a significant cost factor for general or police services. In the case of fire services, structural change directly influences two cost factors, namely the shares of property devoted to services and to manufacturing. Both types of property are relatively inexpensive to protect from fire, however, so a shift from one to the other has virtually no effect on the cost of fire protection. These results indicate that cities need not worry that structural change, defined as a shift from manufacturing to services, will significantly raise their costs for providing public services.

Conclusions

This analysis illuminates the links between one crucial aspect of city's fiscal health, namely its standardized expenditure need, and both its economic health and the economic health of its residents.

The greater the economic health of a city, as measured by its per capita employment, the greater its costs for providing public services, and the greater its standardized expenditure need. Between 1972 and 1982 increases in per capita employment were associated with increases in the cost of general services and in this expenditure need. Thus, although greater

Table 4.5
Changes in Public Service Costs and Standardized Expenditure Need, 1972-1982
(86 Cities)

	of Cities	General Service Number (%)	Police Service Costs (%)	Fire Service Costs (%)	Standardized Expenditure Costs (%)
All cities	86	13.4	52.4	33.9	15.6
City population in thousands					
Less than 100	11	9.0	40.5	22.6	8.3
100-250	20	17.1	55.7	44.6	18.9
250-500	32	15.1	53.7	34.7	17.2
500-1,000	17	12.3	49.7	29.7	14.5
Greater than 1,000	6	3.5	63.6	26.6	12.3
Below-average income, 1971					
Low growth	21	6.1	72.3	44.4	18.9
Medium growth	12	14.1	57.3	42.1	16.4
High growth	10	17.1	47.1	21.9	16.2
Above-average income, 1971					
Low growth	8	5.3	42.1	25.0	8.4
Medium growth	17	15.7	39.7	30.6	12.8
High growth	18	20.8	45.2	29.8	16.7
Below-average economic health, 1972					
Low growth	12	4.7	61.1	25.2	13.4
Medium growth	12	13.1	46.0	36.6	13.3
High growth	20	24.1	51.4	39.8	20.7
Above-average economic health, 1972					
Low growth	17	5.7	56.9	33.7	13.4
Medium growth	17	11.7	50.7	32.9	14.2
High growth	8	20.2	44.9	30.5	17.2
Low employment growth					
Low structural change	5	7.5	49.2	21.7	14.2
Medium structural change	7	2.8	65.4	30.0	15.5
High structural change	17	5.6	58.6	32.8	12.3
Medium employment growth					
Low structural change	13	13.4	48.2	35.9	14.4
Medium structural change	8	10.6	52.0	32.1	13.6
High structural change	8	12.2	46.4	34.3	13.1
High employment growth					
Low structural change	11	24.1	54.8	38.5	21.5
Medium structural change	14	20.9	47.0	33.2	17.3
High structural change	3	28.5	42.0	50.9	24.0

Note: City categories for income change, economic health change, and structural change are defined in tables 3.4, 2.2, and 2.5 respectively. Each entry is an average change for the indicated category of city.

economic health raises a city's potential revenue-raising capacity, it also raises its standardized expenditure need. The overall impact of a city's economic health on its potential fiscal health depends on the balance between these two effects, which is considered in chapter 5.

The higher the economic health of a city's residents, on the other hand, the lower the costs of providing city services, particularly police and fire services, and therefore the lower the city's standardized expenditure need. Greater resident economic health therefore both boosts revenue-raising capacity and lowers standardized expenditure need. Chapter 5 examines the power of this combined effect. Between 1972 and 1982 growth in resident income was associated with lower police and fire costs but higher general service costs. Hence there is no clear link between changes in resident income and changes in standardized need.

Service costs, particularly police costs, are also linked to city size. Larger cities face higher per capita costs and therefore have higher standardized expenditure need. Nevertheless, larger cities did not experience larger increases between 1972 and 1982 in general and fire service costs or in standardized need.

Finally, structural change in a city's economy, namely a shift from manufacturing to service employment, does not lead to any significant changes in its service costs or its standardized expenditure need.

Appendix: Calculating Indexes of Public Service Costs and Standardized Expenditure Need

The city spending model presented in the appendix to chapter 10 yields three city cost functions (for general, police, and fire services) of the following form:

$$(A10.1) \qquad C_j = (I_j)^c \cdot (X_{1j})^{a_1} \cdot (X_{2j})^{a_2} \cdots (X_{Nj})^{a_N},$$

where C_j is the cost per unit of public service quality in city j, I_j is a input cost index in city j, X_{ij} is the value of the ith environmental cost factor in city j, and the c and the a_i's are estimated parameters. Note that I_j is in real terms: that is, it has been deflated for the average national growth in the implicit GNP deflator for state and local purchases, and that the list of X's and the values of the parameters are different for general, police, and fire services.

As is explained in the appendix to chapter 10, the values of I_j and the X_{ij}'s are available for every major central city in four years (1967, 1972, 1977, and 1982), and the parameters are estimated with multiple regression analysis. As a result we can calculate C_j for every city for general, police and fire services in four years.

We use the state manufacturing wage rate to measure the cost of inputs for general and police services, and we use a consumer price index (excluding taxes and housing) to measure the cost of inputs for fire services. The environmental cost variables included for each service are listed in table 4.1. Our method for estimating the parameters is presented in the appendix to chapter 10.

To translate the values of C_j into index form, we calculate the value of C_j in the average city in 1972, divide C_j in each city in each year by this average value, and multiply the result by 100. This procedure, which is carried out separately for the three types of service, ensures that the average cost index equals 100 for each service in 1972. Suppose, for example, that city A has a police cost index of 105 in 1972; this index indicates that city A's police costs were 5 percent higher than those of the average city in 1972. Now suppose that city A's police cost index is 121 in 1982; then city A experienced a 15 percent $[(121-105)/105 = 0.15]$ real increase in its police costs between 1972 and 1982, and its 1982 real costs were 21 percent above those of the average city in 1972.

Our cost indexes for all major central cities are presented in table A4.1. This table includes cost indexes for all three service types in 1972 and 1982.

Standardized expenditure need is a weighted average of the cost indexes for general, police, and fire services, which can be labeled CG_j, CP_j, and CF_j for city j. The weights are the national average service responsibility indexes for each of these services in 1972 (see the appendix to chapter 8), namely \$117.55 for general services, \$21.18 for police services, and \$12.22 for fire services. Thus standardized expenditure need in dollars for city j, SN_j, is:

(A10.2) $SN_j = (117.55)(CG_j) + (21.18)(CP_j) + (12.22)(CF_j)$.

To express standardized expenditure need in index form, we divide SN_j in every city in every year by the value of SN_j in the average city in 1972 and multiply the result by 100. Thus equation (A10.2) and the cost indexes in table A4.1 can be used to calculate a standardized expenditure need index, SNI_j, for each city in 1972 and 1982.

Table A4.1
Indexes of Public Service Costs, 1972 and 1982
(86 Cities)

	1972			1982		
	General	Police	Fire	General	Police	Fire
Akron, OH	116.61	71.19	95.71	130.70	109.75	143.08
Albany, NY	117.01	129.82	122.04	129.32	183.28	156.66
Albuquerque, NM	71.11	49.22	62.30	76.94	63.56	83.23
Anaheim, CA	85.89	64.11	54.38	109.12	93.58	79.93
Atlanta, GA	117.45	175.02	130.33	130.46	386.87	224.38
Austin, TX	58.46	53.41	65.67	79.83	98.31	98.58
Baltimore, MD	98.66	128.49	147.69	108.24	223.97	185.88
Birmingham, AL	97.90	105.70	122.17	117.98	165.17	162.75
Boston, MA	120.74	227.64	138.41	117.93	327.79	165.25
Boulder, CO	68.11	69.44	59.04	92.32	114.67	82.18
Buffalo, NY	112.56	146.58	148.62	116.65	276.12	224.77
Charlotte, NC	72.21	57.14	84.28	97.50	78.44	96.05
Chicago, IL	125.06	210.24	100.31	121.76	341.68	161.29
Cincinnati, OH	132.81	156.09	124.96	144.86	243.79	180.78
Cleveland, OH	133.55	176.96	139.71	150.84	299.83	217.82
Clifton, NJ	93.89	43.99	82.16	113.51	51.36	86.50
Columbus, OH	113.20	95.82	83.45	126.51	152.53	118.86
Dallas, TX	112.44	96.58	72.43	127.80	144.14	94.88
Dayton, OH	132.10	116.35	120.33	155.35	215.76	226.87
Denver, CO	110.88	96.12	98.63	133.42	139.84	116.38
Detroit, MI	148.43	163.11	111.06	154.95	287.66	157.67
El Paso, TX	60.61	57.82	66.95	78.02	102.10	114.77
Everett, WA	121.37	67.14	78.43	126.27	99.51	84.26
Ft. Lauderdale, FL	65.47	63.92	76.92	88.36	118.81	134.40
Fort Worth, TX	117.36	71.86	79.44	143.61	110.95	91.17
Garden Grove, CA	53.81	41.80	38.07	80.95	59.02	72.45
Greensboro, NC	83.19	50.91	72.78	97.23	74.01	95.23
Hartford, CT	114.87	217.30	118.55	114.50	382.44	246.01
High Point, NC	93.55	54.81	89.60	99.92	73.43	103.98
Hollywood, FL	55.19	39.99	51.67	74.24	50.57	69.83
Honolulu, HI	108.01	90.59	123.95	114.47	124.19	156.49
Houston, TX	96.79	79.98	76.81	118.28	130.03	95.42
Indianapolis, IN	121.39	66.77	76.20	127.35	89.49	99.77
Jacksonville, FL	79.24	55.72	74.77	86.71	75.48	95.02
Kansas City, MO	140.13	85.65	101.68	144.35	106.10	99.21
Long Beach, CA	106.18	123.78	89.38	118.40	149.68	120.47
Los Angeles, CA	131.23	148.96	96.43	141.80	230.61	135.34
Louisville, KY	110.62	102.29	120.10	125.34	159.76	197.01
Memphis, TN	76.99	76.23	92.27	90.23	127.10	154.23
Miami, FL	74.79	166.94	168.58	75.22	280.07	193.88

Table A4.1 (Cont.)

| | 1972 | | | 1982 | | |
	General	Police	Fire	General	Police	Fire
Milwaukee, WI	105.72	92.57	78.62	121.54	131.84	118.14
Minneapolis, MN	125.73	104.92	111.58	142.77	153.23	126.70
Nashville-Davidson, TN	93.85	56.91	73.12	107.47	77.50	87.55
Newark, NJ	103.95	272.98	208.43	102.12	709.93	343.89
New Orleans, LA	101.87	258.94	121.64	113.36	461.18	110.15
New York, NY	140.61	297.13	180.50	123.66	474.37	112.88
Norfolk, VA	74.80	76.24	93.36	90.22	119.19	133.33
Oakland, CA	119.29	141.52	139.99	118.68	189.33	187.23
Ogden, UT	94.50	56.30	71.63	112.50	77.31	95.68
Oklahoma City, OK	99.58	57.28	78.77	115.98	77.11	94.14
Omaha, NB	88.13	52.08	77.92	109.70	74.74	104.40
Ontario, CA	86.51	61.88	66.43	90.31	55.26	59.99
Passaic, NJ	82.24	116.00	157.26	80.84	236.24	222.43
Paterson, NJ	78.21	119.19	149.69	84.59	288.30	234.50
Pawtucket, RI	83.15	75.91	111.09	78.81	73.28	118.37
Philadelphia, PA	108.34	122.49	134.53	109.59	203.13	174.60
Phoenix, AZ	91.06	60.89	60.78	106.66	84.59	67.97
Pittsburgh, PA	123.80	125.20	131.16	141.96	172.13	156.93
Portland, OR	129.01	83.39	117.18	144.30	114.40	154.74
Portsmouth, VA	72.76	63.07	84.28	79.60	91.93	110.27
Providence, RI	100.32	137.71	168.05	98.72	192.76	207.10
Richmond, VA	92.36	86.25	121.32	112.26	148.53	187.65
Riverside, CA	89.47	51.23	57.12	109.34	75.17	75.24
Rochester, NY	130.30	113.61	142.95	130.87	203.47	156.23
Sacramento, CA	104.48	88.65	85.68	120.74	122.97	124.97
St. Louis, MO	123.25	175.93	150.75	140.36	285.91	187.64
St. Paul, MN	122.45	80.06	89.16	135.62	108.34	95.85
St. Petersburg, FL	72.22	60.03	70.53	83.16	76.22	81.33
Salt Lake City, UT	134.29	94.88	101.41	163.39	145.35	141.19
San Antonio, TX	71.15	73.10	79.67	94.18	131.47	117.27
San Bernardino, CA	102.49	79.03	87.43	120.75	110.19	120.64
San Diego, CA	100.67	71.17	70.26	114.37	101.28	76.56
San Francisco, CA	121.84	162.39	149.01	116.48	178.55	177.95
San Jose, CA	78.23	48.98	52.34	85.74	60.30	65.66
Santa Ana, CA	85.20	73.64	72.23	93.30	128.90	108.43
Schenectady, NY	119.51	87.82	138.37	112.24	111.03	163.74
Seattle, WA	113.01	77.87	104.27	146.84	113.48	142.10
Tampa, FL	94.77	95.43	108.97	111.51	140.79	137.88
Toledo, OH	113.87	67.00	88.76	116.22	92.37	123.30
Troy, NY	96.04	92.32	126.32	99.02	137.85	159.30
Tucson, AZ	67.27	49.92	61.11	82.94	82.80	94.57
Tulsa, OK	82.66	44.95	68.26	102.98	64.87	96.00
Virginia Beach, VA	57.30	26.25	32.85	69.55	38.03	43.11

Table A4.1 (Cont.)

	1972			1982		
	General	Police	Fire	General	Police	Fire
Warwick, RI	80.27	27.47	65.82	89.64	35.00	83.11
Winston-Salem, NC	90.50	69.78	85.97	108.76	99.80	110.55
Washington, DC	103.05	174.15	117.17	120.13	265.09	157.14
Average	100.00	100.00	100.00	112.00	158.80	133.40

Note: For each type of service, a city's cost index equals its service costs divided by the service costs in the average city in 1972 and multiplied by 100.

5

Standardized Fiscal Health

Economic, social, and demographic factors that are largely outside the control of city officials have a profound impact on a city's potential for raising revenue and on the amount it must spend to obtain a given level of public services. The impact of these factors on a city's ability to deliver services to its residents—that is, on its overall fiscal health—depends on the balance between their effects on the revenue side and on the expenditure side of the city's finances. By bringing together the results from chapter 3 on revenue-raising capacity and those from chapter 4 on expenditure need, we are able to examine this balance and to determine what types of central city face a fiscal squeeze because of recent economic and social trends.

As defined earlier, a city's revenue-raising capacity is the revenue it could raise from three broad-based taxes at a standard tax burden on its residents; and a city's standardized expenditure need is the amount it must spend, given a standardized set of service responsibilities, to provide public services of a standardized quality. These two measures reflect only the economic, social, and demographic factors that constrain a city's finances, not its political or institutional setting. A city's standardized fiscal health is the difference between its revenue-raising capacity and its standardized expenditure need, expressed as a percentage of its capacity. Hence a city's standardized fiscal health summarizes the effect of external economic and social factors on its ability to deliver public services.

A city's actual fiscal health is influenced by institutional factors, such as the assignment of service responsibilities, and by the amount of state intergovernmental aid it receives, as well as by economic and social factors. In part III of this book, we analyze these institutional factors and intergovernmental grants and their effect on the actual fiscal health of cities.

Neither standardized nor actual fiscal health indicates a city's actual budgetary situation. These measures consider aspects of the city's revenue and of its expenditure, but they are detached from its actual decisions about how much to spend or to tax. Instead these measures indicate the severity of the constraints imposed on city finances by economic, social, and demographic factors (and, in the case of actual fiscal health, institutional factors and grants), but they do not reflect the city's response to those constraints. Thus a city with very poor fiscal health—that is, one facing very severe economic or institutional constraints (or both) on its ability to provide services—may make the cuts in service quality or the increases in tax rates that are necessary to balance its budget. Similarly, a city with good fiscal health may manage its finances so poorly that its budget is never balanced. In effect, fiscal health indicates the magnitude of the fiscal challenge facing city officials but does not indicate how well they meet this challenge.

Calculating Standardized Fiscal Health

Standardized fiscal health depends on revenue-raising capacity and on standardized expenditure need, which were explained in chapters 3 and 4. Only two further steps are necessary to calculate an index of standardized fiscal health.

First, revenue-raising capacity is measured in dollars, whereas standardized expenditure need is an index with a value set at 100 for the average city in 1972. To make these measures comparable, we translate standardized need into dollars. This step simply changes the unit of measurement without altering the substance of standardized need. Revenue-raising capacity indicates how much revenue is potentially available to a city at a standard tax burden on its residents. Our approach is to set standardized need so that, on average, cities exactly use up their revenue-raising capacity. This adjustment is carried out for 1972; that is, standardized need is adjusted, by the same proportion in every city, so that the average difference between potential revenue-raising capacity and standardized need is zero in 1972.[1]

This adjustment corresponds to the selection of a constant service quality across cities. As we explained in chapter 4, standardized expenditure need is based on average service responsibilities. In effect, therefore, our procedure is equivalent to determining the quality of public services that could be obtained at the standard tax burden by a central city with 1972 average revenue-raising capacity, 1972 average public service costs, and 1972 average service responsibilities. We define this concept to be the baseline service quality. Remember that revenue-raising capacity is based on own-source revenues and therefore ignores state and federal aid. Thus baseline service quality is the quality of public services that the average city could finance in 1972 from own-source revenues at the standard tax burden on its residents.

---

1. To be precise, the average difference between revenue-raising capacity and expenditure need, expressed as a percentage of capacity, is set equal to zero.

The second step is to express the difference between revenue-raising capacity and standardized expenditure need as a percentage of revenue-raising capacity. The absolute difference between revenue-raising capacity and standardized need depends on the tax burden that is built into the capacity measure. Expressing the difference in percentage form breaks this dependence; the measure is the same whether the tax burden in the capacity measure is set at 3 percent, as it is in chapter 3, or at 10 percent.[2]

The difference between revenue-raising capacity and standardized expenditure need expressed as a percentage of capacity is a summary measure of a city's standardized fiscal health. It reveals the net effect of a city's economic, social, and demographic characteristics on its ability to deliver public services. A positive fiscal health index, which implies that capacity is greater than standardized need, indicates the percentage of its revenue a city would have left over for increases in service quality or for tax cuts after it had provided the 1972 baseline service quality at the standard tax burden. A negative fiscal health index, which implies that capacity is less than standardized need, indicates the percentage increase in revenue the city would have to receive from outside sources to be able to provide the baseline service quality at the standard tax burden. Because the average index in 1972 is defined as equal to zero, the average index in 1982 reveals the change in fiscal health of the average city between these two years. The index for a particular city in 1982 reflects both the change in fiscal health in the average city between 1972 and 1982 and the difference between the fiscal health of that city and that of the average city. To put it another way, a city's 1982 index compares its 1982 fiscal health to that of the average city in 1972.

Standardized fiscal health calculations for 1982 in 10 illustrative cities are presented in table 5.1. Columns 1 and 2 present revenue-raising capacity (see table 3.3) and the standardized expenditure need index (see table 4.3). Column 3 translates standardized need into dollars, using the method described above. The absolute difference between revenue-raising capacity and standardized need appears in column 4, and this difference as a percentage of capacity, which is our summary measure of a city's fiscal health,

---

2. Standardized fiscal health equals [(capacity - need)/capacity]. In applying this formula, need is adjusted so that fiscal health equals zero in the average city. Altering the tax burden on which capacity is based is equivalent to multiplying capacity by a constant. To switch to a 10 percent burden, for example, one must multiply capacity by [(.10)/(.03)]. But if one multiplies capacity by a constant, one also must multiply need by that same constant to ensure that fiscal health still equals zero in the average city. As a result, both the numerator and the denominator of the formula are multiplied by the same constant and the constant cancels.

Table 5.1
Calculating an Index of Standardized Fiscal Health, 1982
(Illustrative Cities)

	(1) Revenue-Raising Capacity ($)	(2) Standardized Expenditure Need Index	(3) Standardized Expenditure Need ($)	(4) Capacity Minus Need ($)	(5) Fiscal Health Index (%)
Atlanta, GA	505	196	640	-136	- 26.9
Baltimore, MD	331	227	483	-152	- 45.7
Boston, MA	501	220	561	- 59	- 11.9
Detroit, MI	341	145	654	-313	- 91.9
Denver, CO	532	265	505	27	5.0
Ft. Lauderdale, FL	649	119	359	290	44.7
Kansas City, MO	388	188	519	-131	- 33.6
Newark, NJ	351	148	737	-386	-109.7
Santa Ana, CA	491	179	374	117	23.8
Virginia Beach, VA	333	126	243	90	27.1

Note: The standardized fiscal health index in column 5 equals column 4 divided by column 1.

appears in column 5.

Table 5.1 reveals a wide range in city fiscal health. Detroit, for example, has a standardized expenditure need that is almost twice as high as its revenue-raising capacity. To be specific, the fiscal health index for Detroit is -92; Detroit would have to receive a 92 percent boost in its revenue-raising capacity, provided by outside sources, to be able to provide services of the quality that the average city could provide out of its own broad-based revenue sources in 1972. In Denver, on the other hand, revenue-raising capacity is slightly greater than standardized expenditure need, and the fiscal health measure is +5 percent. Revenue-raising capacity greatly exceeds standardized expenditure need in Fort Lauderdale; Santa Ana, California; and Virginia Beach, Virginia. Fort Lauderdale, for example, could provide services at the 1972 average quality level and still have over 40 percent of its revenue-raising capacity available for better services or lower taxes.

Table 5.1 also reveals that there is no simple link between revenue-raising capacity and fiscal health. Some cities with relatively high capacity, such as Atlanta, have poor fiscal health, whereas others with relatively high capacity, such as Fort Lauderdale, have excellent fiscal health. Similarly, relatively low capacity can be associated with poor fiscal health, as in Baltimore, or with good fiscal health, as in Virginia Beach. Revenue-raising capacity and standardized expenditure need do not always move together; the balance between them determines a city's overall fiscal health.

Differences Across Cities in Standardized Fiscal Health in 1982

Table 5.2 summarizes the standardized fiscal health in 1982 of the 71 sample cities with complete data. The results for Washington, D.C., are presented separately in the last row of the table.[3] Revenue-raising capacity is in column 2, and standardized expenditure need is in column 3. Standardized fiscal health, which is the difference between capacity and need expressed as a percentage of capacity, is in column 5. The first row of column 5 indicates that in the average city, revenue-raising capacity falls short of standardized expenditure need by 11 percent. In 1982, therefore, the average central city needed revenue from an outside source equal to 11 percent of its own-source capacity to be able to provide the same service quality at the standard tax burden as the average city in 1972.

This standardized fiscal health index varies widely across cities. Its standard deviation is 32 percent, which indicates that most cities fall between -43 percent and +21 percent (the average minus and plus one standard deviation). Standardized fiscal health is negative in 44 cities and positive in the remaining 27. The lowest fiscal health index is -110 percent in Newark, New Jersey, whereas the healthiest city, Hollywood, Florida, has an index of 47 percent. To provide the baseline service quality at the standard tax burden, in other words, Newark would have to more than double its revenue-raising capacity, and Hollywood would have to leave one-half of its revenue-raising capacity untouched.

A city's 1982 standardized fiscal health reflects both changes over time in the fiscal health of the average city and differences across cities in fiscal health in 1982. Because the index is standardized to equal zero in 1972, the average index in 1982 equals the average change in the index between 1972 and 1982. Thus we can eliminate the average 1972-82 change and focus on differences across cities by adding the average decline, 10.9 percent, to the 1982 fiscal health index for each city. The result, namely standardized fis-

---

3. The standardized fiscal health of Washington, D.C., is strictly comparable to that of other cities. Because of its unique institutional setting, however, Washington D.C.'s actual fiscal health is examined separately in chapter 9. To facilitate our investigation of the role of these unique fiscal institutions, which is the difference between actual and standardized fiscal health, we also isolate the District of Columbia's standardized fiscal health.

Table 5.2
Standardized Fiscal Health, 1982
(71 Cities)

	(1)	(2)	(3)	(4)	(5)	(6)	(7)
						Standardized Fiscal Health	
	Number of Cities	Revenue-Raising Capacity ($)	Standardized Expenditure Need ($)	Capacity Minus Need ($)	Standardized Fiscal Health Index (%)	Relative to Average 1982 (%)	Without Costs[b] (%)
All cities							
Average	70	425	458	- 33	- 10.9	0.0	7.4
Standard deviation	70	80	109	128	32.2	32.2	17.2
Maximum	70	649	737	290	47.2	58.1	41.4
Minimum	70	286	243	-386	-109.7	-98.8	-32.6
City population in thousands							
Less than 100	6	457	384	74	16.4	27.3	15.5
100-250	19	473	421	52	9.1	20.0	16.8
250-500	26	420	473	- 53	-13.5	- 2.6	7.6
500-1,000	14	385	466	- 80	-22.9	-12.0	- 2.2
Greater than 1,000	5	341	586	-245	-72.8	-61.9	-12.5
Resident income per capita							
Quintile 1	11	399	567	-169	-46.3	-35.4	2.0
Quintile 2	17	411	433	- 22	- 6.8	4.1	4.5
Quintile 3	15	408	490	- 82	-22.8	-11.9	2.8
Quintile 4	14	427	416	9	2.5	13.4	9.5
Quintile 5	13	481	405	77	13.0	23.9	18.9

Table 5.2 (Cont.)

	(1)	(2)	(3)	(4)	(5)	(6) Standardized Fiscal Health	(7) Standardized Fiscal Health
	Number of Cities	Revenue-Raising Capacity ($)	Standardized Expenditure Need ($)	Capacity Minus Need ($)	Standardized Fiscal Health Index (%)	Relative to Average 1982 (%)	Without Costs[b] (%)
City Economic Health[a]							
Quintile 1	13	375	369	5	- 2.0	8.9	- 3.8
Quintile 2	14	386	449	- 63	- 20.3	- 9.4	- 1.7
Quintile 3	14	394	462	- 69	- 21.0	-10.1	1.7
Quintile 4	14	456	487	- 31	- 8.6	2.3	15.3
Quintile 5	15	505	511	- 7	- 2.5	8.4	23.7
Washington, DC	1	624	535	89	14.3	25.2	39.1

Note: Each entry is an average for the indicated category of city.

[a]City economic health is private employment in the city divided by city population.

[b]The standardized fiscal health index without costs is expressed relative to the 1972 average.

cal health relative to the 1982 average, is presented in column 6 of table 5.2.

Column 6 reveals a clear-cut relationship between city size and standardized fiscal health; on average, larger cities have much poorer fiscal health. This relationship reflects factors on both the capacity side and the expenditure side. As was shown in chapters 3 and 4, larger cities tend to have smaller revenue-raising capacity and higher service costs. Among the smallest cities, standardized fiscal health relative to the 1982 average is almost 27 percent of capacity. Cities with over 1 million people, by contrast, have a standardized fiscal health index relative to the 1982 average of -61 percent, and those with 500,000 to 1 million have an index of -12 percent. To be in comparable fiscal health, the smallest cities would have to give up 27 percent of their capacity, and the largest cities would have to receive revenue from outside sources equal to 61 percent of their capacity.

The economic health of city residents, as measured by per capita income, is also linked to fiscal health. Cities with richer residents tend to have higher revenue-raising capacity and lower costs and hence greater fiscal health. Relative to the 1982 average, cities in the lowest quintile of resident income have a standardized fiscal health index of -35 percent, whereas cities in the highest quintile have an index of +24 percent. The relationship between standardized fiscal health and resident economic health is not smooth, however. Cities in the third quintile of resident income have both higher costs and lower revenue-raising capacity (and hence worse economic health) than cities in the second or fourth quintile.

Another way to illustrate the association between standardized fiscal health and both resident income and population is by plotting the values for individual cities. Figure 5.1 plots city population against standardized fiscal health for the 70 cities included in table 5.2. This figure highlights the strong negative association between population and fiscal health, but it also reveals that fiscal health varies widely at any given population level. Figure 5.2 is the analogous figure for resident income. It highlights both the strong positive association between resident income and standardized fiscal health and the diversity in fiscal health that can occur even across cities with the same resident income.

Per capita employment, which measures the economic health of the city itself, is not closely linked to standardized fiscal health. As was shown in chapters 3 and 4, higher employment is associated with higher revenue-raising capacity and with higher service costs. These two effects are roughly offsetting; for cities in both the highest and the lowest employment quintiles in table 5.2, revenue-raising capacity is approximately equal to standardized expenditure need. However, standardized expenditure need is greater than revenue-raising capacity in the middle of the per capita employ-

Figure 5.1
Population and Standardized Fiscal Health, 1982
(70 cities)

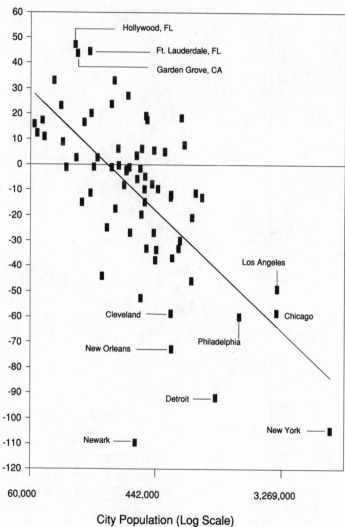

Figure 5.2
Resident Income and Standardized Fiscal Health, 1982
(70 cities)

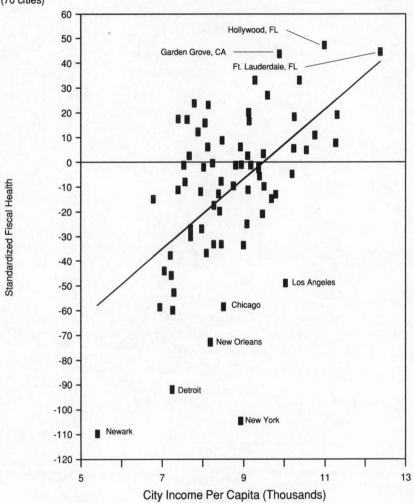

ment range, particularly for cities in the second and third quintiles. Relative to the 1982 average, cities in these two quintiles of city economic health have a standardized fiscal health index of about -10 percent.

The last row of table 5.2 describes the standardized fiscal health of Washington, D.C. The nation's capital has relatively high standardized expenditure need but even higher revenue-raising capacity. As a result, its standardized fiscal health index relative to the 1982 average is 25 percent; economic and social factors alone endow Washington with strong fiscal health.

To provide perspective on the role of public service costs, table 5.2 also presents, in column 7, a standardized fiscal health index, expressed relative to the 1972 average, in which all cities are assumed to have the same costs.[4] The average value of this index is 7 percent; if one ignores the cost increases between 1972 and 1982, in other words, one might conclude that the fiscal health of the average central city improved over this period.

Column 7 also reveals that the links described above between fiscal health and both population and resident income exist even if costs are ignored. The largest cities, for example, have a constant-cost fiscal health index of -13 percent compared to +16 percent for the smallest cities. It also is clear, however, that public service costs magnify these relationships; as was shown in chapter 4, larger cities and those with poorer residents tend to have much higher public service costs.

Finally, column 7 of table 5.2 reveals a strong link between economic health and fiscal health when costs are ignored; cities in the top quintile of economic health have a relatively great ability to export tax burdens to commuters and therefore have a constant-cost index of +24 percent, whereas cities in the bottom quintile, which cannot export their tax burdens, have a constant-cost index of -4 percent. This relationship does not appear in the complete standardized fiscal health index because, as we explained in chapter 4, greater economic health brings with it greater public service costs, which offset the fiscal advantages of an ability to export tax burdens to nonresidents.

Changes in Standardized Fiscal Health, 1972-1982

Between 1972 and 1982 standardized expenditure need increased

---

4. With no variation in service responsibilities or service costs, expenditure need is the same in every city. As a result, a standardized fiscal health index that ignores costs only reflects variation in revenue-raising capacity.

faster than revenue-raising capacity, so standardized fiscal health declined in the average city. As we explained earlier, this decline is measured by the average value of the standardized fiscal health index in 1982, which is in the first row of table 5.2, and by the average change in this index between 1972 and 1982, which is in the first row of table 5.3. The latter table reveals that the average city experienced a 19 percent increase in standardized need, a 9 percent increase in revenue-raising capacity, and hence an 11 percent decrease in standardized fiscal health.[5] These results imply that economic and social trends between 1972 and 1982 caused a significant deterioration in the fiscal health of the average central city. As is shown in the last row of table 5.3, by the way, the nation's capital experienced a decline in fiscal health almost exactly equal to the decline in the average city.

Declines in standardized fiscal health are clearly linked to city size. Cities with populations below 100,000 experienced only a 2 percent decline in fiscal health, thanks to large increases in capacity and modest increases in need, and cities of over 1 million experienced a 27 percent decline in fiscal health, thanks largely to a decline in their revenue-raising capacity. Cities in other size classes experienced intermediate declines in fiscal health.

Table 5.3 also reveals that falling resident income severely undermines a city's standardized fiscal health. Cities with falling resident income, whether they started with below- or above-average resident income in 1971, experienced much larger declines in fiscal health than did cities with growing resident income. Cities with low resident income in 1971 also tended to experience greater declines in fiscal health than those with high income in 1971.

As we explained earlier, city economic health has both fiscal costs and benefits for a city. This point is reinforced by the third panel of table 5.3, which shows that cities with the most rapid growth in employment per capita between 1972 and 1982 also had the most rapid growth both in potential capacity and in expenditure need. Cities in all employment-growth categories encountered declines in fiscal health, but the larger effect of increases in economic health on capacity than on need implies that cities with growing employment encountered smaller declines in fiscal health than did other cities.

Finally, table 5.3 reveals that changes in a city's standardized fiscal

---

5. The change in revenue-raising capacity minus the change in standardized expenditure need does not exactly equal the change in the standardized fiscal health index. This outcome is entirely appropriate; the average change in a variable need not equal the sum of the average changes of its components.

Table 5.3
Changes in Standardized Fiscal Health, 1972-1982
(71 Cities)

	(1)	(2)	(3)	(4)	(5)
		Percentage Change		Percentage Point Change	
	Number of Cities	Revenue-Raising Capacity	Standardized Expenditure Need	**Standardized Fiscal Health Index**	Standardized Fiscal Health with Constant Costs
All cities	70	8.6	19.2	**-10.9**	7.4
City population in thousands					
Less than 100	6	10.3	12.6	**- 1.6**	8.5
100-250	19	10.9	23.2	**- 9.3**	8.3
250-500	26	9.5	20.4	**-11.4**	8.6
500-1,000	14	8.2	17.0	**-10.3**	8.5
Greater than 1,000	5	- 5.6	12.3	**-27.2**	- 6.4
Below-average income, 1971					
Low growth	18	2.1	19.8	**-21.2**	1.4
Medium growth	10	6.4	18.7	**-12.4**	6.5
High growth	6	19.5	16.7	**1.6**	18.9
Above-Average Income, 1971					
Low growth	7	- 1.3	14.3	**-17.4**	- 1.7
Medium growth	17	9.9	19.1	**- 6.7**	8.1
High growth	12	18.9	23.3	**- 2.6**	15.9
Below-average economic health, 1972					
Low growth	11	2.8	13.9	**-15.8**	2.5
Medium growth	9	5.8	17.9	**-12.2**	6.9
High growth	15	16.0	25.4	**- 5.8**	13.6
Above-average economic health, 1972					
Low growth	15	3.9	17.3	**-15.9**	3.5
Medium growth	13	6.6	18.2	**-10.9**	5.5
High growth	7	19.5	22.5	**- 1.5**	14.5
Low employment growth					
Low structural change	5	5.4	17.1	**-10.6**	5.6
Medium structural change	6	1.6	20.1	**-27.1**	0.5
High structural change	15	3.5	13.7	**-13.2**	3.2
Medium employment growth					
Low structural change	9	6.5	19.6	**-12.6**	6.0
Medium structural change	7	10.3	16.6	**- 5.7**	10.4
High structural change	6	1.1	17.6	**-16.6**	1.2
High employment growth					
Low structural change	8	16.6	25.6	**- 5.3**	13.4
Medium structural change	11	17.1	21.7	**- 3.1**	13.8
High structural change	3	18.8	31.7	**- 7.1**	15.3
Washington, DC	1	9.0	24.7	**-10.8**	5.5

Note: City categories for income change, economic health change, and structural change are defined in tables 3.4, 2.2, and 2.5 respectively. Each entry is an average change for the indicated category of city.

health are not linked in any systematic way to structural change in its economy. This outcome reflects the findings in earlier chapters that structural change is not linked to changes in revenue-raising capacity or in standardized expenditure need.

Column 5 of table 5.3 presents changes in standardized fiscal health when changes in public service costs are ignored. As we noted earlier, the constant-cost index increased 7.4 percent; that is, without cost increases, the average city would have experienced an improvement in its fiscal health between 1972 and 1982. Because our fiscal health calculations remove the effects of inflation, this 7.4 percent increase reflects the fact, which was emphasized in chapter 4, that the cost of public services in major central cities increased far more rapidly than the cost of state and local services in general.

Even without cost changes, the largest cities would have experienced a 6 percent decline in their fiscal health over this period, but the constant-cost index rises about 8 percent in all other classes of city, and the difference between the standardized fiscal health index and the constant-cost index is greater for larger cities than for smaller cities. If one ignores cost changes, cities with high growth in resident income have large increases in fiscal health, compared to small increases or declines for cities with low growth in resident income. Finally, changes in constant-cost fiscal health largely reflect changes in revenue-raising capacity, so the relative improvement in the fiscal health of cities with rapid growth in economic health is even greater when costs are ignored than when they are incorporated in the fiscal health index.

Approximating Standardized Fiscal Health

Precisely because it is so comprehensive, our measure of standardized fiscal health is difficult to calculate. For practical applications, therefore, analysts and policy makers may want a more readily calculated approximation. The results in table 5.2 provide a clue to such an approximation; population and resident income are closely correlated with a city's standardized fiscal health. Following this clue, we employ a simple statistical procedure, multiple regression analysis, to obtain a fairly accurate approximation of standardized fiscal health on the basis of three city characteristics: population, resident income, and the poverty rate. The results are presented in column 1 of table 5.4. By adding city population (in millions) multiplied by -12.2, resident income (in thousands) multiplied by 3.5, and the poverty rate (as a percentage) multiplied by -3.1, we obtain an ap-

Table 5.4
Approximating Standardized Fiscal Health

Characteristic	Weight		
	Formula A	Formula B	Formula C
Population (in millions)	-12.2	- 6.8	- 9.5
Per capita income (in thousands)	+ 3.5	+ 3.3	+ 3.1
Poverty rate (in percentages)	- 3.1	- 2.2	- 1.9
Old housing (in percentages)		- 0.6	- 0.3
Share of metropolitan population (in percentages)		-0.5	- 0.5
Unemployment rate (in percentages)			- 2.7
Change in population, 1972-82 (in percentages)			- 0.1
Percentage explained of the variation in standardized fiscal health	61.3	73.5	79.6

Note: These weights are the coefficients of each characteristic in a multiple regression analysis with 1982 standardized fiscal health as the dependent variable. The coefficient of the constant term is not reported. All the coefficients are highly significant statistically.

proximation for city standardized fiscal health that explains over 60 percent of the variation in our comprehensive measure of standardized fiscal health. This approximation can easily be adjusted so that, like our more complex measure, it equals zero in the average city.[6]

Although table 5.2 focuses on population and income, other readily measured city characteristics are closely associated with standardized fiscal health. A city's share of the population of its metropolitan area and the age of its housing stock, for example, are key determinants of its public service costs, and both a city's unemployment rate and its change in popula-

6. To carry out this adjustment, calculate the average value—before adjustment— of (approximated) standardized fiscal health in the set of cities being considered and subtract this average from the pre-adjustment fiscal health of each city.

tion are correlated with both revenue-raising capacity and environmental costs. Thus two other approximations of standardized fiscal health are described in table 5.4. As is shown in column 3, for example, accounting for a city's concentration of old housing, its share of metropolitan population, its unemployment rate, and the percentage change in its population yields an approximation that explains 80 percent of the variation in standardized fiscal health.

The high correlation between standardized fiscal health and several easily observed city characteristics reveals that policy makers could design an aid program specifically directed toward cities in poor fiscal health. Indeed, several programs have made steps in this direction. Federal Community Development Block Grants, for example, provided more money to cities with a higher concentration of old housing. The short-lived Anti-Recession Fiscal Assistance Program of the late 1970s provided unrestricted funds to cities with high unemployment rates. More accurate targeting toward cities with poor standardized fiscal health could be achieved using the weights in table 5.4. We return to this issue in chapter 12.

These correlations also provide some perspective on previous indicators of urban distress. As we noted in chapter 1, for example, per capita income, the poverty rate, and the unemployment rate are among the factors that go into an index of urban hardship constructed by Nathan and Adams (1976). In constructing indexes, however, Nathan and Adams and other contributors to the literature on urban distress place an arbitrary weight, usually one, on each variable in their index, whereas we determined the weights in table 5.4 by a statistical procedure. Thus the two measures yield significantly different rankings for cities. Among the 43 central cities in both Nathan and Adams study and ours, the correlation between their 1970 hardship index and our 1972 standardized fiscal health index is only -0.18; that is, a high degree of hardship does not always correspond to poor standardized fiscal health. Some cities, including Columbus, Los Angeles, Indianapolis, and Kansas City, Missouri, had low standardized fiscal health in 1972 but were relatively healthy according to the Nathan and Adams index; other cities, including Miami and Hartford, Connecticut, had high standardized fiscal health but were relatively unhealthy according to Nathan and Adams. Moreover, New York was among the least healthy cities by our measure but had an average hardship according to the Nathan and Adams index, whereas Newark and Saint Louis were moderately unhealthy by our measure and extremely unhealthy by theirs.

These comparisons should not be interpreted as a criticism of the

Nathan and Adams index, which is designed to summarize a city's overall hardship, not simply its fiscal condition.[7] Instead, they reveal that analysts or policy makers who want to focus on city fiscal health should be wary of any index with arbitrary criteria for selecting variables or a weighting scheme that is not functionally related to fiscal issues.

Conclusions

A city's standardized fiscal health depends on the economic, social, and demographic factors that constrain its ability to raise revenue and determine its costs for public services.

Large cities and those with relatively poor resident economic health have relatively poor fiscal health, both because their revenue-raising capacity tends to be low and because their service costs tend to be high. Indeed, these cities are in critical condition; they must have a large injection of outside resources to achieve the same service quality at the same tax burden as the average city. Furthermore, these cities fell farther behind others between 1972 and 1982.

A city's economic health, as measured by per capita employment, is not clearly linked to the city's standardized fiscal health because the positive effects of economic health on revenue-raising capacity are balanced by its negative effects on standardized expenditure need. Thus the presence of many commuters, which is a key source of good economic health, is a mixed fiscal blessing; commuters provide the potential for exporting tax burdens but also raise the cost of public services. Over the 1972-82 period, however, growth in a city's economic health had a larger positive effect on its revenue-raising capacity than a negative effect on its standardized need, so cities with improving economic health experienced relatively small declines in standardized fiscal health.

Structural change in a city's economy between 1972 and 1982, and in particular a shift from manufacturing to service employment, had little effect either on a city's revenue-raising capacity or on its standardized expenditure need and therefore had little effect on its standardized fiscal health.

---

7. It should be pointed out, however, that ad hoc indexes of city fiscal condition also can yield very different results from our comprehensive measure. For example, the correlation between Cuciti's (1978) index of fiscal need (which is based on tax effort, property tax base, and two measures of service needs) and our 1972 standardized fiscal health index is only -0.15, and the correlation between Cuciti's index and our 1972 actual fiscal health index is only -0.11. These calculations are based on the 32 cities for which both indexes were calculated.

Appendix: Calculating Standardized Fiscal Health

In chapters 3 and 4 we derived a measure of a city's revenue-raising capacity and an index of its standardized expenditure need. Let RRC_j stand for this capacity and SNI_j stand for this need in city j. Remember that SNI_j is an index, not a dollar amount. To express expenditure need in dollar terms, so that it is comparable to RRC_j, one must multiply SNI_j by an indicator of service quality, q, that is the same in all cities.

Standardized fiscal health, SFH_j in city j, reflects the balance between revenue-raising capacity and standardized expenditure need (in dollars), expressed as a percentage of RRC_j; that is,

(A5.1) $SFH_j = [RRC_j - (q)(SNI_j)]/RRC_j = 1 - q(SNI_j/RRC_j)$.

We set the service quality, q, so that the average SFH_j equals zero in the base year, which is 1972. In a set of N cities, therefore, q is determined by the following equation:

$$\sum_{j=1}^{N} SFH_j/N = 0 = \sum_{j=1}^{N} [1 - q(SNI_j/RRC_j)]/N$$

or

(A5.2) $q = N/[\sum_{j=1}^{N} (SNI_j/RRC_j)]$.

This result indicates that q equals the inverse of the average need-capacity ratio in 1972. With this value for q, equation (A5.1) can be used to calculate standardized fiscal health in every city in any year. Remember from chapter 3 that every RRC_j is proportional to K^*, the standard tax burden. According to equation (A5.2), therefore, q also is proportional to K^*, and SFH_j is the same for any standard tax burden.

Table A5.1 presents our standardized fiscal health index for 1972 and 1982 for the 71 major central cities with complete data. The entries for 1972 indicate each city's fiscal health relative to the average city in that year. The entries for 1982 reflect each city's fiscal health relative to the average city in 1982 and the change in fiscal health in the average city between 1972 and 1982.

Table A5.1
Index of Standardized Fiscal Health, 1972 and 1982
(71 Cities)

	Standardized Fiscal Health 1972		Standardized Fiscal Health 1982	
	Index (%)	Rank	Index (%)	Rank
Akron, OH	-10.0	49	- 17.4	49
Albany, NY	16.2	18	8.8	19
Anaheim, CA	42.6	4	33.2	4
Atlanta, GA	2.1	34	- 26.9	54
Baltimore, MD	-14.2	43	- 45.7	44
Boston, MA	-5.1	54	- 11.9	62
Buffalo, NY	-25.7	64	- 52.6	64
Charlotte, NC	25.5	9	3.4	25
Chicago, IL	-38.0	68	- 58.5	65
Cincinnati, OH	-14.4	55	- 33.1	57
Cleveland, OH	-20.4	60	- 58.7	66
Clifton, NJ	31.4	8	11.0	18
Columbus, OH	-19.1	58	- 36.9	59
Dayton, OH	- 1.8	40	- 44.0	61
Denver, CO	4.2	31	5.0	24
Detroit, MI	-50.6	69	- 91.9	69
Ft. Lauderdale, FL	52.8	1	44.7	2
Garden Grove, CA	51.0	3	43.8	3
Greensboro, NC	24.4	11	20.2	9
Hartford, CT	7.0	28	- 15.0	48
High Point, NC	3.2	32	15.9	15
Hollywood, FL	52.2	2	47.2	1
Honolulu, HI	-23.1	63	- 20.9	51
Indianapolis, IN	-26.7	65	- 25.0	52
Jacksonville, FL	-10.9	51	- 12.8	45
Kansas City, MO	-21.0	61	- 33.6	58
Long Beach, CA	11.7	24	- 4.8	36
Los Angeles, CA	-22.7	62	- 48.9	63
Louisville, KY	- 7.2	46	- 26.9	53
Memphis, TN	-11.8	53	- 30.1	55
Miami, FL	22.9	12	17.5	12
Milwaukee, WI	-16.3	57	- 33.1	56
Minneapolis, MN	0.3	36	- 14.8	47
Nashville-Davidson, TN	-11.7	52	- 9.6	40
Newark, NJ	-31.9	66	-109.7	71
New Orleans, LA	-63.8	70	- 72.7	68
New York, NY	-81.5	71	-104.6	70
Norfolk, VA	7.7	27	- 8.1	39
Oakland, CA	- 0.6	37	- 1.6	33
Ogden, UT	13.7	22	12.3	17
Oklahoma City, OK	- 4.0	41	5.6	23
Omaha, NB	1.0	35	- 5.7	37
Ontario, CA	14.6	20	23.2	8
Pawtucket, RI	10.9	25	17.3	13

Table A5.1 (Cont.)

	Standardized Fiscal Health 1972		Standardized Fiscal Health 1982	
	Index (%)	Rank	Index (%)	Rank
Philadelphia, PA	-34.9	67	- 59.9	67
Phoenix, AZ	- 7.1	45	- 11.2	42
Pittsburgh, PA	-10.6	50	- 7.8	38
Portland, OR	- 1.1	39	- 9.8	41
Portsmouth, VA	6.5	30	- 1.2	32
Providence, RI	- 1.1	38	- 11.2	43
Richmond, VA	16.2	17	- 1.2	31
Riverside, CA	13.8	21	2.6	27
Rochester, NY	- 5.4	44	- 0.4	28
Sacramento, CA	8.9	26	- 1.2	30
St. Louis, MO	-14.6	56	- 37.7	60
St. Paul, MN	- 4.6	42	- 2.7	35
St. Petersburg, FL	17.9	14	6.2	21
Salt Lake City, UT	2.1	33	- 1.0	29
San Bernardino, CA	16.3	16	2.7	26
San Diego, CA	- 7.9	47	-13.0	46
San Francisco, CA	7.0	29	7.7	20
San Jose, CA	16.1	19	18.4	11
Santa Ana, CA	31.5	7	23.8	7
Tampa, FL	- 9.0	48	- 2.0	34
Toledo, OH	-19.6	59	-19.8	50
Tucson, AZ	19.0	13	6.2	22
Tulsa,OK	12.8	23	19.2	10
Virginia Beach, VA	34.7	5	27.1	6
Warwick, RI	32.5	6	33.2	5
Winston-Salem, NC	17.7	15	16.6	14
Washington, DC	25.2	10	14.3	16
Average	0.0		-10.9	

Note: A city's standardized fiscal health index equals the difference between its revenue-raising capacity and its standardized expenditure need as a percentage of its revenue-raising capacity.

Part III

Fiscal Institutions and Actual
Fiscal Health

6
The Availability and Form of Taxes

In 1978, California voters passed Proposition 13 and thereby dramatically reduced the ability of local governments in their state to raise revenue from the property tax. Massachusetts voters followed in 1980 with a similar measure that significantly rolled back property taxes in the state's largest cities. Although the media tend to focus on these out-of-the-ordinary events, many less publicized state laws and constitutional provisions also affect the ability of local governments to raise tax revenue. Many states, for example, prohibit their local governments from using income or sales taxes. Others, like Maryland, allow their cities to levy an income tax but prohibit them from taxing commuters. In addition, many states limit the tax rates on one or more of a city's tax bases.

These state laws and constitutional provisions are the topic of this chapter. We contrast the specific broad-based taxes used by cities with the uniformly defined property, sales, and earnings taxes described in chapter 3 and examine how differences between actual and potential tax bases affect the revenue-raising capacity of cities. This is the first of three chapters to address the state-imposed fiscal institutions that affect the ability of central cities in the United States to meet the needs of citizens for public services. Chapters 7 and 8 focus on the fiscal structure of cities; we discuss the role of overlying jurisdictions in chapter 7 and the service responsibilities of cities in chapter 8. Each of these three chapters deals with a single aspect of a larger question: How do fiscal institutions affect the fiscal health of central cities?

In the first three sections of this chapter, we describe which taxes cities are allowed to use, what exemptions they may employ, and what tax rates they may set. Our main concern is how such legal provisions or practices affect a city's ability to tax resident income or to export tax burdens to non-residents. The final section summarizes the effects of these provisions on cities' revenue-raising capacity.

Authorization of Broad-Based Taxes

All central cities in the United States are permitted to use the property tax as a revenue source. Many, however, are not allowed to use other broad-based taxes such as earnings or income taxes or general sales taxes. Because revenue diversification typically raises revenue-raising capacity, cities have an incentive to take advantage of whatever revenue sources they are permitted to use. Hence, in the absence of full information on state laws and how they have changed over time, we rely on city use of particular taxes as an indicator of state laws.[1]

Table 6.1 summarizes the variation in tax use across cities. The table categorizes cities by the combination of taxes they use and reports the average distribution of 1982 tax revenues for each category.

At one extreme are the 29 cities that use no broad-based taxes other than the property tax. This group includes 16 cities—primarily in New England, New York, New Jersey, and North Carolina—in which the property tax accounted for 90 percent or more of all tax revenues, and 13 cities that supplemented property tax revenues with sizable revenues from selective, rather than general, sales taxes and miscellaneous other taxes. At the other extreme are 6 cities, namely Kansas City, Missouri, New York, St. Louis, San Francisco, Washington, D.C., and Birmingham, Alabama. that use both income and sales taxes along with the property tax.

Currently, only 18 of the 86 cities use some form of earnings tax, defined broadly to include earnings, payroll, and income taxes. Six of the 18 are in Ohio, where local governments rely heavily on earnings taxes. The first city earnings tax was adopted by Philadelphia in 1939. Others were adopted throughout the next three decades, the most recent being the adoption by Newark, New Jersey, of the payroll tax in 1971. Many of the 18 cities supplement the personal income or earnings tax with a tax on corporate income. As is shown in table 6.1, 9 cities (those in the earnings and property tax category) derived an average of 71 percent of their tax revenue from earnings taxes in 1982.

Many more cities, but still only 45 of the 86, use a general sales tax. A clear regional pattern emerges here; general sales taxes are quite common in the West and South but are used by only a few cities in the Northeast and Midwest. About one-half of the cities with a general sales tax raise more revenue from it than from the property tax.

What effect does access to a tax have on a city's revenue-raising

---

1. For information on the use of income taxes and sales taxes, see Gold 1982.

Table 6.1
Revenue Mix by Category of Tax Use, 1982
(86 Cities)

Tax Use Category[a]	Number of Cities	Average Percentage of Total 1982 Tax Revenue from:[b]			
		Property Tax	Income, Earnings or Payroll Tax	General Sales Tax	Other Taxes
Property tax only	29	82	0	0	18
Property and earnings	3	66	18	0	16
Earnings and property	9	23	71	0	6
Property and general sales	21	52	0	23	25
General sales and property	18	29	0	48	23
Mixed	6	28	29	18	25
All cities	86	53	10	17	20

Source: U.S. Department of Commerce, Bureau of the Census, *City Government Finances in 1981-82*, GF 82, no. 4 (Washington, D.C.: GPO, 1983).
[a]Tax use categories are defined as follows. Property Tax Only: the property tax is the only broad-based tax the city may use. Property and earnings: the city uses property and income or earnings taxes but not the sales tax; property tax revenue is greater than income tax revenue. Earnings and property: the city uses property and income or earnings tax revenue; income tax revenue is greater than property tax revenue. Property and general sales: the city uses property and general sales taxes but not income or earnings tax; property tax revenue is greater than sales tax revenue. General sales and property: the city uses property and general sales taxes but not income or earnings tax; general sales tax revenue is greater than property tax revenue. Mixed: the city uses property, general sales, and income or earnings taxes.
[b]Simple unweighted averages.

capacity? Recall that a particular tax source influences a city's capacity through its impact on the city's ability to export tax burdens to nonresidents. Hence we measure the impact of access to a tax by its effect on tax exporting. Consider, for example, a city that is authorized to use a property tax but the export ratio for the prohibited earnings tax is smaller than that for the not an earnings tax. If the export ratio (that is, the burden that can be shifted to nonresidents per dollar of burden on residents) for the prohibited earnings tax is greater than the export ratio for the property tax, the prohibition is binding and reduces the city's revenue-raising capacity. If, in contrast, the export ratio for the prohibited earnings tax is smaller than that for the property tax, the prohibition probably has little effect on the city's revenue-raising capacity.[2]

2. The prohibition could still be binding if the *marginal* export ratio for the property tax were below the marginal export ratio for the prohibited tax. This could be the case, for example, if the marginal export ratio of a tax is farther below the average observed ratio for the used tax than for the prohibited tax. The marginal export ratio would be lower than the average export ratio for a particular

A comparison across cities of export ratios for the three potential broad-based taxes shows that the earnings tax dominates property and sales taxes in most cities for most years of this study. The property tax is the most exportable tax in at most 7 of the 86 cities. Six of these 7 (all but Toledo, Ohio) rely more heavily on the property tax than on any other. In only 4 cities does the sales tax have the highest export rate. Three of the 4 use sales taxes; Honolulu, the fourth, has no general sales tax but does employ selective sales taxes.

Our analysis indicates that 60 of the 68 cities not permitted to use an earnings tax would be able to export a higher fraction of their tax burdens to nonresidents if a standard earnings tax were authorized. Moreover, the tendency noted in chapter 3 for export ratios of the earnings tax to grow over time indicates that prohibitions against the use of such a tax are becoming relatively more restrictive. This conclusion is based on our uniformly defined, standard earnings tax, however, which taxes the earnings of both residents and commuters into the city. As we discuss in the next section, the export ratios of some of the income or earnings taxes actually used by cities are substantially lower than those of the standard earnings tax, principally because the earnings of commuters are not included in the tax base.

Tax Bases

Exemptions and exclusions from local tax bases affect a city's revenue-raising capacity by shifting the burden between residents and nonresidents. An example of an exemption that reduces a city's revenue-raising capacity is the widespread exemption of business inventories from the local property tax base. The tax burden on business inventories is more likely to be borne by nonresidents than is the rest of the property tax base. Hence their exemption from the tax base reduces the city's ability to export tax burdens to nonresidents per dollar of burden on residents and, consequently, reduces the city's revenue-raising capacity.

More common are exemptions that lead to greater exporting of tax burdens per dollar of burden on residents and thereby to higher revenue-raising capacity. Widely used examples of this form of exemption are the

---

tax if nonresident taxpayers are more responsive than resident taxpayers to local tax rates.

homestead exemptions, which remove a portion of owner-occupied housing from the property tax base, and the exemption of food purchases from the sales tax base.[2]

Property Tax Exemptions

The property tax is characterized by exemptions and exclusions that vary widely across the states. Universal exemption of government, religious, charitable, and educational property contrasts with diverse treatment of owner-occupied housing and business personal property. Our estimates of actual property tax bases account for two types of exemptions: homestead and business personalty.

Many states have enacted some form of homestead exemption to remove a fraction of the value of owner-occupied houses from the tax base. Exceptions include Colorado, Missouri, and Pennsylvania. Several states, including Washington, Nebraska, and North Carolina, restrict the exemption to limited classes of homeowners, such as the elderly, the blind and disabled, or veterans, and many of these exemptions are income-tested. In contrast, Alabama, California, Louisiana, and others exempt some fraction of the value of all owner-occupied residential property. The fraction of the tax base that is exempted varies widely from state to state; for example, homestead exemptions removed 24 percent of the potential tax base in Louisiana but less than 1 percent in Washington State and North Carolina in 1981.[3]

Homestead exemptions remove a portion of owner-occupied residential property, for which tax exporting is zero, from the tax roll, and thereby shift the tax burden toward renter-occupied property, for which some tax

---

2. A caveat is needed when exemptions remove a large part of the potential tax base. Large exemptions require that the local tax rate be substantially higher than otherwise to generate a given amount of revenue. If nonresident taxpayers are more responsive than resident taxpayers to local tax rates, the higher rate could lead to a reduction in the city's ability to export burdens to nonresidents. Thus the initial increase in the export ratio attributable to the exemption could conceivably be offset by the decrease in the export ratio induced by the higher tax rate.
3. We estimated the size and effects of homestead exemptions in the 86 cities with data published in the *Census of Governments*, vol. 2. These estimates are subject to a number of familiar caveats, the most important being that local officials have little incentive to maintain current and accurate records of exempt property values. In addition we had to assume that all reported exempt real property values were attributable to the homestead exemption and applied to single family owner-occupied housing. State data published in the 1977 *Census of Governments* show that homestead exemptions accounted for over 98 percent of exempt values for more than half the states reporting.

exporting exists. These provisions therefore raise the average export ratio for taxes on residential property. Moreover, they raise the overall export ratio by shifting the composition of the total taxable base away from housing and toward business. For the average city, homestead exemptions in 1976 removed 9 percent of owner-occupied property values and raised the property tax export ratio from 33 to 35 percent. On average, the 29 cities with sizable homestead exemptions (over 5 percent of potential market value) show a 4 percentage point increase in the property tax export ratio. In New Orleans, for example, the exemption of about two-fifths of owner-occupied property in 1976 raised that city's export ratio by 7.5 percentage points.

State practices regarding the taxation of business personal property (such as machines and inventories) vary widely. Unlike the partial homestead exemptions, personalty exemptions typically are complete for a given class of property. Thus, for example, most states exempt all business inventories from the property tax base. The standard property tax bases discussed in chapter 3 incorporate rough estimates of the full market value of business personal property.[4]

The exemption of business personalty from the tax base reduces the exportability of property taxes in most cities, because taxes on business property typically are more exportable than those on residential property.[5] We estimate that over one-half of personal property was exempt from taxation, on average, in 1976, these exemptions amounting to about 9 percent of total property values and reducing the overall export ratio by about 3 percentage points. In the 33 cities with personal property exemptions amounting to more than 10 percent of all property, the reduction in the overall export ratio was about 5 percentage points. At the high end, exemption of business personalty reduced the estimated export ratios by about 8 percentage points in cities in New York and Pennsylvania.

Differential Assessment

Some cities also increase their ability to export property tax burdens by taxing more exportable portions of the tax base, such as business proper-

---

4. These estimates were imputed from data for cities in the few states that substantially tax business personalty and are based on the assumption that the estimated market value of commercial and industrial personal property values is proportional to the estimated market value of real estate.
5. Export ratios for vacant and state-assessed property are usually higher than for business property. Hence, in cities where these two classes of property are an important part of the total, reducing the commercial and industrial taxable values could conceivably raise the overall export ratio.

ty, more heavily than housing. Relatively higher taxes on business property are implemented either directly and explicitly through legal classification of property or implicitly through higher assessment-sales ratios for businesses than for residential property. In one sense, these policies transform the property tax into two or more taxes, depending on the number of property classes—a property tax on housing with one effective tax rate and a property tax on business or other types of property with different effective tax rates.

Classification can take two forms: assessment of various classes of property at different legislated percentages of market value, or uniform assessment, with different tax rates applied to each class. Differential assessment is the more common form. Of the fourteen states with classified property taxes in 1980-81, eleven used different assessment-sales ratios. Some states, such as Minnesota, Alabama, and Arizona, have had classified property taxes for years, but the practice is growing. Louisiana began classification in 1978 and New Mexico in 1982, Massachusetts is phasing in classification at the option of the locality, and Colorado's classification law took effect in 1985.

Much more widespread, but perhaps decreasing as legal classification takes its place, are de facto differential assessment practices that favor housing at the expense of business property. In the metropolitan areas of New York State, for example, which are typical of the cities that use this approach, the assessment-sales ratio in 1976 averaged 34 percent of market value for commercial and industrial property but only 24 percent for residential property.[6]

Our interest here is in the effects of differential assessment, both de jure and de facto, on export ratios and revenue-raising capacity. To simplify the presentation, we focus on only two classes of property, labeled for simplicity housing and business. The latter category includes vacant land, state-assessed property, and personal property along with commercial and industrial real estate.

In 1976 the assessment-sales ratio for housing averaged about four-fifths the ratio for business property and varied across cities from 66 to 102 percent of the ratio for business. The undertaxation of residential property increased the average city's ability to export tax burdens to nonresidents per

---

6. *Census of Governments*, 1977, vol. 2: 63. For a more complete discussion of the impacts of property tax exemption and differential assessment on the relative tax burdens on business and residential property, see Bradbury and Ladd 1987.

dollar of burden on residents by about 3 percentage points. The effect of assessment practices on export ratios ranged from -0.5 to +11 percentage points.

Sales Tax Exemptions and Exclusions

The base of the general sales tax varies substantially from one city to another largely because of the treatment of food consumed at home and the taxation of services. In addition, many cities rely heavily on selective sales taxes as a substitute for or as a supplement to revenues from general sales taxes. Each of these tax base provisions affects the ability of cities to export sales tax burdens to nonresidents. However, data limitations prevent us from quantifying the effects on exporting of any of these provisions other than the treatment of food.

Thirty-two of the 45 major central cities that use the general sales tax exempt food for home consumption. Like the property tax exemption for homesteads, this provision reduces the revenue derived from a given tax rate but at the same time increases the share of the tax burden exported to nonresidents per dollar collected from residents. We find that, on average, existing exemptions raised the export ratio by about 1.5 percentage points in 1977. Thus we conclude that a sales tax base that exempts food contributes slightly more to a city's revenue-raising capacity than one that includes food.[7]

Earnings or Income Tax: Definition of the Tax Base

As we noted earlier, we use the term *city earnings taxes* to describe a variety of income-related taxes. Table 6.2 arrays the 18 existing city earnings taxes in a way that highlights the issue of exportability. With respect to the taxation of resident income, most cities tax only earnings, either with a payroll tax (3 cities) or with an earnings tax that applies to all the earnings of city residents wherever earned (11 cities). Only 4 cities (Detroit, New York, Baltimore, and Washington, D.C.) tax property and investment income as well as earnings.

---

7. According to 1977 information, of the 45 cities with general sales taxes, 23 include in their tax bases room rents in hotels and motels, 9 include admissions and entertainment, and only 5 include personal services such as dry cleaning. We can say with some assurance that the export ratio for hotels and motels is likely to be quite high. Similarly, we presume that the export ratio for admissions is relatively high, but we have no information about the export ratio for personal services such as dry cleaning. The most we can conclude at this point is that cities that are not allowed to tax hotels and motels, and possibly admissions, are not fully exploiting their total revenue-raising capacity.

Table 6.2
Actual City Income and Earnings Taxes
(18 Cities)

	Tax Applies to Wages and Salaries in the City	Tax Applies to All Resident Earnings[a]	Tax Applies to All Resident Income[b]
Nonresident earnings or payroll fully taxed[c]	Louisville, KY (1948) Newark, NJ (1971) San Francisco, CA (1970)	Akron, OH (1962) Birmingham, AL (1970) Cincinnati, OH (1954) Cleveland, OH (1967) Columbus, OH (1947) Dayton, OH (1940) Kansas City, MO (1964) Philadelphia, PA (1939) St. Louis, MO (1948)	
Nonresident earnings partially taxed		Toledo, OH[d] (1946)	Detroit, MI[e] (1962) New York, NY (1966)
Nonresident earnings not taxed or credited to city of residence		Pittsburgh, PA (1954)	Baltimore, MD (1966) Washington, DC (1939)

Note: Year enacted is shown in parentheses.
[a]Earnings include wages and salaries, self-employment earnings, and net profits from unincorporated business.
[b]Income includes earnings plus property and investment income. Local taxes based on income typically include personal exemptions and deductions.
[c]Taxes in the first (second) column apply to all nonresident payroll (earnings) in the city.
[d]Toledo retains only 50 percent of the tax collected from nonresidents who live in jurisdictions that also have income taxes and that grant the same credit to their nonresidents.
[e]Rate for nonresidents is one-half the rate for residents.

Central to our analysis of fiscal capacity is the treatment of the earnings of commuters into the city. Three cities—Detroit, New York, and Toledo, Ohio—tax only partially the earnings of nonresidents, and 3 other cities—Pittsburgh, Baltimore, and Washington—do not tax nonresidents at all, either because such taxation is not allowed or because taxes paid on nonresident earnings are credited to the city of residence rather than to the city of employment.

In general, the more comprehensively defined the resident income tax base, the lower the export ratio. Less than full taxation of nonresident earnings also lowers the export ratio. Hence, all else equal, cities listed in the upper left-hand corner of table 6.2 have the highest export ratios, and those in the lower right-hand corner have the lowest. This observation implies that an earnings tax (as in the middle column) is superior to the mix of an income tax on residents with an earnings tax on nonresidents (as in the bottom right-hand corner of the table) in terms of its contribution to a city's revenue-raising capacity.[8]

In sum, we conclude that 6 of the 18 cities using an earnings or an income tax treat nonresidents in a way that reduces the revenue-raising capacity of the city below what it would be with full taxation of the income earned in the city by commuters.

Summary of Effects on Export Ratios

Table 6.3 reports average export ratios, for both standard and actual tax bases. The ratios for actual tax bases incorporate all the practices discussed in preceding sections: homestead and personalty exemptions as well as differential assessment under the property tax, exemption of food from the general sales tax, and inclusion of resident unearned income or exclusion of nonresident earnings from the local income tax. The table indicates that local exemptions generally increase the exportability of property and general sales taxes. In contrast, the income or earnings taxes used by city governments are less exportable than a simple flat-rate tax on all earnings in the city would be.

Cities appear to have made reasonable choices about the mix of taxes, given the available options, in light of the actual export ratios they face. Consider, for example, the 12 cities that rely on property and earnings taxes. On average, the 9 that rely more heavily on earnings than on property taxes can export a higher proportion of their earnings tax burden than of their property tax burden. This fact justifies these cities' heavier reliance on earnings taxes than on property taxes. In contrast, the 3 cities that rely more heavily on the property tax than on the earnings tax have similar average export ratios for the property and the earnings taxes and therefore have little incentive to expand their use of the earnings tax relative to that of the

---

8. Whether an earnings tax is superior to an income tax on residents combined with an earnings tax on nonresidents in terms of other criteria is an open question. Considerations of horizontal and vertical equity normally argue for taxation of all income of residents, not just earnings. Taxation of all income in this context, however, might induce rich people to leave the city. To the extent that this occurs, equity might be better served by an earnings tax than by an income tax. Out-migration of higher-income households is likely to be less with the earnings tax (provided commuters are taxed) since one must move both one's job and one's residence out of the city to avoid the tax.

Table 6.3
Potential and Actual Export Ratios by Type of Tax, 1982
(79 Cities)

Tax Use Category	Number of Cities	Property Tax	General Sales Tax	Earnings or Income Tax
Property tax only	26			
Potential export ratio		0.55	0.28	1.49
Actual export ratio		0.62	N.A.	N.A.
Property and earnings	3			
Potential export ratio		0.87	0.05	1.90
Actual export ratio		0.75	N.A.	0.75
Earnings and property	9			
Potential export ratio		0.61	0.09	1.47
Actual export ratio		0.61	N.A.	0.99
Property and general sales	19			
Potential export ratio		0.44	0.17	0.93
Actual export ratio		0.48	0.18	N.A.
General sales and property	17			
Potential export ratio		0.50	0.28	1.20
Actual export ratio		0.55	0.32	N.A.
Mixed	5			
Potential export ratio		0.52	0.06	1.45
Actual export ratio		0.70	0.07	0.81
All Cities	79			
Potential export ratio		0.52	0.21	1.30
Actual export ratio (cities with tax)[a]		0.58	0.23	0.89

Note: Export ratios are dollars of nonresident taxes per dollar of resident tax burden. See table 6.1 for definitions of tax use categories. Ratios are for cities with complete data only. N.A. = not applicable.
[a]Property tax average is based on 79 cities, sales tax average on 41 cities, and earnings tax average on 17 cities.

property tax. Similarly, among cities with access to both property and general sales taxes, the sales tax export ratio is higher relative to the property tax export ratio in the category relying more heavily on the sales tax.

Limitations on Tax Rates

The property tax is the traditional mainstay of city governments, but dependence on it has decreased where cities are allowed to use other taxes and where they face restrictions on its use. The restrictions take a variety of forms, including specific limits on either nominal or effective tax rates and ceilings on the rate of growth of property tax revenues. These limits have been subject to extensive analysis in the wake of California's Proposition 13. The question here is a specific one: How do these limits affect a city's revenue-raising capacity?

The effect of a property tax limit depends on the alternative tax sources available to the city. If the limit causes the city to increase its reliance on a general sales tax, the fraction of total tax burdens exported to nonresidents is likely to fall because sales tax burdens are less exportable than property tax burdens in most cities. If the limit forces increased reliance on a tax with a higher export ratio than the property tax, however, the revenue-raising capacity of the city will increase.[9] If the city has no alternative tax sources (or its other sources are also subject to binding limits), a binding property tax limitation is likely to reduce revenue-raising capacity. We return to this issue in chapter 7.

Local circumstances and specific provisions of state law determine whether limits on tax rates or limits on the growth of property tax levies are more restrictive. For example, Proposition 2 1/2 in Massachusetts forced a 40 percent reduction in Boston's property tax levy between 1981 and 1984 and did not authorize any other broad-based tax (see Bradbury and Ladd, 1982a and 1982b; Bradbury and Yinger 1984). Many other cities and towns in Massachusetts face serious consequences of the limitation measure, however, only as the costs of providing local public services outstrip the permitted annual growth of 2 1/2 percent in tax levies. In recent years states wishing to limit local tax collections have moved toward limits on the growth of levies and away from limits on tax rates, because the latter sometimes have been made ineffective by rapid increases in property values. Both California and Massachusetts used rate limits to lower property tax rates, but they also included limits on the growth of levies or assessments to control subsequent tax increases.

Among the 86 major central cities, 17 faced severely binding limita-

---

9. One might ask why the city did not increase its reliance on the alternative tax, given its relatively high export ratio, before the limitation measure was passed. We assume that the answer is imperfect information about exporting or political constraints.

tions on property tax rates in 1982, and another 19 faced some type of limitation that made it difficult for them to increase property taxes. Only 5 of the 29 cities that rely exclusively on property taxes are in states with limitations on city property taxes, and among these, only Boston faces a severely binding limit on both the property tax rate and the growth in the tax levy.

Most of the other cities facing severely binding limits on property taxes are in California, where cities use both property and sales taxes. These limits have two effects. First, they alter the city share of total state and local taxes and hence the share of resident income devoted to city taxes. (We discuss this issue more fully in chapter 7.) Second, they shift the mix of taxes away from property and toward sales taxes, which reduces the ability of cities to export tax burdens to nonresidents.

Most cities using a local sales tax are subject to state-imposed limits on the rate. Cities in California and Texas, for example, are restricted to a 1 percent rate, and this maximum rate remained constant throughout the 1972-82 period. One state, Colorado, imposes a combined rate limit on the sum of state and local sales taxes. In almost all cases, cities using the sales tax appear to tax at the maximum rate allowed.

These limitations kept all but 7 of the 45 cities with general sales taxes from raising their rates between 1971 and 1982. The increase by Tulsa, Oklahoma, from 2 to 3 percent appears to be associated with the removal of a restriction that the local rate not exceed the state tax rate. In 5 cities (New Orleans; Omaha; Nashville-Davidson, Tennessee; Ogden, Utah; and Salt Lake City) rate increases appear to have been associated with increases in the state-imposed limit. The seventh rate increase was in the special case of Washington, D.C.

This brief survey suggests that cities have little freedom to increase sales tax rates. Recall, however, our finding that export ratios for sales taxes typically were declining during the 1970s. This finding implies that rate restrictions alone had little impact on a city's ability to raise revenue. In particular, they did not prevent cities from exploiting more fully over time a tax with a growing export share. Only if restrictions on sales tax rates are combined with binding rate restrictions on all other permitted taxes, do the sales tax rate restrictions limit a city's revenue-raising capacity. California cities illustrate this situation; the combination of Proposition 13's limit on property taxes and the state-imposed limits on sales tax rates effectively restricts the ability of most California cities to raise own-source revenues from broad-based taxes.

States also limit local earnings, income, or payroll tax rates, but they appear to be more flexible with these than with the maximum rates for sales or property taxes. At least 9 of the 18 cities relying on this revenue source raised their tax rates between 1972 and 1982. As a result of these rate increases and the growth of the income tax base, income taxes increased as a percentage of all local tax revenue in most of the 18 cities during this period, in some cases dramatically. In Ohio cities, for example, income tax revenues increased from about 64 to 77 percent of total tax revenues.

Tax Policies and Changes in Revenue-Raising Capacity

In this chapter we have shown how specific tax prohibitions, exemptions, and limits influence a city's ability to export tax burdens and its overall revenue-raising capacity. To determine the combined effects of these tax policies on revenue-raising capacity, we substitute an aggregate export ratio based on actual, rather than potential, tax bases into our expression for potential revenue-raising capacity. The modified expression for revenue-raising capacity, RRC, becomes

$$RRC = K^*Y(1 + e') \quad ,$$

where, as in chapter 3, K^* is the standard tax burden on residents, Y is the per capita income of city residents, and e' is the actual export ratio, namely the tax burden on nonresidents per dollar of burden on residents. We calculate a city's actual export ratio in any given year as a weighted average of the export ratios for the taxes the city uses, where the weights are the proportions of tax revenue from each tax.

Because our overall export ratio is a weighted average, our estimates of changes in the actual export ratio between 1972 and 1982 reflect the city's responses to changes in the export ratios of individual taxes as well as the changes themselves. If a city increases reliance on an earnings tax whose export ratio has increased, for example, our measure of the city's ability to export taxes would increase for two reasons: the rise in the export ratio of the earnings tax and the larger weight given to that export ratio as a result of the city's greater relative reliance on earnings taxes. This approach means that the change over time in the overall ratio approximates the contribution to revenue-raising capacity of tax exporting given all the economic, legal, and political constraints and opportunities faced by the city. Thus the change is not an abstract measure of what the city might have been able to do in the absence of institutional restrictions but rather is a standardized measure of capacity based on the broad-based taxes the city was able to exploit.

In the aggregate, cities fared only slightly better with their actual tax bases than they would have with the standard property tax base alone during the 1972-82 decade. Moreover, they fared substantially less well with their actual bases than they would have with all three standard tax bases if one assumes weights of 50 percent for the property tax and 25 percent for each of the other two taxes. In the average city revenue-raising capacity based on actual tax bases increased by 5.5 percent during the decade compared to 5.4 percent for the property-tax-only base and 8.6 percent for the broader measure of revenue-raising capacity.[10] These results imply that the flexibility to define tax bases and to use taxes other than the property tax has not, on average, provided a major boost to the revenue-raising capacity of cities.

Further analysis suggests, however, that revenue diversification and redefinition of tax bases provided substantial assistance to those cities hit hardest by economic changes during the decade. Actual economic changes combined with exclusive reliance on the standard property tax would have caused declines in the revenue-raising capacity of 25 cities. The use of actual tax bases reduces the number of cities with declining capacity to 20. Moreover, 19 of the 25 cities with declining capacity measured in terms of the property tax base alone fared better with their actual configuration of taxes than they would have with the standard property tax alone.

The use of revenue diversification and redefinition of the tax base to increase revenue-raising capacity appears to be a response to fiscal stringency rather than the typical behavior in U.S. cities during the period. Only 16 of the 46 cities with increasing property tax capacity fared better with their actual tax bases than they did with the potential property tax base alone. This result reflects a complex combination of the effects of explicit choices made by city governments and state laws and limitations that restricted the flexibility of local governments. Cities with growing capacity apparently structured their tax bases in pursuit of goals other than (or in addition to) the maximization of revenue-generating capacity.

Table 6.4 compares the revenue-raising capacity measures by the six groups of cities categorized by tax use. Of the 26 cities restricted to the use of the property tax, 14 were able to improve their fiscal positions by redefin-

---

10. These figures are based on the 71 cities with complete data. All changes are on a per capita basis and are deflated by the state and local price deflator for government purchases. Our measure of capacity based on actual tax bases captures the effect of tax rate limits only to the extent that a limit on one tax causes a city to change its mix of taxes. Chapters 9 and 11 include other effects of tax limitations.

Table 6.4
Measures of Revenue-Raising Capacity Based on Potential and Actual Tax Bases, 1972-1982 (71 Cities)

Tax Use Category[a]	Number of Cities	Number of Cities with Decline, Actual Bases	Average Percentage Change in Capacity			Actual vs. Potential[b] Number of Cities with:	
			Actual Bases	Potential Bases		Positive Difference	Negative Difference
				Property Only	3 Bases 50-25-25[a]		
Property only	26	7	6.43	7.26	9.63	14	12
Property and earnings	3	2	-1.28	0.16	3.06	1	2
Earnings and property	9	2	3.77	-6.58	-0.55	6	3
Property and sales	12	5	4.43	5.25	8.37	6	6
Sales and property	16	3	8.43	13.18	16.22	3	13
Mixed	5	1	1.07	-3.94	-0.34	5	0
Total		20	5.50	5.41	8.63	35	36

Note: See table 6.1 for definitions of tax use categories. All changes are on a per capita basis and are deflated by the price deflator for state and local government purchases. The measures of capacity reported in this table do not incorporate changes in fiscal structure.
[a]Variable is based on a weighted average of the three potential broad-based tax bases, with weights as follows: 0.50 for property tax, 0.25 for earnings tax, and 0.25 for sales tax.
[b]Potential tax base includes property only. Positive difference denotes that percentage change in capacity based on actual bases is greater or less negative than percentage change in potential capacity based on standard property tax.

ing their property tax bases to increase capacity. In several cities, such as Boston, this improvement was accomplished by implicit classification of property that produced higher effective tax rates for business than for residential property. On average, however, the growth in capacity based on actual tax bases was less than the growth based on the other two measures for the 26 cities in this category. This outcome reflects the inability of these cities to shift their tax mix in favor of taxes with high or growing export ratios.

Cities that used all three taxes (category 6) had the most flexibility to shift and apparently used it. Those that relied more heavily on earnings than on property taxes (category 3) also were able to improve their lot by increasing their reliance on the earnings tax during the period. The cities in category 2 (property dominant, with some use of earnings taxes) illustrate the importance of how the earnings base is defined. Two of the 3 cities in this category, Baltimore and Pittsburgh, are in effect not allowed to tax commuters and hence did not benefit from rising export ratios for earnings taxes. Finally, cities with access to the sales tax performed somewhat less well on average in terms of capacity with actual tax bases than in terms of capacity with either potential base, an outcome that reflects the low and falling export ratios for sales taxes.

In summary, we find that fewer cites faced declines in capacity measured in terms of actual tax bases than in terms of the standard property tax alone. This finding provides limited support for the policy recommendation that states should liberalize the use of local revenue instruments. Sales taxes are not a very attractive alternative for this purpose because of their low and typically declining export ratios. Local earnings taxes, in contrast, could make substantial contributions to the revenue-raising capacity of many cities, provided the earnings of commuters are included in the tax base. The benefits of increased tax exporting, however, have to be weighed against possible distortions in the location of local economic activity. We return to these issues in chapter 12.

Most state governments have not been willing to give their local governments the flexibility to use local earnings or income taxes in the past. This observation combined with the finding that the flexibility available to cities throughout the 1970s was insufficient to counter some strong adverse economic trends suggests that revenue diversification may help but is unlikely to solve the fiscal problems of U.S. cities.

Appendix: Accounting for Actual Taxes

As we discussed in the text, restrictions on the taxes that a city is authorized to use affect its revenue-raising capacity through their impact on the city's ability to export tax burdens to nonresidents. Table A6.1 shows both potential and actual export ratios for 71 cities for 1972 and 1982. In all four columns, the export ratio is defined as the amount of the tax burden borne by nonresidents per dollar borne by residents.

The potential export ratio for each city for each year is calculated as a weighted sum of the export ratios for each of the three standard tax bases, with the weights of 50 percent for the property tax, 25 percent for the sales tax, and 25 percent for the earnings tax. These potential export ratios are used in the calculation of each city's revenue-raising capacity (see chap. 3).

The actual export ratio for each city in each year is calculated as the weighted sum of the export ratios for each tax that the city is empowered to use, with weights equal to the city-specific shares of tax revenue from each tax. See the text of this chapter for a discussion of the differences between actual and standardized tax bases for each tax and of the implications of these differences for export ratios. The actual export ratios are used in the calculation of restricted revenue-raising capacity and actual fiscal health in chapter 9. By comparing a city's potential and actual export ratios, one can determine the impact on exporting of the taxing rules under which it operates.

Table A6.1
Potential and Actual Export Ratios, 1972 and 1982
(71 Cities)

	1972		1982	
	Potential (50-25-25)	Actual	Potential (50-25-25)	Actual
Akron, OH	0.54	0.62	0.68	0.68
Albany, NY	1.04	0.88	1.27	1.09
Anaheim, CA	0.93	0.40	0.94	0.34
Atlanta, GA	1.00	1.14	1.12	1.20
Baltimore, MD	0.56	0.60	0.54	0.39
Boston, MA	1.11	1.07	1.12	1.11
Buffalo, NY	0.66	0.54	0.64	0.55
Charlotte, NC	0.37	0.43	0.32	0.42
Chicago, IL	0.47	0.47	0.44	0.36
Cincinnati, OH	0.93	1.08	0.85	1.19
Cleveland, OH	1.16	1.42	1.01	1.41
Clifton, NJ	0.52	0.34	0.38	0.31

Table A6.1 (Cont.)

	1972		1982	
	Potential (50-25-25)	Actual	Potential (50-25-25)	Actual
Columbus, OH	0.55	0.57	0.49	0.60
Dayton, OH	1.23	1.52	1.09	1.59
Denver, CO	0.53	0.32	0.69	0.34
Detroit, MI	0.55	0.42	0.58	0.34
Ft. Lauderdale, FL	0.55	0.36	0.76	0.44
Garden Grove, CA	0.57	0.17	0.78	0.22
Greensboro, NC	0.49	0.56	0.64	0.60
Hartford, CT	1.35	1.25	1.55	1.36
High Point, NC	0.48	0.61	0.81	0.80
Hollywood, FL	0.38	0.34	0.55	0.34
Honolulu, HI	0.22	0.10	0.31	0.08
Indianapolis, IN	0.29	0.36	0.35	0.46
Jacksonville, FL	0.15	0.23	0.15	0.24
Kansas City, MO	0.63	0.75	0.45	0.66
Long Beach, CA	0.54	0.40	0.46	0.24
Los Angeles, CA	0.40	0.33	0.30	0.19
Louisville, KY	0.70	1.02	0.74	1.41
Memphis, TN	0.20	0.23	0.25	0.32
Miami, FL	1.03	0.58	1.26	0.74
Milwaukee, WI	0.39	0.37	0.39	0.22
Minneapolis, MN	0.76	0.54	0.64	0.40
Nashville-Davidson, TN	0.28	0.32	0.36	0.42
Newark, NJ	1.02	0.89	1.18	1.15
New Orleans, LA	0.38	0.41	0.43	0.38
New York, NY	0.22	0.21	0.18	0.19
Norfolk, VA	0.41	0.36	0.50	0.33
Oakland, CA	0.73	0.49	0.76	0.43
Ogden, UT	0.67	0.62	0.97	0.76
Oklahoma City, OK	0.37	0.39	0.44	0.35
Omaha, NB	0.27	0.25	0.34	0.30
Ontario, CA	0.67	0.46	0.71	0.24
Pawtucket, RI	0.59	0.65	0.62	0.71
Philadelphia, PA	0.36	0.47	0.37	0.54
Phoenix, AZ	0.18	0.14	0.28	0.20
Pittsburgh, PA	0.86	0.42	1.05	0.48
Portland, OR	0.69	0.58	0.72	0.47
Portsmouth, VA	0.39	0.31	0.38	0.28
Providence, RI	0.77	0.76	0.80	0.84
Richmond, VA	0.68	0.53	0.72	0.46
Riverside, CA	0.45	0.40	0.48	0.40
Rochester, NY	0.95	0.66	1.18	1.04
Sacramento, CA	0.65	0.44	0.66	0.25
St. Louis, MO	1.10	1.19	1.08	1.25

Table A6.1 (Cont.)

	1972		1982	
	Potential (50-25-25)	Actual	Potential (50-25-25)	Actual
St. Paul, MN	0.63	0.48	0.72	0.41
St. Petersburg, FL	0.32	0.44	0.25	0.29
Salt Lake City, UT	0.94	0.90	1.25	0.86
San Bernardino, CA	1.03	1.07	1.03	1.09
San Diego, CA	0.27	0.24	0.27	0.15
San Francisco, CA	0.65	0.63	0.56	0.59
San Jose, CA	0.30	0.22	0.24	0.12
Santa Ana, CA	0.98	0.54	1.11	0.52
Tampa, FL	0.51	0.71	0.81	0.78
Toledo, OH	0.41	0.27	0.43	0.27
Tucson, AZ	0.33	0.38	0.39	0.45
Tulsa, OK	0.26	0.30	0.36	0.36
Virginia Beach, VA	0.23	0.24	0.17	0.17
Warwick, RI	0.59	0.35	0.68	0.42
Winston-Salem, NC	0.62	0.71	0.80	0.88
Washington, DC	0.92	0.37	0.92	0.28
Average	0.60	0.55	0.66	0.56

Note: Each export ratio is defined as the tax burden borne by nonresidents per dollar borne by residents.

7

The Sharing of Capacity with Overlying Jurisdictions

Boulder must share the taxable resources within its boundaries with an overlying county, an independent school district, and the state government. Denver differs from Boulder in that it is a city-county and therefore does not have to share its taxable resources with an overlying county. Denver's fiscal status also implies, however, that the city must provide its residents with county services along with municipal services. Any analysis of city fiscal health needs to incorporate these differences in fiscal structure.

We use the term *fiscal structure* to refer to two parts of a single package: the sharing of a city's taxable resources with overlying jurisdictions and the assignment of service responsibilities to the city. Although they are parts of the same package, the two components need not balance. For example, a city may have responsibility for a wide range of services, including local schools and health and welfare services, yet find itself with a high-spending state government that uses up a substantial portion of the revenue-raising capacity generated within the city. The possibility of a mismatch between the responsibilities assigned to a city and the revenue available to it means that we need to incorporate both elements of fiscal structure separately into our measures of city fiscal health. In this chapter we focus on the sharing of resources among levels of government. In chapter 8, we turn to the assignment of service responsibilities.

Differences across cities in service responsibilities and in the sharing of revenue-raising capacity largely reflect different patterns of historical development and the fact that cities are creatures of their states. New England cities and towns, for example, historically have had large fiscal responsibilities. In colonial New England, the town was the primary unit of local government, with the counties responsible only for judicial functions. In the Middle Atlantic region, county-townships evolved at the local level. Townships in New York, Pennsylvania, and New Jersey were subordinate to the county governments, in contrast to their independent status in New England. The Southern colonies developed a third pattern of local government, in which counties were the chief unit of local rural government. As settlers moved across the country, the Southern and Middle Atlantic models were transplanted and adapted, but the New England form was not copied (ACIR 1982, 229, 258).

Types of City

The major determinant of a city's fiscal structure is whether it has an overlying county government. Hence we begin our analysis of differences in fiscal structure by dividing cities into two basic categories: *separate cities*, which perform only municipal functions (and which coexist with a separate county government), and *city-counties*, which perform both municipal and county functions. Within each group, we further distinguish between cities that are part of a mixed state system and those that are not. In a mixed state system, some of the study cities within the state have separate overlying counties, but others do not. We differentiate between cities in mixed and "pure" state systems because those that differ from the norm in their state may be treated differently from those with a typical fiscal structure.[1]

Table 7.1 groups major central cities by city type and by Census region. Three-quarters of the 86 central cities have responsibility for municipal functions alone. This group includes all the cities in New Jersey, Ohio, and Texas and most of the cities in New York, Florida, and California. One-quarter of the cities have county responsibilities, including all those in New England and Virginia, selected large cities such as New York and Philadelphia whose fiscal structure differs from the norm in their states, and those, such as Jacksonville, Florida, Nashville-Davidson, Tennessee, and Indianapolis, that have merged with their surrounding counties to form metropolitan governments.

Recognizing the role of counties is just the first step in understanding the variation in fiscal structure across cities. In general, a city-county would be expected to have higher expenditure responsibilities than a city whose residents receive some services from an overlying county, but the magnitude of the difference depends on the division of service responsibilities between the state and its local governments. In some states with city-counties, for example, the state government assumes substantial responsibility

---

1. Furthermore, an additional adjustment to the reported data is needed for cities in states with mixed fiscal systems. See appendix to this chapter for details.

Table 7.1
Separate Cities and City-Counties in Uniform and Mixed State Sytems
(86 Cities)

Region	Separate cities		City-counties	
	Uniform State	Mixed State	Uniform State	Mixed State
New England			Boston, MA[a] Hartford, CT[a] Pawtucket, RI[a] Providence, RI[a] Warwick, RI[a]	
Middle Atlantic	Clifton, NJ[a] Newark, NJ[a] Passaic, NJ[ab] Paterson, NJ[a]	Albany, NY[a] Buffalo, NY[a] Pittsburgh, PA Rochester, NY[a] Schenectady, NY Troy, NY		New York, NY[a] Philadelphia, PA
East North Central	Akron, OH Chicago, IL Cincinnati, OH Cleveland, OH Columbus, OH Dayton, OH Detroit, MI Milwaukee, WI Toledo, OH		Indianapolis, IN	

Table 7.1 (Cont.)

Region	Separate cities		City-counties	
	Uniform State	Mixed State	Uniform State	Mixed State
West North Central	Minneapolis, MN Omaha, NB St. Paul, MN	Kansas City, MO		St. Louis, MO
South Atlantic	Charlotte, NC Greensboro, NC High Point, NC Winston-Salem, NC	Atlanta, GA Ft. Lauderdale, FL Hollywood, FL Miami, FL St. Petersburg, FL	Baltimore, MD[a] Norfolk, VA[a] Portsmouth, VA[a] Richmond, VA[a] Virginia Beach, VA[a] Washington, DC[a]	Jacksonville, FL
East South Central	Birmingham, AL	Louisville, KY Memphis, TN		Nashville-Davidson, TN[a]
West South Central	Austin, TX Dallas, TX El Paso, TX Ft. Worth, TX Houston, TX Oklahoma City, OK San Antonio, TX Tulsa, OK		New Orleans LA	
Mountain	Albuquerque, NM Ogden, UT Phoenix, AZ Salt Lake City, UT Tucson, AZ	Boulder, CO		Denver, CO

Table 7.1 (Cont.)

Region	Separate cities		City-counties	
	Uniform State	Mixed State	Uniform State	Mixed State
Pacific	Everett, WA	Anaheim, CA	Honolulu, HI	San Francisco, CA
	Portland, OR	Garden Grove, CA		
		Long Beach, CA		
		Los Angeles, CA		
		Oakland, CA		
		Ontario, CA		
		Riverside, CA		
		Sacramento, CA		
		San Bernardino, CA		
		San Diego, CA		
		San Jose, CA		
		Santa Ana, CA		

[a]Had responsibility for providing elementary and secondary education during at least one of the years of the study.
[b]Provided education in 1967 only.

for services such as welfare, social services, and courts, which are provided by county governments in other states. This state assumption tends to reduce the responsibilities of city-counties in these states relative to those of city-counties in states where more of these responsibilities are assigned to county governments. Thus an accurate picture of the fiscal structure of U.S. cities requires a detailed analysis that fully incorporates the division of responsibilities among levels of government within each state.

Our goal is to describe the fiscal structure of each city in a way that is independent of the actual choices made by the city government about tax or spending levels. We achieve this goal by using statewide data on taxes and spending to determine the share of responsibilities allocated to city governments within the state, with explicit recognition of the role of counties. To calculate either tax or spending responsibilities for a city with both municipal and county responsibilities, for example, we combine state data for municipalities with state data for counties to estimate a city-county's share of taxes or spending in that state. For cities having responsibility only for municipal functions, in contrast, we rely primarily on data for municipalities.[2] This procedure is discussed in more detail below for the sharing of taxable resources and in chapter 8 for the division of service responsibilities.

Variation Among Regions

States differ dramatically in the proportion of state and local tax revenues that are devoted to the provision of public services in cities. Table 7.2 presents "city" tax shares and "city" aid shares for cities grouped by region. The tax and aid shares indicate the shares of total state and local taxes that are collected as city taxes or that are distributed to cities as intergovernmental aid from the state or other local governments in each city's state. Thus the tax share summarizes cities' access to the taxable resources within their boundaries, and the aid share summarizes the additional resources available to cities through state aid. Together the tax and aid shares indicate the proportion of state and local revenues that serve to finance the services provided by city governments in each state.

---

2. Throughout, we use the term data for municipalities as shorthand for data for municipalities and townships. In most states in which township governments have significant responsibilities, municipalities and townships do not overlap, yet they provide a similar range of public services. Only in the special case of Indiana do we exclude townships from the analysis.

Table 7.2
Average City Shares of Taxes and State Aid by Region, 1982
(86 Cities; as Percentages of State and Local Taxes)

	City Tax Share (minimum to maximum)	City Aid Share (minimum to maximum)	City Tax and Aid Share (minimum to maximum)
New England	40.6 (38-43)	18.7 (16-22)	59.3 (59-61)
Middle Atlantic	21.3 (8-51)	15.3 (1-40)	36.5 (9-91)
East North Central	13.8 (12-15)	5.8 (3-17)	19.5 (17-30)
West North Central	13.1 (7-24)	5.3 (1- 8)	18.4 (15-28)
South Atlantic[a]	22.5 (11-41)	12.1 (1-29)	34.6 (12-70)
East South Central	21.8 (10-39)	11.3 (1-29)	33.1 (12-70)
West South Central	15.5 (15-20)	1.4 (0- 8)	16.9 (16-27)
Mountain	13.9 (8-25)	6.8 (1-13)	20.8 (12-36)
Pacific	14.1 (12-23)	4.7 (3-24)	18.7 (17-26)

Note: Each entry is the average share (expressed as a percentage) for cities in each region. City tax share was calculated as taxes paid to jurisdictions performing the same functions as each city as a percentage of total state and local taxes in the relevant state. City aid share was calculated as state and local aid to jurisdictions performing the same functions as each city as a percentage of total state and local taxes in the relevant state. See text for additional explanation.
[a]Averages exclude Washington, D.C.

The figures for each specific city from which the averages are calculated represent all taxes (or aid) in the relevant state raised by (or distributed to) all local governmental jurisdictions performing the functions comparable to the particular city. Thus the shares vary across cities in states with mixed systems because county taxes are included in the calculation for some cities but not for others. Differential treatment of taxes for elementary and secondary education account for the remaining variation among cities within a state. The city shares of taxes or aid are larger in a state for those cities that operate local public schools than they are for other cities where the school district is independent of the city government.

Table 7.2 shows that the three New England states with major cities (Massachusetts, Connecticut, and Rhode Island) devote almost 41 percent of state and local taxes to local governments that provide the same types of services as these cities. These services include county services, local public schools, and traditional municipal services. On average, an additional 18.7 percent of state and local taxes is distributed to city governments in the form of state aid. The data confirm the importance of city and town governments relative to state and other local governments in New England; the 59 percent tax plus aid share in the New England region exceeds the average share in each of the other regions by a large margin. Moreover, as is indicated by the entry in parentheses, tax and aid shares do not vary much across the New England cities.

At the other extreme in terms of tax share are the states in the North Central regions, both the East (Ohio and others) and the West (Minnesota and others); the Mountain region (Colorado, Arizona, and others), and the Pacific region (California and others), all with 13 or 14 percent of state and local taxes accruing directly to cities. These low percentages reflect the large proportion of cities in these states with responsibility for municipal functions alone and the correspondingly large role for county and state governments and special districts. The aid share is lowest in the West South Central region, which reflects extremely low aid shares for the Texas cities. At 1.4 percent of total state and local taxes, the average aid share for this region is significantly lower than the aid shares of 5-6 percent in four regions, 11-12 percent in two regions, and 15-18 percent in the Middle-Atlantic and New England regions.

Implications for Revenue-Raising Capacity

Standardizing tax burdens as a percentage of resident income is a central feature of our approach to measuring the capacity of cities to raise revenue from their own sources. As we discussed in chapter 3, a standard burden of 3 percent means that revenue-raising capacity would be measured as the maximum revenue a city could raise with a tax burden on city residents equal to 3 percent of resident income. Differences in fiscal structure among cities complicate the standardization procedure. Where overlying jurisdictions such as counties or school districts are important, part of the ability of city residents to pay taxes is "used up" by these jurisdictions. Consequently, careful comparisons across cities require that the standard burden in such cities be adjusted for the role of overlying governments. In addition, a complete notion of revenue-raising capacity must include all nonfederal intergovernmental aid to the city. We exclude federal aid from this calculation in order to focus on the state-specific fiscal institutions that influence the fiscal health of cities. We consider federal aid in chapter 11.

Thus a city's restricted revenue-raising capacity depends on the proportion of capacity claimed by overlying jurisdictions, the income of city residents, the city's ability to export tax burdens to nonresidents, and the amount of state aid it receives. We can express restricted revenue-raising capacity, RRRC, of a city as

$$RRRC = (KC)(Y)(1 + e') + AID^*,$$

where KC is a city-specific standard burden that accounts for the capacity claimed by overlying jurisdictions, Y is the per capita income of city residents, e' is an export ratio based on the taxes the city is allowed to use, and AID^* is standardized state aid to the city. Export ratios based on actual, in contrast to standard, taxes were discussed in chapter 6. We begin our discussion of the role of fiscal structure with the derivation of the city-specific standard burden, KC.

The logic behind the city-specific standard burden is straightforward. First, we specify a uniform standard burden, K^*, for the sum of all state and local taxes. Second, we calculate a city-specific standard burden, KC, that reflects both this overall standard burden and the differing distribution of claims upon that burden across states. To be more specific, we define KC as the fraction of city resident income that the city government can tap given the standard total state and local tax burden on city residents. Thus K^* is the same for all cities, whereas KC varies from one city to another depending on the type of city and the division of responsibilities among levels of government in the state. Ideally K^* and KC should apply to revenues from both taxes and user charges, but empirical and conceptual problems lead us to exclude user charges from the calculation. In chapter 8 we compensate for this exclusion by measuring service responsibilities net of user charges.[3]

We use actual tax decisions of state and local officials to set the standard burden K^*. We begin by calculating, for each state, the ratio of state and local taxes paid by residents to state income. Assuming that state and local

---

3. This approach is reasonable to the extent that they are payments for services residents choose to "buy" in addition to tax-supported services. It misleads by suggesting that user-charge financing is free to the city. In many cases, user charges represent a claim on the income of city residents just as taxes do, and, consequently, the more a city relies on user charges, the greater is the drain on its capacity to levy broad-based taxes. Much of the state data we require does not separate user charges from a host of miscellaneous revenues, such as interest earnings, that generally do not reduce the ability of residents to pay city taxes. In addition, inclusion of user charges would require that they be treated the same way as taxes, namely that such revenues be divided into resident and nonresident portions. This division is difficult to implement.

taxes are borne in proportion to income within each state, this ratio is equivalent to the average burden of state and local taxes on the residents of each city in the state.[4] Second, we rank the state-specific tax burdens assigned to each city from low to high, and we select as K^* the burden at the 75th percentile. Thus, instead of imposing our own value judgments about what K^* ought to be, we let it reflect actual state and local tax burdens; in particular, it is the tax burden that is exceeded in only 25 percent of the cities.

The uniform state and local tax burden translates into the following city-specific standard burden for city-level taxes alone (see appendix to this chapter for details of the derivation):

$$KC = K^* \left(\frac{\text{"City" taxes paid by residents in state j}}{\text{State and local taxes paid by residents in state j}} \right) .$$

In other words, the city-specific standard burden for city taxes alone is simply the standardized state and local burden for residents in all cities multiplied by the "city" share of total state and local tax burdens on residents of a specific city. The quotation marks around the word *city* are a reminder that cities have differing fiscal responsibilities. For cities with county functions, the calculation is based on the sum of taxes collected by both municipalities and counties within the appropriate state, but for cities without county functions, the calculation is based on municipalities' taxes alone. The city-specific standard burden varies across cities because of differences in the importance of state taxes relative to local taxes and of taxes levied by cities relative to taxes levied by other local governments.[5]

The basic idea here is that the ratio of city taxes to total state and local taxes reflects the fraction of all state and local taxes not claimed by state government and noncity local governments. Thus KC represents the fraction of resident income that would be available for city taxes if the com-

4. To calculate the average burden in each state, we used data on state and local taxes from the *Census of Governments* and data on tax exporting from Donald Phares as updated by Steven Barro. Specifically, we used Phares's 1976 estimates by states for 1972 and 1977, and Barro's 1981 estimates for 1982. All estimates are based on the methodology initially developed by McLure 1976. Barro's estimates were made available to us on a computer printout. Initially calculated by Phares, the export ratios were modified by Barro to treat severance taxes uniformly across states.
5. It also should vary with differences in the relative exportability of state and local taxes, but, in practice, we ignore this variation.

bined burden on resident income of all state and local taxes in the state were K^*.

An example may clarify the importance of calculating city-specific standard burdens. Consider two different cities, one in a state where cities have responsibility for financing schools and the other in a state where independent school districts finance schools. Assume further that the two cities have exactly the same resident income and ability to export tax burdens to nonresidents and that the boundary of the independent school district coincides with that of the second city. Hence both cities have the same capacity to finance the combined total of municipal and school services. This implies that the revenue-raising capacity available to the city without responsibility for schools must be less than that of the other city; part of its capacity is used up by the overlying school district. Because this study focuses on the city government as the unit of observation, in contrast to the geographic area defined by the city, we must adjust for such claims on capacity made by overlying governments. For the city without responsibility for schools, statewide data on the fraction of all state and local revenues raised by school districts and other overlying governments, including state government, indicate the fraction of the total standard resident burden used up by other governments and therefore not available to the city government. For the city with responsibility for schools, revenues raised for schools are not treated as capacity used up, so a greater share of income remains available for the city's larger responsibilities.

This approach correctly captures the possibility that tax decisions by higher levels of government may adversely affect the revenue-raising capacity of cities. For example, an increase in state government taxes not accompanied by an increase in city taxes reduces the measured capacity of a city in the state to finance public services; a smaller share of a fixed pie is available for city taxes. If, on the other hand, the taxes levied by cities statewide increase at the same rate as those levied by the state and all non-city local governments, the calculated fiscal capacity of a city in the state remains unchanged, all other factors held constant. This outcome reflects the standardizing procedure; a uniform total state and local tax burden is used for all states regardless of actual tax levels.

High state taxes relative to city taxes lower a city's standard burden and hence reduce its ability to raise revenues from its own resources. To the extent that high state taxes are used to provide aid to the city, however, the low standard burden for a specific city gives a misleading picture of its total ability to finance public services, where total ability includes both its ability to raise local taxes and its receipt of state aid.

Because our measure of a city's actual revenue-raising capacity incorporates the negative effects on the city's revenue-raising capacity of the state's claim on local resources, it should also include state aid to the city.

We measure the contribution of state aid to the revenue-raising capacity of a particular city by actual aid to that city, adjusted to make it consistent with other components of revenue-raising capacity. The adjusted aid approximates the per capita aid the city would receive if the state-local system of which it is a part were imposing the standard state-local burden on all its residents. If the standard burden, K^*, were 14 percent, for example, but state and local taxes paid by residents in the state were 16 percent of income, we would scale actual aid to the particular city down to 14/16 of its actual value. Analogously, aid in a low-tax state is scaled up.

Patterns across Cities and over Time

In chapters 9 and 11 we examine how the whole set of fiscal institutions affects the fiscal health of U.S. cities and look for patterns across cities grouped by size, economic health of residents, and economic health of the city itself. Because this chapter focuses on only two of the components of fiscal institutions—the city-specific standard burden and state aid—the reader must be careful not to attach too much policy significance to the variations across cities and over time reported below. These results contribute to our understanding of one part of a complex phenomenon, but because they exclude other components of the package of fiscal institutions, such as the division of service responsibilities and rules about what taxes cities are empowered to use, they tell us little about the net effect of the whole package of fiscal institutions.

Table 7.3 summarizes variation in city tax shares (the key determinant of variation in city-specific tax burdens) and adjusted per capita aid by groups of cities in 1982. All else equal, the higher the city tax share, the higher the own-source revenue-raising capacity of the city. Similarly, the higher adjusted aid, the higher the city's total revenue-raising capacity.

No clear patterns emerge for cities grouped by size or by their economic health. The clearest and most interesting pattern emerges for cities grouped by the income of residents. With one exception to the pattern, state fiscal institutions boost the revenue-raising capacity of cities with poorer residents more than they boost that of cities with richer residents. Cities with the poorest residents can tap about 22.6 percent of the total state and local burden for their own taxes in contrast to the 16 percent that those with higher resident income can tap. And the poorest cities receive about

Table 7.3
City Shares of Taxes and State Aid, 1982
(85 Cities)

	Number of Cities	1982 City Share of State and Local Taxes[a] (%)	1982 Standardized Per Capita Aid[b] (1982 dollars)
All Cities			
Average	85	18.6	173
Standard Deviation	85	10.6	191
Minimum	85	7.4	8
Maximum	85	50.6	950
City population in thousands			
Less than 100	11	19.1	118
100-250	20	20.0	187
250-500	31	16.9	147
500-1,000	17	19.3	227
Greater than 1,000	6	20.6	210
Resident income per capita			
Quintile 1	17	22.6	288
Quintile 2	17	20.0	190
Quintile 3	17	18.3	167
Quintile 4	17	16.1	122
Quintile 5	17	20.9	93
City economic health[c]			
Quintile 1	17	10.0	161
Quintile 2	17	20.4	225
Quintile 3	16	23.4	158
Quintile 4	17	13.5	76
Quintile 5	18	20.6	233
Washington, DC	1	100.0	16

Note: Each entry is an average for the indicated category of city.

[a]Calculated from statewide data, the city share is defined as the taxes collected in jurisdictions performing the same functions as each city as a percentage of total state and local taxes in the relevant state.

[b]Per capita state aid to each city adjusted to approximate the per capita aid the city would receive if the state and local system of which it is a part were imposing the standard state and local tax burden on its residents. "State" aid includes small amounts of aid from other local governments.

[c]Measured as private sector jobs in the city per city resident. See chapter 2 for discussion of city economic health.

$288 in state aid in contrast to $93 for the those with the richest residents. Recall from chapter 3 that standardized revenue-raising capacity is higher for cities with richer residents than for those with poorer residents. This new finding implies that state fiscal institutions tend to counteract the effects of income on revenue-raising capacity, thereby making actual revenue-raising capacity more equal across cities grouped by resident income than it would be if it were based on local economies alone.

Table 7.4 indicates changes in city tax shares and in per capita aid for the 1972-82 period for cities grouped by size, changes in the income of city residents, and changes in the economic health of the city. If one assumes no change over time in the standard state and local tax burden, reductions in city tax shares translate directly into comparable percentage reductions in the capacity of cities to raise revenue from their own taxes. Reductions in state aid reduce a city's total revenue-raising capacity, but the proportional reductions depend on the amount of aid relative to own-source fiscal capacity.

In contrast to the cross-sectional results, changes in fiscal structure appear to have reinforced the adverse effects of changes in local economies. Consider first the categories that represent changes in the economic health of city residents. A clear pattern emerges for changes in city tax shares: those where resident income grew most slowly experienced over 8.6 percentage point declines in city tax shares, and consequently in own-source revenue-raising capacity, whereas those where resident income increased the most benefited from rising city tax shares. A similar pattern emerges across cities grouped by changes in city economic health: those with less job growth per resident experienced larger declines in their ability to tap local resources than those with more job growth. The pattern of changes in per capita aid is less clear. In some categories of city it reinforces the changes in city shares, but in others it counteracts them. We return to this issue in chapter 11, where we provide a more complete analysis of state aid in the context of our full measures of fiscal health.

The Tax Revolt

During the late 1970s and early 1980s, voters became increasingly reluctant to levy state and local taxes. California gained national attention in 1978 as its citizens voted to roll back local property taxes, but many other states also joined the revolt either by passing referenda to limit state or local taxes or both or by the reluctance of elected officials to vote for tax increases. In chapter 6, we discussed the effect of the tax revolt on the mix of taxes

Table 7.4
Changes in City Shares of Taxes and State Aid, 1972-1982
(85 Cities)

Cities	Number of Cities	1972-82 Percentage Change		
		City Share of Taxes[a]	Aid (1982 dollars)[b]	KC (with Tax Revolt)[c]
Average	85	- 1.2	- 0.4	-12.3
Standard Deviation	85	19.4	94.3	17.2
Minimum	85	-67.7	-318.8	-71.3
Maximum	85	63.0	316.6	44.6
City population in thousands				
Less than 100	11	0.4	6.2	-11.0
100-250	20	- 2.8	- 2.6	-13.8
250-500	31	- 0.1	- 3.1	-11.3
500-1,000	17	- 2.8	11.5	-13.8
Greater than 1,000	6	0.1	- 24.3	-11.2
Below-average income, 1971				
Low growth	21	- 8.9	32.2	-19.2
Medium growth	12	- 2.6	- 48.5	-13.6
High growth	10	2.2	13.7	- 9.3
Above-average income, 1971				
Low growth	8	- 8.6	- 47.2	-18.9
Medium growth	17	- 0.3	2.8	-11.6
High growth	17	10.0	4.1	- 2.4
Below-average economic health, 1972				
Low growth	12	- 2.3	- 40.4	-13.4
Medium growth	12	1.5	0.9	- 9.9
High growth	20	9.3	3.0	- 3.0
Above-average economic health, 1972				
Low growth	17	-10.6	14.6	-20.7
Medium growth	16	- 5.7	14.0	-16.4
High growth	8	- 0.7	- 10.8	-11.9

Note: City categories for income change and economic health change are defined in tables 3.4 and 2.2.
[a]Based on statewide data. See definition in table 7.3.
[b]Standardized aid per capita to each city. See definition in table 7.3.
[c]City-specific tax burden, defined as the product of the state and local standard tax burden and the city share of state and local taxes. "With tax revolt" means that the standard tax burden is permitted to decline from its 1972 value of 14.5 percent of income to its 1982 value of 12.9 percent.

used in each city. Here we focus on the effects of the nationwide decline in the propensity of voters to levy state and local taxes.

Figure 7.1 indicates the power of the national tax revolt by presenting standard state and local tax burdens on residents as a percentage of income. The figure shows that voters were least willing to tax themselves for state and local services in 1967, that they became substantially more willing to do so during the late 1960s and early 1970s, but that between 1978 and 1982 they reversed the upward trend. The 40 percent increase in the state and local tax burden between 1967 and 1972 financed the rapid growth of the state and local public sector at that time. The leveling off of the growth and then the 11 percent decline between 1978 and 1982 indicate the strength of the tax revolt movement, which had its origins in the mid-1970s and accelerated after the success of California's tax limitation measure in 1978. On average, U.S. citizens paid approximately 13 percent of their income in state and local taxes in 1982.

The decline in voter support for state and local taxes does not bode well for the provision of public services in U.S. cities. We have chosen not to incorporate this national decline into our basic measure of city revenue-raising capacity, however. Instead, we measure a city's revenue-raising capacity in 1982 as the amount of revenue the city could raise given the 1972 standard state and local tax burden of 14.5 percent.

If the fall in the standard burden from 14.5 percent in 1972 to 12.9 percent in 1982 is included in the analysis, the revenue-raising picture of cities looks bleaker than it does when based on changes in city tax shares alone. This result is shown in the final column of table 7.4. The national decline in voters' willingness to tax themselves means that the average proportion of resident income available for city taxes declined in all categories of city. This decline in turn translates into much larger declines in own-source revenue-raising capacity than is given by the percentage changes in the city tax shares alone. Our basic measure of changes in fiscal health holds tax effort constant at the 1972 level. In chapter 11, however, we supplement the basic analysis with separate analysis of the effects of the nationwide tax revolt.

Although the national effects of the tax limitation movement are not incorporated into our measures of changes in revenue-raising capacity, state-specific effects of tax limitations are included—partly through their impact on the mix of taxes, as we discussed in chapter 6, and partly through their impact on city tax shares. Consider, for example, a tax limitation provision that initially applies to city but not state taxes in a particular state. This provision will reduce the revenue-raising capacity of the state's cities

Figure 7.1
Standard State and Local Tax Burdens on City Residents, 1967-1982

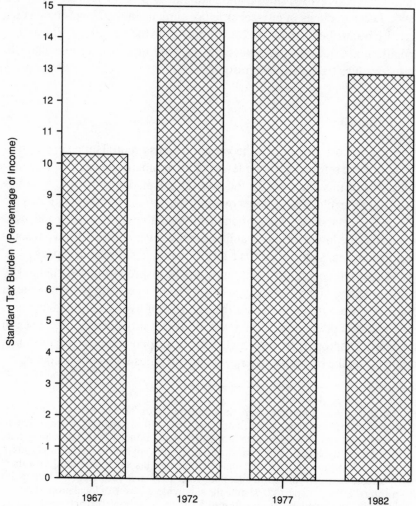

by reducing the city share of state and local taxes. This type of reduction shows up most clearly in the data for Boston. Reflecting the stringent limitation on local property taxes passed by Massachusetts in November 1980, the calculated city share of state and local taxes (based on data for all municipalities and townships in the state) fell 31 percent between 1978 and 1982. Large declines in city-specific tax burdens in the New Jersey cities can also be attributed to local expenditure lids in the late 1970s. Thus state-specific limitations clearly reduce the capacity of cities in these states to raise revenues from their own resources.[6]

Conclusions

This chapter documents the variation across central cities in the sharing of taxable resources among levels of government and examines the implications of this variation for the revenue-raising capacity of U.S. cities. The larger the role of overlying governments, the smaller the fraction of the standard state and local tax burden that is available for city taxes and, consequently, the lower the city's ability to raise revenue from its own resources. In addition, state aid boosts a city's total revenue-raising capacity.

Cities with poorer residents appear to be disproportionately helped by below-average claims on taxable resources of overlying governments in 1982. But we remind the reader that the role of overlying jurisdictions is only part of a package of fiscal institutions that influence the fiscal health of cities. Disproportionately high service responsibilities, for example, might offset the favorable revenue picture in cities with poor residents.

---

6. Tax limitations sometimes have the opposite effect. That is, they sometimes increase the city tax share of state and local taxes within a state. This occurs whenever the limitation reduces state government and noncity local taxes more than it reduces city taxes. Somewhat surprisingly, this appears to be the situation for most California cities. We calculate that the city tax share increased by almost 9 percent in most California cities between 1977 and 1982 (and by 16 percent during the 1972-82 period) despite the statewide rollback of local property taxes in 1978 mandated by Proposition 13. Because school districts and county governments were more dependent on local property taxes than were the cities, municipal taxes grew relative to other local taxes. Also contributing to the growth in the city tax share were the limitations on state government tax revenues imposed by referenda passed after Proposition 13. Consistent with this explanation are the contrasting results for San Francisco, the only California city with responsibility for both municipal and county functions. Our calculations indicate a 15 percent decline in the city tax share for San Francisco because of the fall in the share of state and local taxes accruing to local jurisdictions performing county functions throughout the state.

Changes over time present a less encouraging picture than the cross-section findings for cities with weak or declining economies. Those with the weakest economies appear to have experienced disproportionately large reductions between 1972 and 1982 in their capacity to tap resident income and, in some cases, in state aid.

Our basic analysis in subsequent chapters assumes that voters were equally willing to tax themselves in 1982 and in 1972. This assumption means that our basic measures of changes in fiscal health do not reflect the observed decline in the willingness of voters to levy state and local taxes between 1972 and 1982, but a separate analysis highlights the fiscal effects of the national tax revolt.

Appendix: Accounting for Overlying Jurisdictions

As was explained in chapter 3, the notion of revenue-raising capacity incorporates a single standardized tax burden, K^*, that applies to the residents of all cities. To calculate a city's actual revenue-raising capacity, however, we adjust the standardized tax burden in each city to account for the importance of that city in its state's tax system—that is, to account for the portion of each city's revenue-raising capacity that is claimed by over-lying jurisdictions. In this appendix we explain how to calculate the standardized city tax burden, KC, for different types of city.

Remember that K^* is the standardized total state and local tax burden, expressed as a percentage of resident income. We define the standardized city tax burden in a city m in state j, KC_{mj}, to be equal to K^* multiplied by the fraction of state and local taxes in state j that are city taxes. In other words, KC_{mj} is the share of the overall standardized tax burden that is not claimed by overlying jurisdictions in state j and is therefore available to a city in that state.

The calculation of KC is not the same for all cities because some have county or school functions in addition to municipal functions. To simplify the presentation, we define the following taxes paid by residents of state j:

ST_j = total state taxes

M_j = total municipal, that is, city government, taxes

C_j = total county taxes

SD_j = total school district taxes

O_j = total other local taxes.

Different components of this list belong with "city" taxes depending on a city's assigned responsibilities.

Separate Cities

Separate cities, by definition, do not have responsibility for county functions. Assume for the moment that they also have no responsibility for local schools. For cities of this type, the standardized city tax burden on residents can be written:

$$(A7.1) \qquad KC_{mj} = K^* \left(\frac{M_j}{ST_j + M_j + C_j + SDj + O_j} \right).$$

City-specific information is not available for calculating this expression. We would not want to use such information even if it were available, however, because it would inappropriately reflect the actual level of taxes in city m. Instead we rely on statewide data. The denominator of the expression in parentheses is total state and local taxes in state j. To calculate the numerator, one possibility is to use total taxes in all municipalities and townships in the state, with townships included because they are indistinguishable from municipalities in most of the states in which township governments have significant responsibilities. (Indiana must be treated differently because townships play a different role there than elsewhere.) This approach is reasonable for states in which all residents live in areas incorporated either as municipalities or townships.

This approach is not appropriate, however, for states in which a substantial portion of the population lives in unincorporated areas. Because people in unincorporated areas often receive municipal type services from county governments, taxes in municipalities and townships understate the total amount of taxes collected for municipal type services. Two options emerge for dealing with the problem of unincorporated areas.

1. Use statewide taxes collected by municipalities and townships (M_j) in the numerator, just as above.
2. Use M_j multiplied by 1 plus a population adjustment factor (the ratio of population in unincorporated areas to population in municipalities and townships) to blow up taxes collected by municipalities and townships to cover all state residents.

Option 1 is more appropriate than option 2 if counties provide limited municipal type services to residents of unincorporated areas. By averaging municipal taxes over all residents of the state, option 1 produces results that are comparable to those for states in which rural areas are incorporated but municipal services in such areas are limited. Option 2, in contrast, is more appropriate when per capita spending on municipal type services to unincorporated areas is the same as per capita municipal and township spending statewide. This option essentially treats the observed taxes of municipalities and townships as applying only to people in incorporated areas and grosses them up in line with the share of population in unincorporated areas. Because neither extreme is fully correct, we compromise by making one-half the adjustment required by option 2. Thus, to calculate KC for separate cities, we use statewide data to replace M_j with

$$(A7.2) \qquad M_j^* = M_j \frac{(1 + \text{Population adjustment factor})}{2}.$$

Note that the population adjustment factor is 0 in states with no unincorporated areas.

City-Counties

For cities with county responsibilities we add county taxes to the numerator of equation (A7.1) to obtain

$$(A7.3) \qquad KC_j = K^* \left(\frac{M_j + C_j}{ST_j + M_j + C_j + SO_j + O_j} \right).$$

Because all residents in all states live in counties, problems related to unincorporated areas do not arise in this case. We simply use statewide data on the sum of municipal, township, and county taxes in the numerator of the "city" share component of the expression.

Cities in States with Mixed Fiscal Systems

One additional adjustment is needed in the calculation of KC for separate cities in states where some cities perform county as well as municipal functions. Statewide taxes collected by municipalities and townships as a share of total state and local taxes overstate the "city" share for separate cities (if one ignores the problem of unincorporated areas), because such taxes include some taxes for the county functions provided by the city-counties in the state. Hence we adjust M_j downward for separate cities in mixed state systems to correct for this problem.

Cities with Responsibility for Local Public Schools

The treatment of cities with responsibility for local public schools is straightforward. We simply add statewide school taxes, SD_j, to the numerator of equation (A7.2) or (A7.3). In several cases this number is quite small, because much of the local school spending statewide is already included in municipal taxes (M_j).

8
Service Responsibilities

One of the most striking facts to emerge from the 1975 fiscal crisis in New York City was the wide range of services provided by the city. Not only was the city providing basic public services such as sanitation and public safety, but it was also paying part of welfare costs, providing elementary and secondary education, and financing both a municipal hospital and a city university (for a detailed discussion see Gramlich 1976). This wide range of services required a high level of public spending and hence led to a high tax burden on residents. It also raised questions about the extent to which a city government is able to provide redistributive services given the potential for upper income-households and firms to move out of the city.

Certainly cities have some control over the range of services they provide. Some cities choose, for example, to provide housing subsidies for the poor and others do not. But to a large extent, the scope of a city's service responsibilities is outside its control. New York City has little choice about welfare spending, for example; the New York State government decides how the nonfederal portion of welfare costs is to be allocated among state and local governments. Similarly, a city has little choice about local public schools. State governments typically determine whether elementary and secondary education is to be provided by the city or by an independent school district. Less obvious, but also important, is the division of responsibilities among levels of government for spending categories such as parks and roads. The greater the share of responsibility given to overlying governments, the lower the remaining burden on city governments.

Our measure of the scope of a city's service responsibilities is intended to reflect statewide decisions about the division of service responsibilities among levels of government, but not the actual spending decisions of a particular city. Because a city's service responsibilities affect how much it must spend to provide a given quality of public services, they are a key component of the set of fiscal institutions that, along with economic and demographic factors, determine the city's actual fiscal health.

An Index of Service Responsibilities

City spending depends on the quality of services the city chooses to provide, the cost of providing an average quality of services, and the scope of service responsibilities assigned to the city. As a measure of scope, our index of service responsibilities indicates how much the city would have to spend to provide services of average quality if it faced average costs, given the division of responsibilities within the city's state.

Consider first the extreme case of a city that has exclusive responsibility, if one ignores the role of the federal government, for providing a particular service, say health and social services. Washington, D.C., best exemplifies this situation in that it has no overlying state or other local governments with which to share the burden of providing services to its residents. In this case, national average per capita spending on health and social services by state and local governments can serve as a measure of how much the city would have to spend to provide average service quality if it had average costs.

More generally, spending responsibilities are shared between city and noncity state and local governments. In some cases a city has little responsibility for health and social service programs relative to other levels of government. This situation arises, for example, if the state assigns primary responsibility for such services to county governments and if the city has an overlying county. In other cases a city has extensive responsibility for health and social services because it has no overlying county and its state government plays little role in the provision of these services.

We can measure these differences by the "city" share of total state and local spending on the specified service in the city's state. The quotation marks around the word *city* emphasize that "city" refers to all governmental jurisdictions in the state that perform the same functions as the particular city. If, for example, the city in question is a city-county, the numerator of the fraction would include spending by all counties in the state as well as that by municipalities.

This logic implies that the scope of a city's responsibility for health and social services can be measured as national average spending per capita multiplied by the "city" share of state and local spending in the state. The national average spending level indicates the per capita spending requirement that would fall on each city if all spending on that service were assigned to city governments in the state. In practice we reduce this amount by the average proportion of spending that is recovered from fees and charges so that it represents the amount of state and local spending to be financed out of general revenues.[1] The city share indicates the proportion of the per capita spending on the service that is allocated to cities in the state. If city governments account for 40 percent of total state and local spending on health and social services in the state, for example, we measure the scope of the city's responsibility for these services as 40 percent of the national average per capita spending (minus fees) of state and local governments on health and human services.[2]

This approach to measuring service responsibilities is analogous to that for the city-specific tax burden in chapter 7. In both cases we start with a national average and adjust it downward using data on the division of taxes or spending between city and all noncity governments within the state.

We calculate a city-specific responsibility index for each of the fourteen general services listed in table 8.1. Because the index for each service is expressed in dollars per capita, the sum over the fourteen services is simply the total spending required to meet the city's general spending responsibilities, if one assumes services of average quality produced at average cost. One can view the index as a weighted average of the fourteen city shares (which correspond to the 40 percent share in our earlier example), where the weights are per capita national average spending by state and local governments on each service. For example, if city governments in state X spend 90 percent of the money appropriated by all state and local governments for police services and 60 percent of the money appropriated for libraries, the overall index would give greater weight to the 0.9 city share for police spending than to the 0.6 library share because of the higher per capita national spending on police than on libraries.[3]

Three services—elementary and secondary education, higher education, and hospitals—require special treatment. In contrast to its role in providing the other fourteen services, a city either has or does not have spending responsibility for local schools, higher education, or a city hospital. Hence we first determine which cities provide these services and then calculate responsibility measures only for those providing each service in a specific year.

---

1. For the user charge adjustment, we use published data for cities with population over 300,000 to calculate a coverage ratio defined as the average percentage of expenditures on each service covered by user fee revenues. Thus for each service we adjust national average spending downward by the proportion of spending that a city could expect to receive from fees. See also chap. 7 n. 3.
2. A detailed description of our calculations can be found in appendix to this chapter.
3. In 1982 average per capita spending on libraries was $8.88 and on police was $72.88.

Table 8.1
Services Included in the Index of Service Responsibilities

General services responsibility index
Libraries
Public welfare
Health
Highways
Parking
Police
Fire
Corrections
Sewerage
Sanitation other than sewerage
Parks and recreation
Housing and urban development
Air transportation
Water transportation

Special services
Elementary and secondary education
Higher education
Hospitals

Total service responsibility index
General and special services

The cities that had responsibility for local schools in at least one of the study years are indicated in table 7.1. These cities are concentrated in New England and along the Atlantic coast. In the South and West, elementary and secondary education are always provided by independent school districts and not by the city. Because the magnitude of required spending varies with public school enrollment, we base our calculation of spending for this service on U.S. average per pupil, rather than per capita, spending. The education responsibility index is then converted back to per capita terms by multiplying average per pupil spending by the city's ratio of pupils to population. If a city does not have responsibility for local schools, its index for this category is zero.

Only Washington, D.C., and New York City devoted substantial resources to higher education in 1982.[4] The index of responsibilities for

---

4. Because Baltimore spends some money for higher education, we included it as one of the cities with responsibility for higher education. Its low spending in this category suggests, however, that its responsibility is not comparable to that of New York City and Washington, D.C.

higher education for these cities is simply the average net spending per capita of the study cities that provide this service. Similarly, the index of hospital responsibilities is the average per capita spending on hospitals minus direct hospital revenues by the study cities. The 7 cities responsible for municipal hospitals in 1982 are Austin, Boston, Indianapolis, New York, San Francisco, St. Louis, and Washington, D.C.

Combining the general services responsibility index based on the fourteen general services with the indices for the three special services yields a total service responsibility index for each city. This comprehensive index of a city's responsibilities for current operating expenditures can be compared across cities and over time. General administrative expenses are omitted from the index, but this omission has little effect on our subsequent analysis because a city's administrative costs are approximately proportional to its total spending on the measured categories.[5]

Our measure of service responsibilities is intended to indicate the scope of services to be provided by each central city, given the division of responsibilities in the city's state. As such, service responsibilities are a major, but not the only determinant, of a city's expenditure need. As was shown in chapter 4, city-specific environmental factors such as population density or the incidence of poverty significantly affect the cost to the city of providing public services. We have excluded these cost factors from the service responsibility index in this chapter to focus on the state-specific division of spending responsibilities among levels of government. In chapter 9, we explore how city-specific cost factors interact with service responsibilities to determine the overall expenditure need of a city.

Variation across Cities

Compared to separate cities, city-counties typically have more extensive responsibilities because they must provide county as well as municipal services. We capture this difference in our index by using the city-county or separate city status of the city to determine the "city" share component of the index. To calculate the index for a city-county such as San Francisco, for example, we use data on statewide spending by both counties and municipalities to determine the "city" share of total state and local spending. For the other California cities, all of which have overlying counties, in

---

5. We would have liked to include transit assistance, which is a sizable expenditure item in some cities, but data were available for this spending category only for cities with population over 300,000.

contrast, we use spending by municipalities alone. Consequently, San Francisco has substantially higher responsibilities according to our measure than the other California cities.

Higher spending associated with the provision of county functions accounts for only part of the variation in our index across cities. An active state government or extensive reliance on special districts reduces city responsibilities whereas city provision of local schools, a hospital, or a college all increase its service responsibilities. The combined average effects of these factors are illustrated in figure 8.1 for cities grouped by city-county status. The four categories of city are the same as those listed in table 7.1. The first two categories are separate cities, that is, cities without overlying counties. They differ only in that the second group of cities are in states in which at least one other central city is a city-county. The second two categories are city-counties, with the same distinction between the two categories as for the separate cities.

The figure shows that the average service responsibilities in city-counties are more than double those in separate cities. Some of the difference ($20-30 per capita) is accounted for by broader responsibilities in the city-counties for general services other than welfare and health. A larger share ($40-85) is due to the concentration in city-counties of responsibility for health and welfare. These redistributive types of service tend to be assigned to county governments, if they are assigned to the local level at all. Hence cities providing county functions are more likely to have responsibility for these functions than are separate cities. Spending on higher education or hospitals increases average responsibilities by $10 to $60 per capita more in the city counties than in the separate cities.

Responsibility for local schools has the largest impact on these average figures. On average, the provision of schools increases service responsibilities by $300 per capita in a city-county in a nonmixed system but only by $32 per capita in a separate city in a nonmixed system. These figures reflect differences across cities in pupils as a proportion of the population and, more importantly, differences across categories of city in the proportion of cities that have responsibility for local schools. Thus the large burden of local schools in the city-counties (in nonmixed systems) reflects the fact that 10 of the 14 cities in this category have responsibility for local schools (as shown in table 7.1, excluding Washington D.C.). In contrast, only 6 of 64 cities without overlying counties had responsibility for schools in 1982.

Figure 8.2 provides a somewhat different perspective by restricting the sample to the 19 cities with responsibility for local schools in 1982. In all

Figure 8.1
Composition of Service Responsibilities, 1982
(86 Cities)

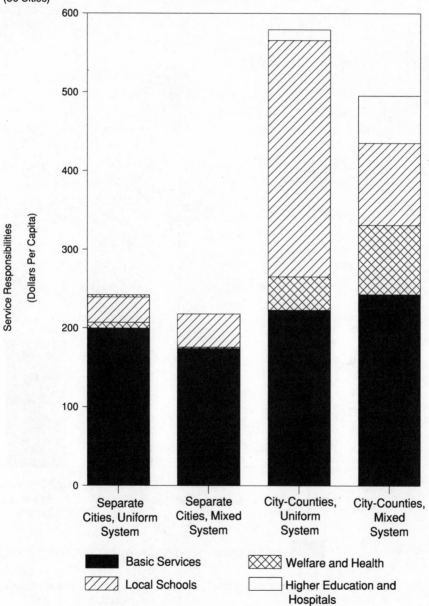

Figure 8.2
Composition of Service Responsibilities Including Schools, 1982
(19 Cities with Responsibility for Schools)

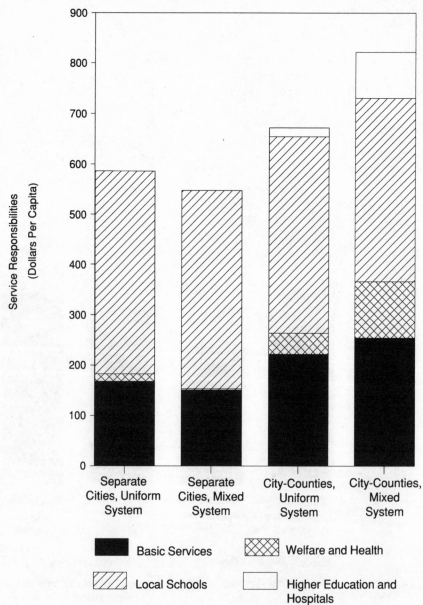

Basic Services

Local Schools

Welfare and Health

Higher Education and
Hospitals

four categories of city, average school responsibilities substantially exceed responsibilities for basic services (excluding health and welfare). Only in the city-counties in mixed systems does the total of all other service responsibilities exceed those for local schools.

These patterns by city type help explain some of the variation in service responsibilities across regions. (The patterns by region are not shown in a separate table because they are quite similar to those shown for taxes and aid shares in table 7.2.) Because all 5 New England cities have responsibility for both county functions and local schools, it is not surprising that they top the list with average service responsibilities of $617. If one controls for city-county status, however, their responsibilities for the fourteen general services are lower than those in all other regions.[6] This result reflects the large role of New England state governments, relative to other states, in health and welfare spending. The lowest average service responsibilities are found in cities in the East North Central states of Ohio, Illinois, Michigan, and Wisconsin ($209) and in the Pacific states of Washington, Oregon, California, and Hawaii ($219). Both regions have separate counties and independent local school districts.

Historical accident, rather than rational planning, appears to be the main determinant of variation in service responsibilities across states. This observation makes it difficult to develop specific hypotheses about how service responsibilities are likely to vary across cities grouped by the characteristics of central interest for this book: population, the income of residents, and a city's economic health. The best we can do is to try to understand the patterns we observe.

Table 8.2 shows that relatively clear patterns emerge across cities grouped by size and income, but not by the city's economic health. In terms of size, those with larger populations have higher per capita service responsibilities than those with smaller populations. The service responsibilities in cities with population over 1 million, for example, exceed those in the smallest cities by over 25 percent.

---

6. This statement is based on a regression of general service responsibilities on dummy variables for eight Census divisions (using New England as the base) and dummy variable for three city types (using separate cities in mixed fiscal systems as the base). The coefficients of all the regional dummies are positive, and most are significantly different from zero. These results imply that service responsibilities are higher in other regions than they are in New England, when one controls for city type. The regression also shows that all other city types have higher responsibilities than separate cities in mixed systems, when one controls for region; separate cities have responsibilities that are higher by $37, city-counties by $102, and city-counties in mixed systems by $166.

Table 8.2
Service Responsibilities, 1982
(86 Cities; in Dollars per Capita)

	Number of Cities	Basic Services (without Health and Welfare)	Health and Welfare	Local Schools	Higher Education and Hospitals	Total Service Responsibilities
All Cities						
Average		198.2	17.3	82.6	8.5	306.6
Standard deviation		21.3	36.2	162.5	37.8	197.1
Minimum		117.8	0.0	0.0	0.0	117.8
Maximum		270.1	203.0	508.2	184.4	998.9
City population in thousands						
Less than 100	11	178.2	6.8	91.3	0.0	276.2
100–250	20	190.6	11.9	121.6	0.0	324.1
250–500	31	195.2	10.2	67.1	7.6	280.1
500–1,000	17	219.6	31.7	68.4	17.8	337.4
Greater than 1,000	6	215.1	50.1	56.9	30.7	352.8
Resident income per capita						
Quintile 1	17	191.1	15.5	145.4	10.8	362.9
Quintile 2	17	202.9	13.0	133.3	6.9	356.1
Quintile 3	17	190.5	27.9	64.4	10.8	293.7
Quintile 4	17	210.1	9.5	54.1	6.9	280.6
Quintile 5	17	196.3	20.4	15.8	6.9	239.4

Table 8.2 (Cont.)

	Number of Cities	Basic Services (without Health and Welfare)	Health and Welfare	Local Schools	Higher Education and Hospitals	Total Service Responsibilities
City economic health[a]						
Quintile 1	17	197.9	17.6	109.3	0.0	324.8
Quintile 2	17	205.6	14.7	118.8	10.8	349.9
Quintile 3	16	191.3	23.4	84.8	11.5	311.0
Quintile 4	17	192.9	4.1	0.0	0.0	197.0
Quintile 5	18	202.6	26.3	99.3	19.6	347.9
Washington, D.C.		376.5	295.1	392.4	184.4	1248.4

Note: See text for explanation of service responsibilities.

[a]City economic health is defined to be private employment in the city divided by city population.

The range is even greater for health and welfare services; average responsibilities in the largest cities are more than seven times those in the smallest cities. Somewhat surprisingly, this range for welfare and health cannot be explained by a higher proportion of city-counties among the large cities; the largest are only slightly more likely to be city-counties than are the smallest cities. The larger cities simply tend to be located in states where state governments play below-average roles in paying for welfare services. The presence of a large city in the state may help explain this below-average state role. If a large proportion of the state's needy households live in the city, legislators from other parts of the state may be reluctant to provide additional assistance for what appears to many to be primarily a city problem.

An even more pronounced pattern emerges across cities grouped by resident income. Cities with the poorest residents have average responsibilities that exceed those in the cities with the richest residents by 50 percent. Here the explanation is found in special services; cities with lower-income residents are much more likely to have responsibility for local schools than are those with higher-income residents. Many of the cities with below-average income are in older metropolitan areas. Unlike more rapidly growing cities in the South and West, they typically do not have the power to raise the average incomes of their residents by annexing their wealthier suburbs. By historical accident these older cities are more likely to have responsibility for providing elementary and secondary education than are their western counterparts.

The above-average service responsibilities found in the largest and poorest cities are potentially important for the fiscal health of those cities, but they are only one part of the whole fiscal picture. For example, a city with extensive service responsibilities also may have above-average revenue-raising capacity and below-average costs for providing a given quality of public services. These cost and revenue-raising considerations could offset, in part or in full, the negative effects on the city's fiscal health of large service responsibilities. We examine the combined effects of these fiscal institutions in chapters 9 and 11.

Changes Over Time

How much have state governments done to reduce the expenditure burdens on their city governments over time? For at least one expenditure category, welfare, the answer is, quite a lot, although more remains to be done in some states.

Table 8.3 lists all cities that had relatively high responsibilities for welfare in 1967. To make the responsibilities comparable over time, they all are expressed in terms of 1982 spending levels.[7] In other words, the difference between the 1967 and 1982 levels measures changes in the intrastate division of responsibilities alone and is not confounded by increases in national welfare spending. Cities not included in the table all had welfare burdens below $15 per capita in 1967, and most of them had essentially no responsibility for welfare.

Topping the list in 1967 was Washington, D.C., which, unlike other cities, has no overlying governments to pick up some of the responsibility for welfare. New York, Boston, 4 Virginia cities, and Indianapolis also had extensive responsibility for welfare in 1967. The biggest change during the 1967-72 period was the assumption by Massachusetts of welfare responsibilities. This takeover reduced Boston's welfare burden by 95 percent between 1967 and 1972. Large changes in welfare also occurred in Maryland and Virginia. By 1982, Baltimore's welfare responsibilities were inconsequential, and those of the Virginia cities had been reduced by 70 percent. Most states appear to have made some effort to reduce the burden of welfare on their cities, but 1982 welfare responsibilities still exceed $100 per capita in Washington, D.C., New York, Denver, and San Francisco.

Turning now to the set of general services provided by city governments, which includes all the services in our index other than local schools, higher education, and hospitals, we find that, on average, service responsibilities remained approximately constant between 1972 and 1982. A small increase in average responsibility for basic services (all general services other than health and welfare) of 3.6 percent was almost exactly offset by a decline in average responsibility for the more redistributive services of health and welfare.

But underneath this average are widely differing changes across cities. Table 8.4 lists the central cities experiencing the greatest declines and those experiencing the greatest increases in general responsibilities. The upper panel of the table shows that about one-half of the cities with the largest declines started the period with heavy health and welfare burdens. Baltimore's 33 percent reduction, for example, reflects the dramatic drop in its welfare burden, combined with a small increase in its responsibilities

---

7. Thus, for example, the 1967 figures indicate how much each city would have had to spend on welfare, given the state's division of spending responsibilities in 1967, in order for the sum of state and local spending to equal the 1982 national average.

Table 8.3
Changes in Welfare Responsibilities, 1967-82
(Cities with Significant Welfare Responsibilities; in 1982 Dollars per Capita)

		1967 Welfare Burden	Change in Welfare Burden		1982 Welfare Burden
			1967-72	1972-82	
	Washington, D.C.	248	0	0	248
New York	New York City	237	8	- 75	171
Massachusetts	Boston	224	-212	- 5	6
Virginia	Norfolk	214	- 52	-102	60
	Portsmouth	214	- 52	-102	60
	Richmond	214	- 52	-102	60
	Virginia Beach	214	- 52	-102	60
Indiana	Indianapolis	208	- 86	- 34	87
Colorado	Denver	196	- 44	- 36	116
Maryland	Baltimore	169	- 23	-144	2
California	San Francisco	169	- 11	- 45	114
Pennsylvania	Philadelphia	48	- 19	3	32
Florida	Jacksonville	29	- 4	- 6	18
Rhode Island	Pawtucket	25	- 4	- 6	15
	Providence	25	- 4	- 6	15
	Warwick	25	- 4	- 6	15
New Jersey	Clifton	22	- 16	0	7
	Newark	22	- 16	0	7
	Passaic	22	- 16	0	7
	Paterson	22	- 16	0	7
Connecticut	Hartford	22	- 1	2	24
Tennessee	Nashville-Davidson	15	1	- 2	14

Note: A city's welfare burden is calculated as the share of the state and local spending accounted for by cities in the city's state in the specified year, multiplied by national per capita welfare spending in 1982. Thus the 1982 spending weight is used for each year.

for other basic services. Similarly, declines in the 4 Virginia cities and in New York City are attributable to declines in health and welfare responsibilities. In Boston, the 5 Florida cities, and Louisville, Kentucky, in contrast, the drop in service responsibilities is attributable fully or partially to a drop in responsibilities for basic services.

The lower panel of table 8.4 indicates that the largest responsibility increases occurred primarily in cities with limited responsibility for health and welfare services. In these cities increases in responsibility for basic services ranged from 12 to 29 percent. The 12 percent increase in the California cities is somewhat surprising in light of Proposition 13's rollback of local property taxes. It apparently reflects tighter limits on taxes and spending at the county and state level than at the city level. Because county governments were more dependent on local property taxes than were the cities, Proposition 13 apparently forced them to cut back on their spending relative to that of city governments. Similarly, limits on state government revenues forced expenditure cutbacks at the state level. With California state and county governments cutting back on spending, a greater share of the spending on each category remains for city governments.

A city's responsibility for special services changes over time only if it stops providing the service or if it starts providing a new service.[8] One city, Albany, New York, that was providing local schools in 1972 was no longer doing so by 1982. Cincinnati lost its responsibility for higher education and its municipal hospital during this period, but Indianapolis and Austin gained municipal hospitals. Although only a few cities are affected, these types of change can have large effects.

Conclusions

This chapter focuses on the division of spending responsibilities among levels of government within a state. The division determines the scope of a city's service responsibilities, defined as how much the city would have to spend to provide services of average quality if it had average public service costs. Our index of responsibilities is designed to be independent of a city's choices about the quality of services to provide. It is also independent of the harshness of the city environment and thus does not in-

---

8. This statement is not quite right for our measure of responsibilities for elementary and secondary education. An increase or a decrease over time in the city's ratio of pupils to population will lead to a proportionate increase or decrease in the city's education responsibilities.

Table 8.4
Changes in Service Responsibilities, 1972-1982
(Cities with Large Changes)

		Basic General Services		Health and Welfare		Total General Services	
		1972 Level (1982 dollars)	1972-82 Change (%)	1972 Level (1982 dollars)	1972-82 Change (%)	1972 Level (1982 dollars)	1972-82 Change (%)
Cities with largest declines in service responsibilities							
Maryland	Baltimore	231	3	169	-82	400	-33
Virginia	Virginia	211	6	178	-59	389	-23
	Richmond	211	6	178	-59	389	-23
	Portsmouth	211	6	178	-59	389	-23
	Norfolk	211	6	178	-59	389	-23
Kentucky	Louisville	238	-24	0	149	239	-23
New York	New York City	277	0	279	-29	555	-15
Massachusetts	Boston	251	-9	28	-64	279	-15
Florida	Tampa	190	-12	1	-15	191	-12
	St. Petersburg	190	-12	1	-15	191	-12
	Miami	190	-12	1	-15	191	-12
	Hollywood	190	-12	1	-15	191	-12
	Fort Lauderdale	190	-12	1	-15	191	-12
Cities with largest increases in service responsibilities							
Colorado	Boulder	124	29	1	281	124	31
Utah	Ogden	141	21	0	95	141	21
	Salt Lake City	141	21	0	95	141	21
Louisiana	New Orleans	204	21	23	2	226	19
Missouri	Kansas City	148	16	6	11	154	16

Table 8.4 (Cont.)

		Basic General Services		Health and Welfare		Total General Services	
		1972 Level (1982 dollars)	1972-82 Change (%)	1972 Level (1982 dollars)	1972-82 Change (%)	1972 Level (1982 dollars)	1972-82 Change (%)
California	Anaheim	177	12	1	-17	178	12
	Garden Grove	177	12	1	-17	178	12
	Long Beach	177	12	1	-17	178	12
	Los Angeles	177	12	1	-17	178	12
	Oakland	177	12	1	-17	178	12
	Ontario	177	12	1	-17	178	12
	Riverside	177	12	1	-17	178	12
	Sacramento	177	12	1	-17	178	12
	San Bernadino	177	12	1	-17	178	12
	San Diego	177	12	1	-17	178	12
	San Jose	177	12	1	-17	178	12
	Santa Ana	177	12	1	-17	178	12
Pennsylvania	Pittsburgh	114	12	2	-30	116	11
	Philadelphia	203	12	62	5	265	10

corporate variation across cities in the costs of providing a given quality of public services. In chapter 9, we combine our service responsibility indexes with the cost indexes from chapter 4 to measure a city's expenditure needs.

Cities have relatively uniform responsibilities for many typical city services. They have widely differing responsibilities, however, for services such as health and welfare, local schools, and municipal hospitals. Total service responsibilities are quite closely related to type of city; city-counties typically have higher responsibilities than separate cities both because they perform county functions as well as city functions and because they are more likely than separate cities to have responsibility for local schools, municipal hospitals, or higher education.

State governments actively worked to reduce welfare burdens on city governments between 1967 and 1982, but welfare burdens remain high in a few cities, such as Denver, New York, and San Francisco. Thirteen cities have benefited from reductions in service responsibilities of between 12 and 33 percent, but on average, the 86 study cities experienced no change in their service responsibilities between 1972 and 1982.

Appendix: Calculating Service Responsiblities

In this appendix we describe our measure of service responsibilities. As we discussed in the text, we use spending data from the city's state rather than from the city itself to calculate the measure for each city. This approach assures that the measure is not directly affected by the city's choice about service quality or by the costs that it faces.

General Services

Consider the fourteen general services listed in table 8.1. For each service i, we define the "city" share of responsibility, F_{ij}, for a city in state j as follows:

$$F_{ij} = \frac{\text{"City" spending on service i in state j}}{\text{All state and local spending on service i in state j}} .$$

Consistent with our approach to tax burdens (see appendix to chapter 7), we calculate "city" spending as the sum of spending by municipalities and townships for separate cities and as that amount plus spending by counties for city-counties.

In states with uniform fiscal systems, the "city" shares for all cities within a state are the same, with statewide spending by counties included or excluded from the numerator as appropriate. In states with mixed fiscal systems (that is, with some separate cities and some city-counties), the "city" shares will be higher for the city-counties than for the separate cities because the numerator of the "city" share expression includes spending by counties in the former case but not the latter. Because statewide spending by municipalities and townships in these states includes in these states includes the spending on county functions by the city-counties, it overstates the spending by separate cities on municipal type services. Hence we adjust municipal and township spending downward before using it to calculate F_{ij} for separate cities in mixed state systems.

In sum, the F_{ij}s for each city are calculated from statewide data but vary from one city to another within state j on the basis of the type of city. Hence the j subscript should be interpreted as referring to a city.

We next weight the "city" shares by national average state and local spending per capita on the ith service, net of average user fees. This weighting converts the share into the per capita dollar amount the city would have to raise from general revenues to assure its residents of average spending levels, given the division of responsibilities between city and noncity governments in the city's state. Each national spending weight, S_{in}, is calculated as follows:

$$S_{in} = (\text{U.S. average per capita state and local spending})(1 - c_i) ,$$

where the coverage ratio, c_i, is the average percentage of spending for service i covered by user fees, based on data from cities with population over 300,000.

Thus our measure of service responsibilities for the ith service, S_{ij}, for the jth city is simply

$$S_{ij} = (F_{ij}) (S_{in}) ,$$

where F_{ij} varies among cities within a state in line with their city-county status. Summing this expression over the fourteen general services listed in table 8.1 for each city yields the general responsibility index, GSRI:

$$\text{GSRI}_j = \sum_{i=1}^{14} S_{ij} .$$

The GSRI is the per capita spending that would be required by a city to achieve its assigned share of the national average state and local spending per capita on the fourteen general services, given the state's assignment of responsibilities among all state and local governments and the city's status as a city-county or a separate city.

Special Services

We modify this approach for elementary and secondary education, higher education, and hospitals. We first determine which cities provided these services in each year on the basis of a threshold level of per capita spending. The threshold is selected to ensure that we identify cities with primary responsibility for these services (for example, running a school system), not those with incidental responsibility (for example, providing crossing guards for an independent school district).

For cities with responsibility for elementary and secondary education, spending varies with public school enrollments. We therefore base our calculation of spending for this service on U.S. average spending per pupil. For consistency with the general service responsibility index, the education responsibility index, ERI, for a city is then converted back to per capita terms:

$$\text{ERI} = (\text{U.S. average spending per pupil}) \frac{(\text{School enrollment in city})}{(\text{Population of city})} .$$

If the city government does not provide schools, its ERI is set to zero.

In cities that provide higher education, the service responsibility index for higher education, HERI, is the average net spending per capita by major central cities that provide this service. Similarly, in cities that run hospitals the index for hospital responsibilities, HRI, is the average per capita net spending on hospitals by cities that provide them. Both of these indexes equal zero if the city does not provide the service.

Total for All Services

Summing the indexes for general and special services in each city produces an index of total services responsibilities, TSRI:

$$\text{TSRI} = \text{GSRI} + \text{ERI} + \text{HERI} + \text{HRI}.$$

Table A8.1 reports total service responsibilities by city broken down by the categories discussed in the text.

Table A8.1
Index of Service Responsibilities, 1982
(86 Cities)

	Basic Services	Welfare and Health	Local Schools	Hospitals and Higher Education	Total Service Responsibilities
Akron, OH	189	4	0	0	194
Albany, NY	117	1	0	0	118
Albuquerque, NM	228	3	0	0	231
Anaheim, CA	199	1	0	0	200
Atlanta, GA	197	3	0	0	200
Austin, TX	210	15	0	118	343
Baltimore, MD	237	30	417	67[a]	751
Birmingham, AL	220	2	0	0	221
Boston, MA	228	10	294	118	650
Boulder, CO	160	3	0	0	163
Buffalo, NY	117	1	359	0	477
Charlotte, NC	244	0	0	0	244
Chicago, IL	171	17	0	0	188
Cincinnati, OH	189	4	0	0	194
Cleveland, OH	189	4	0	0	194
Clifton, NJ	168	16	268	0	452
Columbus, OH	189	4	0	0	194
Dallas, TX	210	15	0	0	225
Dayton, OH	189	4	0	0	194
Denver, CO	229	139	0	0	368
Detroit, MI	206	6	0	0	213
El Paso, TX	210	15	0	0	225
Everett, WA	194	2	0	0	196
Ft. Lauderdale, FL	167	1	0	0	168
Fort Worth, TX	210	15	0	0	225
Garden Grove, CA	199	1	0	0	200
Greensboro, NC	244	0	0	0	244
Hartford, CT	217	38	459	0	715
High Point, NC	244	0	0	0	244
Hollywood, FL	167	1	0	0	168
Honolulu, HI	212	7	0	0	219
Houston, TX	210	15	0	0	225
Indianapolis, IN	221	100	0	0	322

Table A8.1 (Cont.)

	Basic Services	Welfare and Health	Local Schools	Hospitals and Higher Education	Total Service Responsibilities
Jacksonville, FL	247	26	0	0	273
Kansas City, MO	171	7	0	0	178
Long Beach, CA	199	1	0	0	200
Los Angeles, CA	199	1	0	0	200
Louisville, KY	182	1	0	0	183
Memphis, TN	218	6	451	0	675
Miami, FL	167	1	0	0	168
Milwaukee, WI	201	6	0	0	208
Minneapolis, MN	183	8	0	0	191
Nashville-Davidson, TN	232	27	388	0	646
Newark, NJ	168	16	472	0	655
New Orleans, LA	246	23	0	0	269
New York, NY	277	196	341	184	999
Norfolk, VA	224	74	354	0	652
Oakland, CA	199	1	0	0	200
Ogden, UT	170	1	0	0	171
Oklahoma City, OK	187	2	0	0	189
Omaha, NB	192	7	0	0	199
Ontario, CA	199	1	0	0	200
Passaic, NJ	168	16	0	0	183
Paterson, NJ	168	16	469	0	653
Pawtucket, RI	212	17	325	0	554
Philadelphia, PA	227	65	0	0	291
Phoenix, AZ	234	4	0	0	238
Pittsburgh, PA	127	1	0	0	129
Portland, OR	189	1	0	0	190
Portsmouth, VA	224	74	470	0	767
Providence, RI	212	17	297	0	526
Richmond, VA	224	74	366	0	664
Riverside, CA	199	1	0	0	200
Rochester, NY	117	1	372	0	490
Sacramento, CA	199	1	0	0	200
St. Louis, MO	227	15	0	118	360
St. Paul, MN	183	8	0	0	191
St. Petersburg, FL	167	1	0	0	168
Salt Lake City, UT	170	1	0	0	171
San Antonio, TX	210	15	0	0	225
San Bernardino, CA	199	1	0	0	200
San Diego, CA	199	1	0	0	200
San Francisco, CA	262	146	0	118	526
San Jose, CA	199	1	0	0	200
Santa Ana, CA	199	1	0	0	200
Schenectady, NY	117	1	0	0	118
Seattle, WA	194	2	0	0	196

Table A8.1 (Cont.)

	Basic Services	Welfare and Health	Local Schools	Hospitals and Higher Education	Total Service Responsibilities
Tampa, FL	167	1	0	0	168
Toledo, OH	189	4	0	0	194
Troy, NY	117	1	0	0	118
Tucson, AZ	234	4	0	0	238
Tulsa, OK	187	2	0	0	189
Virginia Beach, VA	224	74	508	0	806
Warwick, RI	212	17	411	0	640
Winston-Salem, NC	244	0	0	0	244
Washington, DC	376	295	392	184	1248

[a]This figure may overstate Baltimore's responsibility for providing higher education. Compared to other cities that appropriate funds for higher education, Baltimore's spending is quite low.

9
Actual Fiscal Health

Fiscal institutions, which vary enormously from one central city to another, have a profound impact on city fiscal health. The tax on commuter earnings in Philadelphia and Cleveland, the extensive service responsibilities of New York City, and the important role of overlying counties in many cities in the South and West clearly affect the ability of these city governments to deliver high-quality public services at a reasonable tax burden on their residents. Although economic and social factors are the foundation of a city's fiscal health, their influence must filter through the fiscal institutions—such as the availability and form of taxes, taxes levied by overlying jurisdictions, and the assignment of service responsibilities that guide the city's fiscal behavior.

Fiscal institutions influence a city's capacity to raise revenue and the amount it must spend to provide any given quality of public services. To determine a city's actual fiscal health, therefore, we must develop new measures of revenue-raising capacity and of expenditure need that account for the role of fiscal institutions. It is important to recognize that intergovernmental grants, institutions affecting capacity, namely those that determine taxing authority, and institutions affecting need, namely those that determine the division of service responsibilities, are all parts of the same package. Some states assign heavy responsibilities to their cities but offset the burden by extending city taxing authority or giving generous intergovernmental grants. Other states retain responsibility for many services but limit cities' taxing authority and provide little intergovernmental aid. In determining overall actual fiscal health, therefore, we can no longer consider the revenue-raising capacity of a city to be independent of that city's expenditure need, as we did in the case of standardized fiscal health. We can measure *restricted revenue-raising capacity*, which reflects access to taxes and intergovernmental grants, and *actual expenditure need*, which reflects service responsibilities, but we must recognize that the role of fiscal institutions is revealed only in the balance between these two concepts, not in either one alone.

In this chapter we define restricted revenue-raising capacity and actual expenditure need and combine them into an index of *actual fiscal health*. This index measures a city's capability to deliver public services given its economic and social circumstances, the grants it receives, and the fiscal rules under which it must operate. Because restricted revenue-raising capacity and actual expenditure need are not independent of each other, we do not present the analog to chapter 3, on revenue-raising capacity, or to chapter 4, on standardized expenditure need. Instead we concentrate on actual fiscal health, which reveals the balance between restricted capacity and actual need. We show how actual fiscal health varied across central cities in 1982 and how it changed between 1972 and 1982. Because a city's actual fiscal health index reflects fiscal institutions and grants as well as the economic and social factors that determine its standardized fiscal health index, the difference between these two indexes measures the net effect on the city's fiscal health of state intergovernmental grants and the key state-determined fiscal institutions, including tax availability, taxes collected by overlying jurisdictions, and service responsibilities. This comprehensive measure of the role of state assistance to cities is examined in detail in chapter 11.

Restricted Revenue-Raising Capacity

A city's restricted revenue-raising capacity depends on the economic factors reflected in its full revenue-raising capacity and on the availability and form of its taxes, taxes levied by overlying jurisdictions, and the grants it receives from its state. In general terms, revenue-raising capacity depends on resident income and on the ability to export tax burdens to nonresidents. As we discussed in chapter 3, revenue-raising capacity is based on the assumption that all cities have access to three uniformly defined broad-based taxes. Restricted revenue-raising capacity, in contrast, is based on only those taxes and tax bases that a city is empowered to use. Consider, for example, a city with many commuters but without the authority to levy an earnings tax on them. Its restricted revenue-raising capacity, which reflects its inability to export tax burdens to nonresidents, is below its full revenue-raising capacity, which includes the potential tax payments by commuters. The first step in calculating restricted capacity, therefore, is to determine the ability of a city to export tax burdens to nonresidents through the taxes it actually is allowed to levy. This step is described in chapter 6.

As we explained in chapter 3, our revenue-raising capacity measure is comparable across cities because it indicates how much revenue a city could raise at a selected tax burden on its residents. This tax burden is selected to be typical; in particular, we rank states by tax burden in 1972, which is total state and local taxes borne by residents as a fraction of resident income, and we select the tax burden that is exceeded in one-quarter of the states. We employ this standard tax burden to calculate revenue-raising capacity in all cities in both 1972 and 1982.

Our measure of restricted revenue-raising capacity begins with this standard tax burden but also must account for the taxes imposed by overlying local jurisdictions. Our objective is to determine how much revenue a city could raise at a standard tax burden on its residents. To make a sensible comparison across cities, this standard tax burden must be interpreted as the total state and local tax burden on city residents, not just that imposed by the city government. It follows that the tax burden available to a city is the overall state and local tax burden minus the tax burden imposed by other local governments and by the state. As we explained in detail in chapter 7, our measure of the standard tax burden in a city is the standard overall state and local tax burden multiplied by city taxes as a share of total state and local taxes in that city's state.

A city's restricted revenue-raising capacity also depends on the intergovernmental grants it receives from its state. It is not appropriate, however, simply to add actual grants to own-source revenue-raising capacity. Some cities receive relatively more state grants, in part because their state taxes and the level of their state services, including grants, are relatively high. In other words, they receive more grants, but their residents also make a higher sacrifice to receive them. In our calculations, therefore, state grants are standardized so that they reflect the same level of sacrifice in every state. The details of this standardization procedure are presented in chapter 7. Note that the standardization retains most of the variation in state grants; standardized grants are higher for cities in states that spend a larger share of their budget on aid or tilt their aid more heavily toward large cities.

To focus on the role of state and local fiscal institutions, we exclude federal grants from our measure of restricted revenue-raising capacity. Federal grants obviously play an important role in central city finances, however, so we examine them and their impact on city fiscal health in chapter 11.

In summary, a city's restricted revenue-raising capacity is its revenue-raising capacity adjusted to account for the taxes it is allowed to levy, the taxes levied by overlying local jurisdictions, and the intergovernmental grants it receives from its state.

Actual Expenditure Need

Standardized expenditure need, which is based on the assumption that all cities have the same service responsibilities, depends only on a city's public service costs. Actual expenditure need, however, also depends on a city's service responsibilities. Our approach is to divide each city's total service responsibility index, which is presented in chapter 8, into three parts: general, police, and fire. Each of these parts is based on national average spending and on the division of spending responsibilities within the city's state and therefore does not reflect the city's own public service costs. To combine the city's costs and its service responsibilities, we multiply each part of the service responsibility index by the cost index for that type of service. The product of the fire responsibility index and the fire cost index, for example, indicates how much a city must spend to meet its fire protection responsibilities given its costs for providing this protection. A city's expenditure need equals the sum of its cost-weighted service responsibilities for general, police, and fire services.

As we explained in chapter 3, the level of expenditure need cannot be examined without specifying the quality of public services. Our approach is to select the service quality that is consistent with our measure of restricted revenue-raising capacity. To be specific, we adjust actual expenditure need so that it embodies the service quality that the city with average restricted revenue-raising capacity and average cost-weighted service responsibilities could afford in 1972.[1] We call this the *baseline service quality*. In other words, our measure of actual expenditure need is the amount a city must spend to obtain the baseline service quality.

Actual Fiscal Health

Actual fiscal health is the balance between restricted revenue-raising capacity and actual expenditure need. To form an index of actual fiscal health, we find the difference between restricted revenue-raising capacity and actual expenditure need and express this difference as a percentage of restricted capacity.[2] Our method for adjusting actual need ensures that the

---

1. As in the case of our standardized fiscal health index, we adjust expenditure need until the average difference between capacity and need as a percentage of capacity equals zero. Washington, D.C., is not included in calculating this average.
2. See the appendix to this chapter for a more precise, algebraic statement of these calculations.

average central city has an actual fiscal health index of zero in 1972. A negative actual fiscal health index indicates the percentage increase in its restricted capacity a city would have to receive from outside sources to be able to provide the 1972 baseline service quality with the standard tax burden on its residents. Before federal aid or management skill is accounted for, therefore, cities with negative fiscal health indexes either must impose higher tax burdens on their citizens than the average city or must settle for lower service quality than the average city, or both. A positive fiscal health index indicates what share of its capacity a city would have left over for better-than-baseline service quality (or for lower-than-standard tax burden) after it has provided the baseline service quality.

Table 9.1 illustrates the calculation of our actual fiscal health index for selected cities in 1982. Column 1 contains restricted revenue-raising capacity per capita, which includes state but not federal aid. In these 10 cities this capacity ranges from $258 in Santa Ana, California, to $1,476 in Baltimore. Column 3 contains actual expenditure need per capita, which ranges from $245 in Fort Lauderdale to $1,596 in Newark. Column 4 contains the difference between restricted capacity and actual need. This difference is the revenue per capita that would have to be raised from outside sources to bring a city up to the baseline service quality at the standard tax burden. Our method ensures that this difference equals zero in the average

Table 9.1
Calculating an Index of Actual Fiscal Health, 1982
(Illustrative Cities)

	(1) Restricted Revenue- Raising Capacity ($)	(2) Actual Expenditure Need Index	(3) Actual Expenditure Need ($)	(4) Capacity Minus Need ($)	(5) Actual Fiscal Health Index (%)
Atlanta, GA	368	169	610	-242	-65.9
Baltimore, MD	1,476	382	1,375	101	6.8
Boston, MA	1,421	385	1,388	33	2.3
Denver, CO	711	207	745	- 35	- 4.9
Detroit, MI	442	160	578	-136	-30.8
Ft. Lauderdale, FL	442	68	245	-196	44.5
Kansas City, MO	370	94	339	32	8.6
Newark, NJ	1,314	443	1,596	-282	-21.5
Santa Ana, CA	258	84	302	- 44	-17.2
Virginia Beach, VA	995	231	833	162	16.3

Note: The actual fiscal health index in column 5 equals column 4 divided by column 1.

city in 1972. Column 5 presents our actual fiscal health index, which is the difference between capacity and need (column 4) divided by capacity (column 1). In these selected cities, this index ranges from +45 percent in Fort Lauderdale to -66 percent in Atlanta. In the case of Atlanta, for example, restricted capacity would have to increase by two thirds for the city to be able to provide the baseline service quality at the standard tax burden.

Actual fiscal health is determined by the balance of restricted capacity and actual need, not by either one separately. Some cities with relatively low actual need, such as Fort Lauderdale, have a positive fiscal health index, whereas others, such as Santa Ana, have a negative index. Baltimore, with high restricted capacity, has an index somewhat above zero, whereas Newark, also with a high restricted capacity, has an index well below zero.

The actual fiscal health index in table 9.1 can be compared with the standardized fiscal health index in table 5.1. Remember that the two indexes differ because the actual indexes account for grants and fiscal institutions, whereas the standardized indexes do not. Indeed, the difference between the two indexes is a measure of the impact of state grants and state-imposed institutions on the fiscal health of a city. We postpone a detailed analysis of the impact of state policies on city fiscal health until chapter 11. At this stage we simply point out that grants and fiscal institutions can have a significant impact on a city's fiscal health. Comparing tables 9.1 and 5.1 reveals that the combined effect of tax availability and form, taxes collected by overlying jurisdictions, intergovernmental aid, and service responsibilities weakens the fiscal health of some cities, such as Atlanta and Santa Ana, but strengthens that of others, such as Baltimore, Detroit, and Newark.

Differences across Cities in Actual Fiscal Health, 1982

Actual fiscal health for various categories of city in 1982 is presented in table 9.2. Restricted revenue-raising capacity is in column 2, actual expenditure need is in column 3, and the actual fiscal health index is in column 5. This actual fiscal health index reflects variation in fiscal health both across cities and over time. Remember that the index is standardized so that its average value in 1972 equals zero. As a result the average change in actual fiscal health between 1972 and 1982 equals the average value of the index in 1982. As is shown in the first row of column 5, this average value is -5 percent; in other words, the average city would need to receive a 5 percent boost in its capacity from outside sources to be able to achieve the 1972 baseline service quality at the standard tax burden. This average actual fiscal health is somewhat better than the average standardized fiscal health

Table 9.2
Actual Fiscal Health, 1982
(71 Cities)

	(1)	(2)	(3)	(4)	(5)	(6)	(7)
		Actual Revenue-raising Capacity ($)	Actual Expenditure Need ($)	Capacity Minus Need ($)	Actual Fiscal Health Index (%)	Actual Fiscal Health	
	Number of Cities					Relative to 1982 Average (%)	With Constant Costs[b] (%)
All cities							
Average	70	548	571	- 23	**- 4.9**	- 0.0	13.1
Standard Deviation	70	345	396	160	**26.8**	26.8	19.2
Maximum	70	1,546	2,251	282	**56.4**	61.2	51.4
Minimum	70	208	162	-872	**-79.7**	-74.9	-54.2
City population in thousands							
Less than 100	6	618	509	109	**14.6**	19.5	14.4
100-250	19	541	518	23	**6.4**	11.3	13.5
250-500	26	473	513	- 40	**- 9.0**	- 4.1	12.2
500-1,000	14	653	668	- 14	**- 5.5**	- 0.6	14.8
Greater than 1,000	5	582	879	-297	**-48.1**	-43.2	9.9
Resident income per capita							
Quintile 1	10	814	890	- 76	**-13.0**	- 8.1	26.5
Quintile 2	17	550	595	- 46	**-10.3**	- 6.5	3.8
Quintile 3	15	544	592	- 48	**- 3.6**	1.3	21.0
Quintile 4	14	431	419	12	**- 2.6**	2.3	5.2
Quintile 5	13	450	409	41	**6.5**	10.4	13.2

Table 9.2 (Cont.)

	(1) Number of Cities	(2) Actual Revenue-raising Capacity ($)	(3) Actual Expenditure Need ($)	(4) Capacity Minus Need ($)	(5) Actual Fiscal Health Index (%)	(6) Actual Fiscal Health Relative to 1982 Average (%)	(7) Actual Fiscal Health With Constant Costs[b] (%)
City economic health[a]							
Quintile 1	13	475	456	19	3.7	8.5	0.3
Quintile 2	14	607	645	- 38	- 9.1	- 4.2	9.7
Quintile 3	14	540	623	- 83	-14.1	- 9.2	8.6
Quintile 4	14	368	356	12	3.2	8.1	22.3
Quintile 5	15	730	755	- 24	- 7.3	- 2.4	22.8
Washington, DC	1	3,543	3,189	-355	10.0	14.9	32.9

Note: Each entry is an average for the indicated category of city.
[a]City economic health is defined to be private employment in the city divided by city population.
[b]The actual fiscal health index without costs is expressed relative to the 1972 average.

index in table 5.2 of -11 percent; as is explained more fully in chapter 11, changes in grants and fiscal institutions between 1972 and 1982 boosted the ability of the average central city to deliver public services.

The variation in actual fiscal health across cities is summarized in the next three rows of column 5 of table 9.2. The standard deviation of the actual fiscal health index is 27 percentage points, which indicates that most cities have indexes between -32 percent and +22 percent. In fact, 17 cities have indexes below -20 percent. Because of economic, social, and institutional factors that are outside their control, officials of cities in these categories must choose significantly lower service quality or higher tax burdens or both than officials of other cities. On the other hand, 31 cities have positive indexes. The large differences in actual fiscal health across cities also are revealed by the wide range in fiscal health, from -80 in Los Angeles, the least healthy city, to +56 in Hollywood, Florida, the healthiest. In other words, Los Angeles would have to receive revenue from outside sources equal to four-fifths of its restricted revenue-raising capacity to be able to provide the baseline service quality at the standard tax burden, whereas Hollywood can provide this service quality at this tax burden and still have over one-half of its restricted capacity left over for higher service quality or lower taxes.

Although these differences in actual fiscal health across cities appear to be large, they are smaller than the differences in standardized fiscal health in table 5.2. This comparison suggests that grants and fiscal institutions tend to provide more assistance to (or at least to inflict less harm on) cities in worse fiscal health. We examine this conclusion more fully in chapter 11.

To highlight the relative fiscal health of various types of city, we also present, in column 6 of table 9.2, actual fiscal health relative to the 1982 average. The numbers in this column simply equal the actual fiscal health index in column 5 minus the average change in this index between 1972 and 1982, namely -4.9 percent.

Column 6 reveals that actual fiscal health is markedly poorer in central cities with large populations than in those with small populations. The average actual fiscal health of cities with populations below 100,000 is 20 percentage points above the 1982 average, whereas the average actual fiscal health of the largest cities is 43 percentage points below the average. A comparison of tables 9.2 and 5.2 reveals that the largest cities face a less severe disadvantage in restricted revenue-raising capacity than in full revenue-raising capacity but a larger disadvantage in actual expenditure need than in standardized expenditure need. The former effect is somewhat stronger, so that grants and fiscal institutions mitigate, but do not remove, the severe overall fiscal disadvantage of the largest cities.

A city's actual fiscal health also is clearly linked to the income of its residents, but the range across city categories is not as pronounced as it is for city size. Cities with the poorest residents are in the poorest actual fiscal health, with an index of -8 percent relative to the 1982 average, and cities with the richest residents are in the best actual fiscal health, with an index of +11 percent. Throughout the per capita income range, the higher the income of a city's residents, the lower its restricted capacity, the lower its actual expenditure need, and the better its actual fiscal health.

The fact that restricted revenue-raising capacity is higher for cities with poorer residents is a dramatic turnaround from the findings in chapter 3. Economic factors alone imply that cities with poorer residents have a lower revenue-raising capacity. Fiscal institutions and intergovernmental grants reverse this relationship, so that cities with poorer residents have higher restricted revenue-raising capacity. The turnaround on the revenue side is offset to some degree by reinforcement on the expenditure side. As was shown in chapter 4, cities with poorer residents tend to have higher public service costs and hence higher expenditure need. Furthermore, they tend to have more service responsibilities. The net effect is that actual fiscal health is poorer in cities with poorer residents, but the fiscal health gap between cities with rich and poor residents is not as large as it is in the case of standardized fiscal health.

Figures 9.1 and 9.2 illustrate these results for the 70 cities included in table 9.2. Figure 9.1 highlights the negative association between population and actual fiscal health, and figure 9.2 highlights the positive association between resident income and actual fiscal health. Analogous figures for standardized fiscal health, figures 5.1 and 5.2, appear in chapter 5. A comparison of figure 9.1 with figure 5.1 (or of figure 9.2 with figure 5.2) reveals that, on average, the difference in actual fiscal health between large and small cities (or between rich and poor cities) is considerably smaller than the analogous difference in standardized fiscal health.[3] In other words, fiscal institutions and intergovernmental grants lessen, but do not eliminate, the fiscal disadvantages of large and poor cities.

Table 9.2 reveals no clear link between city employment per capita and actual fiscal health. Cities in the first and fourth employment quintile are in

---

3. The lines in these four figures are regression lines, which highlight the "average" relationship between the population (or resident income) and fiscal health. Another way to make the point in the text is that the regression lines are much flatter in figures 9.1 and 9.2 than in figures 5.1 and 5.2.

Figure 9.1
Population and Actual Fiscal Health, 1982
(70 cities)

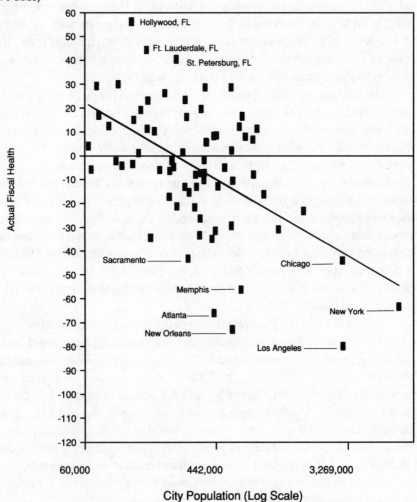

Figure 9.2
Resident Income and Actual Fiscal Health
(70 cities)

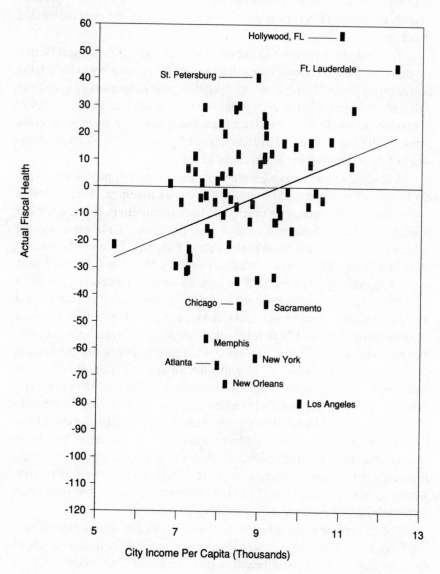

the best fiscal health relative to the 1982 average (about +8 percent), and those in the middle quintile are in the worst fiscal health (-9 percent). With some exceptions, both actual need and restricted capacity tend to be higher in cities with more employment per capita; these two tendencies produce roughly offsetting effects on actual fiscal health, as they did on standardized fiscal health.

To highlight the impact of public service costs on actual fiscal health, we calculate a constant-cost index that ignores variation across cities in the cost of providing public services. In this index, which is presented in column 7 of table 9.2, all variation in expenditure need is determined by variation in service responsibilities. Because it excludes the large increase in costs between 1972 and 1982, the average constant-cost index is +13 percent instead of the -5 percent for actual fiscal health.[4]

A comparison of the constant-cost index (column 7) and the actual fiscal health index (column 5) in table 9.2 reveals that high costs impose a severe fiscal disadvantage on cities with large populations, those with poor residents, and those with high employment per capita. To be specific, cost factors reduce the actual fiscal health index of the largest cities, the poorest ones, and those with the best economic health by 58, 40, and 30 percentage points respectively. Among the five resident income categories, the cities with the poorest residents have the highest constant-cost fiscal health and the lowest actual fiscal health. Costs have such a dramatic effect on these cities because they have both relatively high costs and relatively high service responsibilities. Expenditure need is the product of responsibilities and costs, so high responsibilities magnify the impact of high costs on actual fiscal health. The relatively high service responsibilities of the cities with the poorest residents do not lead to relatively poor constant-cost fiscal health because states tend to enhance the revenue-rising capacity of these cities, by allowing them to tax nonresident earnings, for example, to help them finance these responsibilities. Overall, these capacity enhancements are sufficient to compensate cities with the poorest residents for their high responsibilities, but not nearly sufficient to compensate them for their high responsibilities weighted by their relatively high costs.

Public service costs affect both standardized and actual expenditure need, so it is not surprising that these results are similar to the effects of costs on standardized fiscal health, which were described in table 5.2. In particular, public service costs have approximately the same effect on the

---

4. Like the actual fiscal health index, this constant-cost index is standardized so that it equals zero in the average city in 1972.

actual and standardized fiscal health of large cities and of those with high employment per capita. Because cities with relatively poor residents have relatively high service responsibilities, however, costs play a larger role in determining their actual fiscal health than in determining their standardized fiscal health.

Changes in Actual Fiscal Health, 1972-1982

Changes in actual fiscal health are described in table 9.3. Because actual expenditure need increased more on average than did restricted revenue-raising capacity, the actual fiscal health index declined by 5 percentage points between 1972 and 1982. To prevent a decline in service quality or an increase in tax burden over this period, the average city required a 5 percent increase in its capacity from outside sources. This result also appears in table 9.2; because the 1972 average index equals zero, the average value of the index in 1982 measures the average 1972-82 change.

Changes in actual fiscal health differed widely for cities with different populations. The fiscal health index declined 21 percent for cities with a population above 1 million but increased 7 percent for those with a population below 100,000. This difference is primarily due to events on the expenditure side. Both classes of city faced little change in their restricted capacity, but the largest faced a 19 percent increase and the smallest faced a 9 percent decline in actual expenditure need.

Table 9.3 reveals a weak link between changes in resident income and changes in actual fiscal health. Cities with lower growth in resident income encountered somewhat greater declines in fiscal health than did others, but not by a large amount. Rapid growth in resident income boosts restricted revenue-raising capacity, but it also raises actual expenditure need. Between 1972 and 1982, the capacity effect tended to be somewhat greater than the need effect, thereby leading to somewhat smaller declines in actual fiscal health for cities with higher growth in resident income.

We also find no clear link between changes in a city's economic health and changes in its actual fiscal health. High employment growth tends to boost both actual need and restricted capacity; these two effects were roughly offsetting during the 1972-82 period. Indeed, all employment growth categories except one experienced declines in actual fiscal health of between 6 and 12 percent.

Column 5 of table 9.3 presents 1972-82 changes in the constant-cost index. Changes in costs serve to magnify the fiscal disadvantages of the largest cities and in those in which resident income is not growing and

Table 9.3
Changes in Actual Fiscal Health, 1972-1982
(71 Cities)

	(1)	(2)	(3)	(4)	(5)	(6)
		Percentage Change			Percentage Point Change	
	Number of Cities	Actual Revenue-raising Capacity	Actual Expenditure Need	Actual Fiscal Health Index	Actual Fiscal Health with Constant Costs	Actual Fiscal Health with Tax Revolt
All cities	70	6.9	12.7	- 4.9	13.1	- 3.8
City population in thousands						
Less than 100	6	-4.1	- 8.5	**7.0**	18.4	- 1.1
100-250	19	8.1	19.8	**- 9.2**	9.8	-17.9
250-500	26	5.9	11.8	**- 4.4**	14.9	-13.9
500-1,000	14	14.4	11.5	**0.8**	16.7	- 6.9
Greater than 1,000	5	0.3	18.7	**-20.8**	0.0	-32.0
Below-average income, 1971						
Low growth	18	3.1	12.6	**- 9.1**	10.5	-18.0
Medium growth	10	-2.7	2.2	**2.2**	15.1	- 6.3
High growth	6	17.6	20.3	**- 4.8**	13.3	-14.9
Above-average income, 1971						
Low growth	7	-13.2	0.2	**-13.2**	2.8	-23.7
Medium growth	17	13.5	15.3	**- 2.8**	14.5	-11.3
High growth	12	18.1	21.2	**- 2.5**	19.1	-10.8

Table 9.3 (Cont.)

	(1)	(2)	(3)	(4)	(5)	(6)
		Percentage Change		Actual	Percentage Point Change	
	Number of Cities	Actual Revenue-raising Capacity	Actual Expenditure Need	Fiscal Health Index	Actual Fiscal Health with Constant Costs	Actual Fiscal Health with Tax Revolt
Below-average economic health, 1972						
Low growth	11	- 1.7	9.1	-10.7	2.4	-19.5
Medium growth	9	8.8	16.6	-12.4	9.1	-21.3
High growth	15	17.3	27.4	- 7.8	16.4	-16.9
Above-average economic health, 1972						
Low growth	15	6.5	11.3	- 6.2	12.3	-15.2
Medium growth	13	2.2	- 3.5	11.3	21.5	2.9
High growth	7	5.9	14.8	- 7.0	13.7	-16.1
Washington, DC	1	6.7	5.7	0.9	12.2	- 5.1

Note: City categories for income change and economic health change are defined in tables 3.4 and 2.2, respectively. Each entry is an average change for the indicated category of city.

roughly to offset the relatively high growth in restricted capacity of cities with rapidly growing economic health.

One major fiscal event between 1972 and 1982, namely the nationwide tax revolt, is not fully reflected in our actual fiscal health index. The tax revolt in particular states affects the restricted capacity, and hence the actual fiscal health, of cities in those states in two ways: it alters the "city" share of state and local spending, both of which directly enter our capacity calculations, and it alters the mix of taxes used by cities, which determines their ability to export taxes to nonresidents. However, the nationwide decline in state and local tax burdens between 1972 and 1982 does not affect our index because restricted revenue-raising capacity is based on the same overall state and local tax burden in both 1972 and 1982. It is instructive, therefore, to recalculate our 1982 actual fiscal health index incorporating the nationwide decline in tax burdens between 1972 and 1982.[5]

The decline in tax burdens represents a voter preference for lower tax rates, which is an additional constraint on the ability of a city to provide public services. Some people have argued that the tax revolt led to increased attention to good management and cost-effectiveness in state and local governments. To the extent that this argument is true, the decline in tax burdens exaggerates the negative impact of the tax revolt on the ability of cities to deliver public services. We know of no way to measure managerial improvements, however, and we do not attempt to incorporate them into our analysis. It follows that our approach provides an upper bound on the impact of the tax revolt on cities' actual fiscal health.

Changes in actual fiscal health that account for the nationwide tax revolt are presented in column 6 of table 9.3. The 1972-82 change in the fiscal health with the tax revolt is -14 percent. Comparing this change with the change without the revolt, -5 percent, reveals that on average the tax revolt caused a 9 percentage point decline in the fiscal health of cities.

---

5. Remember that our calculation of restricted revenue-raising capacity begins with the actual nationwide state and local tax burden, as a percentage of income, in 1972. Our actual fiscal health index holds this burden constant—that is, the 1972 burden is used in 1982. Our index with the tax revolt uses the actual national 1982 burden in 1982. In both cases the service quality is held constant, at the level that the average city could afford in 1972.

The nationwide tax revolt did not have the same impact on every type of city, but differences in its impacts are not large.[6] In cities with populations over 1 million, for example, actual fiscal health fell by 11 percentage points more (32 - 21) the tax revolt is accounted for, whereas in the smallest cities fiscal health fell by 8 percentage points more with the tax revolt. Because the nationwide tax revolt had a similar effect on all types of city, the relationships between actual fiscal health and city size, resident income, and city economic health are similar whether or not one accounts for it.[7]

Conclusions

A city's actual fiscal health depends on the economic and social factors that influence its revenue-raising capacity and public service costs, on the grants it receives from its state, and on its state-determined fiscal institutions. These institutions include its access to taxes, the taxes collected by overlying jurisdictions, and its service responsibilities.

Across all major central cities in 1982, the average actual fiscal health index was -5 percent, which indicates a modest deterioration in fiscal health between 1972 and 1982. Average actual fiscal health is somewhat better than average standardized fiscal health; in other words, changes in grants and fiscal institutions between 1972 and 1982 added to the ability of the average city to provide public services. The role of grants and institutions is examined in detail in chapter 11.

Although the 1972-82 decline in average actual fiscal health was modest, some cities found themselves in extremely poor fiscal condition in

---

6. By lowering the acceptable tax burden, the tax revolt lowers a city's restricted revenue-raising capacity, which is in both the numerator and the denominator of our actual fiscal health index. To determine the net effect of the tax revolt on fiscal health, note that our index takes the form [(capacity - need)/capacity], which is the same as [1 - (need/capacity)]. This formula indicates that cities with a larger need-capacity ratio, and hence with a lower actual fiscal health, are more affected by a change in capacity. In other words, any decline in the acceptable tax burden has the greatest effect on the cities that have the poorest fiscal health to begin with.
7. Remember that the average fiscal health index in 1982 equals the average change in the index between 1972 and 1982. Hence the average 1982 actual fiscal health index with the tax revolt is -14 percent. Furthermore, to approximate the 1982 actual fiscal health index with the nationwide tax revolt for a particular category of city, one can simply subtract 9 percentage points from the actual fiscal health indexes in table 9.2. To be more exact, one must subtract slightly more than 9 points from categories of city in poor fiscal health and slightly less than 9 points from cities in good fiscal health.

1982. Actual fiscal health, like standardized fiscal health, is worse in larger cities than in smaller ones, and this difference grew over the 1972-82 period. By 1982 cities with populations over 1 million would have to receive outside resources equal to almost one-half of their restricted revenue-raising capacity to be able to obtain the same quality of public services at the same tax burden as the average city. Cities with poorer residents also have relatively poor actual fiscal health, although their need for outside resources is not as great as that of the largest cities. Neither small and large cities nor cities with rich and poor residents differ as much in actual fiscal health as they do in standardized fiscal health; grants and fiscal institutions, in other words, narrow the fiscal gap between the healthiest and the least healthy cities.

Cities with poor economic health, which we measure with per capita employment, do not appear to have poorer actual fiscal health than other cities, just as they do not appear to have poorer standardized fiscal health. After one accounts for fiscal institutions, the positive effects of economic health on both revenue-raising capacity and expenditure need still tend roughly to offset each other, both across cities and over time.

Finally, the nationwide tax revolt lowered the acceptable tax burden for state and local governments. We estimate that the decline in the acceptable tax burden between 1972 and 1982 more than offset the positive contributions to city fiscal health of fiscal institutions and state intergovernmental grants.

Appendix: Calculating Actual Fiscal Health

This appendix is a guide to our calculations for restricted revenue-raising capacity, actual expenditure need, and actual fiscal health.

Restricted Revenue-Raising Capacity

As we explained in chapter 7, city j's restricted revenue-raising capacity, $RRRC_j$, reflects the income of its residents, its ability to export tax burdens to nonresidents, the taxes collected by overlying jurisdictions, and its standardized state aid. To be specific, let Y_j stand for resident income per capita, KC_j be the city's standard tax burden after the capacity claimed by overlying jurisdictions is accounted for, e_j' be the city's export ratio based on the taxes it is allowed to use, and A_j^* be the city's standardized state aid. Then,

(A9.1) $\quad RRRC_j = (KC_j)(Y_j)(1 + e_j') + A_j^*$.

Actual Expenditure Need

Actual expenditure need is the sum of cost-weighted service responsibilities for police, fire, and general services. Let CP_j, CF_j, and CG_j be the cost indexes for police, fire, and general services in city j, which were defined in chapter 4, and let SRP_j, SRF_j and SRG_j be the service responsibility indexes for these three services, which were defined in chapter 8. Then our index of actual expenditure need in city j, ANI_j, is

(A5.2) $\quad ANI_j = (CP_j)(SRP_j) + (CF_j)(SRF_j) + (CG_j)(SRG_j)$.

(The reader may recall that we adjusted the standardized expenditure need index in chapter 4 to be equal to 100 in the average city in 1972. The purpose was to highlight differences across cities and changes over time in standardized expenditure need. Because we do not examine actual expenditure need separately, we do not make this adjustment in our actual expenditure need index. Our standardized fiscal health index is not affected by this adjustment, and our actual fiscal health index would be the same even if this adjustment were carried out.)

Actual Fiscal Health

Actual fiscal health in city j, AFH_j, is the balance between the city's restricted revenue-raising capacity and its actual expenditure need. Let Q be the baseline service quality. Then

(A5.3) $\quad AFH_j = [AC_j - (Q)(ANI_j)]/AC_j = 1 - Q(ANI_j/RRRC_j)$.

As we explained in the text, we set Q equal to the service quality that the average city could afford in 1972. Thus, in 1972, we set

$$\sum_{j=1}^{N} AFH_j/N = 0 = \sum_{j=1}^{N} [1 - Q(ANI_j/RRRC_j)]/N$$

or

(A5.4) $\quad Q = N/[\sum_{j=1}^{N} (ANI_j/RRRC_j)]$

In other words, Q is set equal to the inverse of the average need-capacity ratio in 1972. With this value for Q, we can calculate AFH_j in every city in both 1972 and 1982 using equation (A5.3).

Table A9.1 presents our actual fiscal health index for 1972 and 1982 for the 71 major central cities with complete data. The entries for Washington, D.C., reflect federal assistance through institutions and grants.

Table A9.1
Index of Actual Fiscal Health, 1972 and 1982
(71 Cities)

	Actual Fiscal Health, 1972		Actual Fiscal Health, 1982	
	Index (%)	Rank	Index (%)	Rank
Akron, OH	12.5	19	- 4.5	38
Albany, NY	9.9	24	30.2	4
Anaheim, CA	19.1	12	- 2.0	34
Atlanta, GA	0.2	43	-65.9	69
Baltimore, MD	5.9	64	6.8	30
Boston, MA	-28.8	34	2.3	26
Buffalo, NY	-19.0	60	-26.2	58
Charlotte, NC	24.2	7	- 7.8	46
Chicago, IL	-15.7	58	-43.8	66
Cincinnati, OH	-66.6[a]	70[a]	5.9	27
Cleveland, OH	- 2.7	45	-29.3	59
Clifton, NJ	30.0	6	17.0	13
Columbus, OH	1.9	40	-10.4	48
Dayton, OH	22.6	8	- 5.9	41
Denver, CO	- 1.3	44	- 4.9	39
Detroit, MI	-18.0	59	-30.8	60
Ft. Lauderdale, FL	49.5	2	44.5	2
Garden Grove, CA	38.1	3	15.1	16
Greensboro, NC	22.4	9	23.2	10
Hartford, CT	3.5	36	1.3	32
High Point, NC	4.3	35	4.2	29
Hollywood, FL	55.4	1	56.4	1
Honolulu, HI	16.3	13	- 7.8	45
Indianapolis, IN	-38.9	67	26.5	8
Jacksonville, FL	20.5	11	28.8	6
Kansas City, MO	6.4	32	8.6	23
Long Beach, CA	3.3	37	- 7.1	43
Los Angeles, CA	-28.0	63	-79.7	71
Louisville, KY	-21.2	61	-15.3	52
Memphis, TN	-22.8	62	-56.1	67
Miami, FL	- 5.5	51	5.6	28
Milwaukee, WI	22.3	10	12.3	18
Minneapolis, MN	- 5.4	50	- 1.5	33

Table A9.1 (Cont.)

	Actual Fiscal Health, 1972		Actual Fiscal Health, 1982	
	Index (%)	Rank	Index (%)	Rank
Nashville-Davidson, TN	-34.7	65	-12.7	49
Newark, NJ	7.6	30	-21.5	56
New Orleans, LA	-42.0	68	-72.8	70
New York, NY	-71.1	71	-63.2	68
Norfolk, VA	14.6	15	1.6	31
Oakland, CA	-12.9	55	-33.2	62
Ogden, UT	6.8	31	- 5.6	40
Oklahoma City, OK	-14.1	56	8.4	24
Omaha, NB	10.4	22	-12.9	51
Ontario, CA	8.3	27	- 2.1	35
Pawtucket, RI	9.8	25	29.5	5
Philadelphia, PA	- 3.6	47	-23.1	57
Phoenix, AZ	- 4.5	48	11.4	19
Pittsburgh, PA	- 5.3	49	-34.7	64
Portland, OR	-10.6	54	-10.2	47
Portsmouth, VA	8.1	28	- 4.0	37
Providence, RI	2.0	39	11.3	20
Richmond, VA	13.2	17	- 6.2	42
Riverside, CA	13.6	16	10.4	21
Rochester, NY	-35.8	66	-21.1	55
Sacramento, CA	3.1	38	-43.0	65
St. Louis, MO	-65.1	69	-31.3	61
St. Paul, MN	1.0	41	-12.9	50
St. Petersburg, FL	31.1	4	40.6	3
Salt Lake City, UT	0.6	42	-34.3	63
San Bernardino, CA	13.1	18	- 3.3	36
San Diego, CA	- 6.0	52	-16.0	53
San Francisco, CA	- 7.3	53	8.0	25
San Jose, CA	15.7	14	16.7	14
Santa Ana, CA	8.1	29	-17.2	54
Tampa, FL	12.2	20	23.6	9
Toledo, OH	- 3.6	46	- 7.2	44
Tucson, AZ	30.9	5	19.8	11
Tulsa, OK	6.3	33	28.8	7
Virginia Beach, VA	10.0	23	16.3	15
Warwick, RI	-15.0	57	12.5	17
Winston-Salem, NC	10.6	21	19.2	12
Washington, DC	9.1	26	10.0	22
Average	0.0		- 4.9	

Note: A city's actual fiscal health equals the difference between its restricted revenue-raising capacity and its actual expenditure need as a percentage of its restricted revenue-raising capacity.

[a]This figure may understate Cincinnati's fiscal health in 1972. Because of a small amount of unidentified spending on education, Cincinnati was assigned some responsibility for schools.

Part IV

The Roles of City, State, and Federal Governments

10

Spending Decisions by Central City Governments

A city's fiscal health summarizes the fiscal constraints facing it but does not reveal the budgetary choices it makes. Even cities that are severely constrained by economic, social, and institutional factors outside their control can decide either to provide high-quality public services by levying high taxes or to keep taxes low by cutting service quality. By design our measures of fiscal health are not affected by actual city government decisions. Influence does run in the other direction, however: the components of our fiscal health measures, such as resident income, ability to export tax burdens, public service costs, state and local fiscal institutions, and intergovernmental grants influence the expenditures and tax rates selected by the city. In this chapter we break from the focus of parts II and III on measuring external constraints; here we explore city spending decisions and the impact on them of the components of a city's actual fiscal health.

Although a city's fiscal health, as we measure it, is not affected by its actions, the analysis of its spending decisions presented in this chapter provides the basis for the cost indexes reported in chapter 4. The impact of environmental factors, such as population and the poverty rate, on the cost of public services is determined by measuring their impact on expenditures in the average central city—but only after identifying and controlling for other determinants of expenditure.

Looking at city spending decisions also provides insight into several questions asked by state and federal policy makers: Do intergovernmental grants induce a city to improve service quality or to cut taxes, or both? Does an ability to export taxes to nonresidents induce a city to improve service quality or to cut taxes, or both? Does the extent of service responsibilities assigned to a city affect the quality of the services it provides? In this chapter we provide answers to these and related questions; in chapter 12 we use these answers to design our suggestions for state and federal policy toward cities.

A Framework for Analyzing City Spending Decisions

Evidence about the spending decisions made by city governments can be seen in police patrols, the patching (or neglect) of potholes, the hiring of teachers, and other governmental activities. The decisions are determined by the complex interaction between citizens' demands for public services and the political and institutional environment of the city. Citizens' demand for public services reflects the same economic trade-offs as the demand for private goods and services but is articulated in different ways. In the case of private goods, households express their preferences by the goods they purchase. In the public sector, however, direct purchasing is the exception. Instead, individuals express their preferences primarily by the way they vote. Furthermore, the expression of demand via voting is mainly indirect, through the election of public officials. Only occasionally do city voters make a direct decision about a public service level through a referendum.

Thus our analysis of city spending decisions accounts both for the citizens' preferences for public services and for the city political and bureaucratic institutions through which those preferences are implemented and sometimes altered. We begin with a discussion of the basic determinants of citizens' demand for city services and with an analysis of the political institutions of cities. We then bring the components of city fiscal health into this framework to determine how each of these components affects city spending decisions.

The results in this chapter are based on an empirical analysis of the spending decisions of the 86 major central cities in the United States in the years 1967, 1972, 1977, and 1982. Detailed explanations of our data, our estimating technique, and our results are provided in the appendix to this chapter.

The Basic Determinants of Citizens' Demand for City Services

An individual voter's demand for city public services, like her demand for any other good or service, depends on that voter's income and the price she must pay to obtain another unit of these services. The higher a voter's income and the lower the price she must pay, the more public services she prefers to have.

The price residents pay for city services takes a different form from the price of a private good. City governments do not set a single price for their services and allow citizens to purchase as much of the service as they want at that price. Instead, they establish a tax system to pay for public services. The provisions of the tax system determine each citizens' share of an increase in taxes. When the property tax rate increases, property owners with higher-than-average assessed values face a larger tax increase than those with lower-than-average assessed values. To be more specific, a voter's share of a property tax increase equals the ratio of her assessed value to the per capita property base in the jurisdiction.[1] From the perspective of a single taxpayer, therefore, the price of another unit of local services equals the resource cost of that unit multiplied by that taxpayer's share of each dollar of additional taxes. This product of resource cost and tax share is known as the taxpayers tax price.

The starting point for our analysis of city expenditures is a simple demand relationship, which states that a voter's desired service level depends on her income and her tax price. A voter's preferences vary from one public service to another. It is appropriate, therefore, to carry out separate analyses for three broad types of city services: police, fire, and general. The general category includes schools, hospitals, and higher education, if the city provides them, plus airports, city administration, corrections, libraries, health, highways, housing and urban renewal, parks and recreation, public welfare, sanitation, sewers, and water transportation.

Demand for public services also varies from one voter to another. The role of the political process is to reconcile these differing demands. One approach, which has been employed by many previous studies, is to assume that expenditure decisions reflect only voters' demand and are decided by majority rule.[2] This assumption implies that citizens' demand for services can be adequately represented by the income and tax price of the median voter. In practice, this approach usually involves the additional simplifying assumption that the median voter is the voter with the median income.[3]

---

1. More formally, a voter's tax share equals the assessed value of her property divided by assessed value per capita in her city. With uniform assessment procedures, assessed value is a constant fraction of property value, so the voter's tax share also equals her property value divided by property value per capita. For a more complete discussion, see the appendix to this chapter.
2. This approach assumes that all political institutions other than voting are neutral, in the sense that they simply implement voters' preferences, and that all residents vote, or at least that nonparticipation is unrelated to income.
3. Bergstrom and Goodman 1973 have shown that under certain conditions the median voter is the one with the median income and median house value in the city. In this case, therefore, the outcome of the voting process is given by the demand function of a single voter who has the median income and the median house value. This approach, which is known as the median voter model, has been employed by many studies. For reviews of this literature, see Inman 1979b or Rubinfeld 1985.

Our approach is more pragmatic. Thanks to complex electoral and bureaucratic institutions, the decision-making process in major cities involves more than simple majority rule. Nevertheless, citizens' preferences for services remain an important influence on city spending decisions and need to be considered. We do not attempt to specify precisely the way in which citizens' preferences and political institutions interact to generate spending outcomes. Instead, we identify summary measures of citizens' demand for public services and, as is explained in the next section, control for key political institutions. Because they are averages, which summarize the underlying distributions, and because they are linked to the logic of voting, we use the median income of city residents and the city's property tax base per capita, which is the denominator of every voter's tax price, to summarize citizens' demand.[4]

This demand framework focuses on voters' desired service level, not on their desired public expenditure. The service level is the quality of the public services received by residents, such as the caliber of the protection against crime or fire. Public expenditure, of course, is the amount of money a city spends. The link between these two concepts is the cost per unit of public services. By definition, expenditure equals the service level multiplied by the cost per unit of service. This distinction is important because the resource cost of public services differs from one city to another and changes over time. As we explained in chapter 4, two cities that spend the same amount per capita on public services do not necessarily provide the same level of public services to their residents. These observations imply that we cannot accurately determine the impact of voters' income and tax price on city spending without controlling for public service costs. We return to this issue in a later section.

Median income and tax price had significant effects on voters' desired service level, and hence on observed city spending, in the 86 cities between 1967 and 1982. Our results are presented in the first panel of table 10.1. For both income and tax price the results are in elasticity form—that is, they indicate the percentage difference in spending between two cities that accompanies a 1 percent difference in income or tax price.

---

4. Because of data limitations we were not able to measure the numerator of tax price for the voter with median income—or for any other voter. However, we account for this numerator indirectly by bringing the demand for housing into our analysis. See the appendix to this chapter.

Table 10.1
Determinants of Spending by Central Cities

Determinant	Service		
	General	Police	Fire
Basic demand factors			
Median income[a]	0.57	1.61**	0.98[h]
Tax price[b]	-0.20***	-0.08*	-0.08*
City political institutions			
Lagged adjustment parameter	0.44***	0.54***	0.60***
City manager[c]	-0.05**	-0.02	-0.003
Severe property tax limitation[c]	-0.09**	-0.03	0.07**
Percent elderly[d]	-0.03**	0.01	0.002
Percent homeowners[d]	0.01**	0.01	0.002
Components of city fiscal health			
Exported earnings taxes[e]	0.19*	0.03**	(g)
Exported sales taxes[e]	0.20	0.04	0.04*
Overlying tax take[a]	(g)	-0.45	-0.43
Service responsibilities[a]	0.80***	0.15	0.21**
State aid[f]	0.32***	0.002	0.02***
Federal categorical aid[f]	0.49***	0.02*	0.01[h]
Federal general revenue sharing[f]	0.30	(g)	(g)

Note: All dollar variables are in per capita terms.
*Impact is significant at the 10 percent level.
**Impact is significant at the 5 percent level.
***Impact is significant at the 1 percent level.
[a]Entry is the elasticity of spending with respect to the variable.
[b]Entry is the elasticity of spending with respect to tax share, which is the coefficient of the per capita property tax base times minus one.
[c]Entry is the percentage difference in spending between cities with city manager or a severe property tax limit and other cities.
[d]Entry is the percentage impact on spending of one percentage point increase in the elderly population or homeowners.
[e]Entry is the dollar impact on spending of $1.00 of exported taxes; calculated assuming the tax share, spending, and income equal the 1982 average and 5 percent tax rate. Dollar impact of $1.00 of resident income is $0.04, $0.02, and $0.008 for general, police, and fire services respectively.
[f]Entry is the dollar impact on spending of $1.00 of aid; calculated assuming the tax share, spending, and income equal the 1982 average.
[g]Estimated impact has the wrong sign and is not significantly different from zero.
[h]Impact is significant at the 11 percent level.

The income elasticity differs across services. For police this elasticity is 1.61 and is statistically significant. In other words, a 1 percent difference in the median resident income between two cities leads to a 1.61 percent difference in spending on police services between those two cities. This elasticity is higher than that found by previous studies.[5] The income elasticities for fire and general services are 0.97 and 0.57 respectively, but they are not statistically significant.[6]

These results imply that a one standard deviation difference in median income would lead to a 10 percent difference in spending on general services, a 35 percent increase in spending on police services, and a 23 percent increase in spending on fire services. These impacts can also be expressed in dollar terms. A city with a median income $100 above the 1982 average for the 86 cities spends $4 per capita more on general services, $2 per capita more on police, and $0.80 per capita more on fire than a city with a median income equal to the average.

The price elasticities are small and negative for all three categories of spending. Indeed, these elasticities are at the low end of the range found by previous studies. For police and fire spending, the price elasticity of demand is about -0.08; that is, a 10 percent increase in the property tax base per capita (and hence a decrease in the median voter's tax share) leads to a 0.8 percent decrease in spending.[7] The price elasticity for general services is -0.20, or over twice as large in absolute value, and is highly significant statistically.[8]

To place these results in perspective, consider the variation in the property tax base per capita—the main component of tax price other than resource cost.[9] In 1982 a city with a per capita property tax base one standard deviation above the mean spent about 3 percent more on police and fire services and about 6 percent more on general services than a city with a per capita tax base equal to the 86-city mean, solely because of the tax price effect.

---

5. Previous studies have tended to focus on more homogeneous jurisdictions than on major central cities. As a result, they have not identified and controlled for the wide range of factors, such as service responsibilities and costs, that are considered in our analysis. Thus our study has the advantage of having more controls and the disadvantage of a situation in which it may be more difficult to estimate price and income elasticities with precision.
6. The income elasticity for fire services is significant at the 11 percent level.
7. The results in this chapter apply both over time and across cities. Whenver we say, "a 10 percent increase," we could also say, "a 10 percent difference between city A and city B."
8. The price elasticities are significant at the 10 percent level for police and fire and at the 0.5 percent level for general services.
9. The median tax share equals the median house value divided by the property tax base per capita. As is explained in the appendix to this chapter, our analysis estimates the effect on spending of the per capita tax base and controls indirectly for the median house value.

Political Institutions in the City

City spending outcomes are influenced by political and bureaucratic institutions as well as by citizens' demand for services. We account for these institutions in four ways.

First, political institutions do not adjust instantaneously to a change in citizens' demand for services. Before they actually lead to a change in spending, changes in voters' incomes or tax prices must filter through city council elections, referenda, and other features of a city's political system. To account for this factor, we employ a "lagged adjustment" assumption, which allows us to estimate how long it takes for a change in demand factors to show up in a change in spending. The length of adjustment is summarized by a lagged adjustment parameter, which is the inverse of the time it takes to make the adjustment voters would like to have in one year.

This lagged adjustment process is powerful. As is shown in the second panel of table 10.1, the lagged adjustment parameter is about 0.5 and highly significant statistically for all three service types. The result indicates that political institutions are indeed slow to adjust to changes in demand factors; it takes ten years to make the adjustment voters would like to have in five years. The lagged adjustment parameter is somewhat larger (that is, adjustment is somewhat faster) for police (0.54) and for fire (0.60) than for general services (0.44).

Second, city spending may depend on the form of the city government. All major central cities in the United States have an elected city council, but some also have an elected mayor whereas others have an appointed city manager.[10] The translation of demand factors into expenditure may be different in these two cases. In attempting to please various voting blocks, for example, mayors may spend more than city managers on certain services, all else equal. Consequently we estimate the average spending differences between cities with mayors and those with city managers.

We find that, on average, cities with city managers spend almost 5 percent less than those with mayors on general city services, but we cannot tell whether this difference represents a difference in service level or in managerial efficiency. On the other hand, cities with city managers and those with mayors do not differ significantly in their spending for police or fire services.

Third, voters and government officials in large cities face various direct restrictions on their ability to tax or spend. The most important type of

---

10. Three cities also have a commission form of government. These cities are included in the same category as those with city managers.

restriction is a severe property tax limitation, which we define as a law that makes it difficult or impossible for a city to raise its property tax rates.

We find that, on average, a severe property tax limit lowers spending on fire services by 7 percent and spending on general services by 9 percent. The effect of such a limit on spending for police services is small and not statistically significant. We cannot determine whether this impact on spending for fire and general services represents a cut in service quality or an increase in governmental efficiency or some combination of the two.

Finally, voting outcomes in cities also may be influenced by the characteristics of voters or by regional variation in institutions or preferences. With a few minor exceptions, these factors do not prove to be important in major central cities. For general services, elderly voters prefer a slightly lower service level and homeowners a slightly higher service level than do other voters, but these groups have the same demand as other groups for public safety. Furthermore, city spending does not vary significantly by region, when one controls for other things, for any type of service.

City Fiscal Health and City Spending

The key components of a city's actual fiscal health, namely restricted revenue-raising capacity (including intergovernmental aid), public service costs, and service responsibilities, all influence citizens' demand for services and thereby influence city spending. The influence is not accidental; the concept of city fiscal health is designed to measure the constraints on a city's spending decisions, and the demand framework explains how voters respond to constraints. When fiscal health improves—that is, when constraints loosen—one would expect voters' demand for services, and hence actual spending, to increase. By introducing the components of fiscal health into the above framework, we can determine their impact on city spending.

Resident Income and Tax Exporting

As we explained in chapter 9, a city's restricted revenue-raising capacity is the income of its residents augmented by its ability to export its tax burden to nonresidents and by intergovernmental grants. These three factors are also key elements of citizens' demand for city services, although in somewhat different form. The first two factors are considered here; intergovernmental grants are considered in a later section.

Per capita income is the base of revenue-raising capacity, whereas median income is used to help summarize citizens' demand for services. These two income variables are highly correlated, and for practical purposes the income elasticities presented earlier describe the impact on city spending of the income component of revenue-raising capacity.[11]

In the case of exporting, the median voter's tax share is related to the ability of a city to export the burden of its property taxes to nonresidents. To be specific, a voter's tax share can be thought of as the property tax burden falling on residents as a share of total property taxes, whereas the export ratio for the property tax is the dollars of property tax borne by nonresidents for every dollar of taxes borne paid by residents.[12] Because they contain the same elements, these two concepts are algebraically related, and the impact of tax share on spending can be translated into an impact of export ratio on spending.[13] Because a higher tax share is associated with a lower export ratio, the small, negative price elasticities described earlier indicate that, all else equal, cities with a relatively high ability to export property taxes, and hence with a higher restricted revenue-raising capacity, will spend slightly more than other cities on all three types of services.

In most central cities, the property tax is not the only available broad-based tax. So one also must consider the impact on city spending of city earnings taxes and city general sales taxes. From a voter's point of view, earnings and sales taxes paid by residents do not represent new resources; instead they represent alternative ways of collecting taxes from the same resource, namely resident income. Because they do not represent new resources, the resident portion of these taxes will have no effect on the demand for city services. On the other hand, income and sales taxes exported to nonresidents do represent new resources; they raise the revenue available to a city without increasing the tax burden on residents. As a result, income and sales taxes paid by nonresidents boost spending on city services. As in the case of the property tax, there is a clear link between this demand framework and the concept of revenue-raising capacity. Earnings and sales taxes on nonresidents, but not on those residents, add to a city's restricted

---

11. In our data for 1982 the correlation between per capita income and median income is 0.82.
12. A voter's tax share also reflects the value of her property relative to the value of other voters' property. For a discussion of this issue, see the appendix to this chapter.
13. The export ratio, ER, equals resident taxes, R, divided by nonresident taxes, N. The tax share, TS, equals resident taxes divided by total taxes, (R+N). It follows that $ER = (1 - TS)/TS$ or $TS = 1/(1 + ER)$.

revenue-raising capacity and therefore loosen the revenue constraint on voters.[14] As this constraint loosens, spending goes up.

For two reasons exported taxes do not have exactly the same effect on the demand for services as does resident income. First, earnings and sales taxes paid by nonresidents raise a voter's desired level of services because they allow the voter to purchase the same level of city services at a lower property tax rate. The value to the voter of a lower property tax rate depends on that voter's property tax share: the higher her tax share, the greater the value to her of the property tax cuts that exported earnings and sales taxes can bring. Thus the impact of exported earnings and sales taxes on the demand for services, unlike the impact of resident income, is weighted by property tax share.

Second, exported taxes, unlike resident income, flow directly into the city treasury. Several studies have found that this difference matters: money flowing directly into a city's treasury has a greater effect on spending than an equivalent increase in resources given directly to voters (see Inman 1979b; Rubinfeld 1985; or Hamilton 1983). This so-called "flypaper" effect must be considered in interpreting the impact on spending of exported taxes.

We find that an ability to export earnings tax burdens does indeed boost city spending. Of course, voters do not care about the exportable earnings tax base as such; instead they care about actual exported taxes, which equal the base multiplied by the tax rate.[15] Actual tax rates on nonresident earnings are below 5 percent in every city with an earnings tax. So $1.00 of exportable tax base corresponds to less than $0.05 of exported tax burden. Estimates of the dollar impact on spending of $1.00 of exported earnings tax burden based on a 5 percent tax rate are presented in the third panel of table 10.1.[16] A $100.00 increase in exported earnings taxes leads to a $19.00 increase in spending on general services and a $3.00 increase in spending on police services but has no significant effect on fire spending. The rela-

14. Because we are trying to explain actual spending, this link is between actual demand and restricted revenue-raising capacity, not full revenue-raising capacity. A city's potential for exporting tax burdens to commuters does not affect voters' demand for services—unless the city actually is allowed to tax nonresident earnings.
15. One might ask why we do not estimate the impact of exported earnings taxes instead of that of the earnings tax base on spending. The reason is that the earnings tax rate, unlike the tax base, is endogenous, that is, it is selected by the city government. See the appendix to this chapter.
16. In these calculations, the assumed tax share is based on the 1982 average property tax export ratio, and spending and income are assumed to be at the 1982 average.

tively small effects on police and fire spending are not surprising, given that they make up relatively small portions of the typical city's budget.

The comparable effects on spending of a $100.00 increase in resident income are $4.00, $2.00, and $0.80 for general, police, and fire services, respectively. These results imply, therefore, that there is a flypaper effect for exportable earnings taxes. With a 5 percent tax rate, each $1.00 of actual earnings tax revenue from nonresidents has 4.9 times the impact on spending for general services and 1.4 times the impact on spending for police as $1.00 of resident income.

The impact on city spending of exporting through the sales tax is somewhat larger, but less significant statistically, than the impact of exporting through earnings taxes. With a 5 percent tax rate, a $100 increase in exported sales taxes leads to spending increases of $20 for general services and $3 each for police and fire services.[17] Only the impact on fire spending is statistically significant, however. The flypaper effect in this case is quite large; a $1.00 increase in exported sales taxes has 4.6 times the effect on fire spending as $1.00 of resident income.

Although some of these impacts cannot be estimated with precision, the general pattern is very similar for exported earnings taxes and exported sales taxes. An increase in a city's ability to export tax burdens to nonresidents, either through earnings taxes or through sales taxes, leads to an increase in city spending, and hence to an increase in city service quality. This increase in spending is greater for services that form a larger part of the average city's budget, and it is greater than the increase that would ensue from adding an equivalent amount to resident income.

The final element of restricted revenue-raising capacity is taxes collected by overlying jurisdictions. The higher the taxes collected by overlying jurisdictions, the lower the share of resident income left over for city services, and the lower a city's restricted revenue-raising capacity. The parallel logic in the demand framework begins with the observation that the demand for city services depends on a voter's income after taxes paid to the state and to other local governments.[18] Voters in a city with relatively high overlying taxes have relatively low disposable incomes, all else equal, and therefore demand a lower level of city services.

As we expected, we find that the effect of overlying taxes on police

17. Like those above, these calculations employ 1982 averages.
18. This demand also depends on taxes paid to the federal government, but voters in all cities face the same federal tax system, so federal taxes do not help to explain variation in public spending across cities.

and fire spending is negative; a 1 percentage point increase in overlying taxes relative to income has about the same effect on spending for these services as a 0.5 percent decline in resident income. This effect is not statistically significant, however. The effect of overlying taxes on spending for general services is close to zero and also not significant.

The Cost of Providing City Services

As was discussed in chapter 4, higher input prices or a harsher environment raise the cost of providing city public services. Because expenditure equals the service level multiplied by the average cost of services, input costs and environmental factors also directly influence city spending.

The relevant environmental factors are quite diverse. For all types of services, population, the city's share of the metropolitan population, and the ratio of employment to population all have a significant impact on service costs. Other environmental factors that affect the cost of city services include poverty (for police and fire services), the quantity of old housing (for fire and general services), density (for general services), and type of property (primarily for fire services). Thus, for example, cities with a higher percentage of poor residents must spend more to achieve the same quality of police services.

A voter's tax price equals her tax share multiplied by the resource cost of another unit of service quality. Consequently a higher cost, whether due to higher input prices or a harsher environment, leads to a higher tax price and hence lowers the voter's demand for city services. By the logic of the demand analysis, in other words, voters in a city with higher input prices or a harsher environment will select lower-quality city services. According to the price elasticities estimated earlier, a 1 percent increase in costs leads to a 0.08 percent decline in service quality for police and fire services, and a 0.20 percent decline for general services.

Remember that city public expenditure equals the service level multiplied by the cost per unit of service. If the price elasticity were zero, therefore, a 1 percent increase in cost would lead to a 1 percent increase in spending. Because of the behavioral response to a higher tax price, however, a 1 percent increase in cost leads to a slightly less than 1 percent increase in spending. To be precise, a 1 percent increase in the cost of police or fire services leads to a $(1 - 0.08) = 0.92$ percent increase in spending, and a 1 percent increase in the cost of general services leads to a $(1 - 0.20) = 0.80$ percent increase in spending on general services.

These results imply that cost differences across cities have a minimal effect on differences in service quality but lead to large differences in tax burdens. Cities apparently do not respond to high input or environmental costs by cutting back on service quality; instead they respond by raising taxes.

It is important to emphasize that the cost factors considered here are outside a city's control. Environmental factors, such as poverty and property type, are determined largely by economic and social forces at the national level. Similarly, our indexes of input costs, the state manufacturing wage and the metropolitan consumer price index, are independent of city government actions.[19]

Service Responsibilities

As we indicated in chapter 8, some cities provide schools, hospitals, and higher education, whereas others do not. Similarly, responsibility for other local public services (namely police, fire, sewers, sanitation, highways, parks and recreation, public welfare, health, housing and urban renewal, airports, water transportation, parking, corrections, and libraries) is divided in different ways among cities, counties, special districts, and states. Consequently one cannot account for variation in spending across cities without accounting for variation in their spending responsibilities.

Our index of service responsibilities, which was described in chapter 8, indicates how much each city must spend to reach national average state and local spending for each type of service given the division of service responsibilities among levels of government in that city's state. This index is independent of a city's actual decisions about service provision.

To understand the impact of service responsibilities on spending, one must distinguish between the quantity or scope of city services and their quality. The scope of services is determined by the service responsibilities assigned to a city, whereas the quality is determined by voter demand and various institutional factors. In other words, each state decides which services its cities must provide, and the voters in each city decide how good those services will be.

Voters' decisions about service quality may depend on service respon-

---

19. City governments do, of course, influence the compensation of their employees, and some cities raise the cost of providing city services by making generous wage or pension settlements with city employee unions. As a result, it is inappropriate to employ actual compensation rates for public employees as a measure of the costs imposed on a city. In the long run, city policies also may have some effect on the city environment. But even in the long run the impact of city policies is small relative to the impact of national economic and social trends.

sibilities. For example, voters who must provide an extensive set of services may select a somewhat lower quality for each service. This phenomenon is a kind of fiscal overburden. Because spending equals the scope of services multiplied by service quality multiplied by the cost per unit of services, we can measure the impact of extensive service responsibilities on service quality by determining the effect on spending of greater service responsibilities, holding constant the cost per unit of services.

As is shown in table 10.1, service responsibilities have a significant impact on spending for each of the broad service types. In the case of general services, a 1 percent difference in service responsibility between two cities leads to a 0.80 percent difference in spending—that is, spending does not increase proportionately with responsibilities. This result has two possible interpretations. First, cities with extensive responsibilities may cut back on the quality of the services for which they are responsible. Under this interpretation, extensive responsibilities impose a kind of fiscal overburden on cities, forcing them to cut back service quality. Second, extensive responsibilities may be accompanied by economies of scope. Administrative costs may not increase proportionately with service responsibilities, so that the cost per unit of service responsibilities is lower with high than with low responsibilities. Unfortunately, we cannot determine which of these interpretations is appropriate.

Although not shown in table 10.1, school and hospital responsibilities, which unlike the others are of the all-or-nothing variety, are not included in the overall service responsibility measure. Not surprisingly, school and hospital responsibilities prove to have a large and statistically significant effect on city spending.

In the case of police and fire services, the service responsibility effects are not as large. A 1 percent difference in police responsibilities between two cities leads to a 0.15 percent difference in police spending, but this effect is not statistically significant. A 1 percent difference in fire responsibilities leads to a 0.21 percent difference in fire spending. All cities have police and fire responsibilities, but these are shared to various degrees among city, other local, and state governments. As in the case of general services, this result may imply that cities with a larger share of the state and local police or fire responsibility provide lower-quality police or fire services than do other cities, or it may imply that police and fire services are characterized by economies of scope.

Intergovernmental Aid

Intergovernmental aid provides a city with more revenue for services without any increase in the tax burden imposed on residents; that is, aid adds to a city's restricted revenue-raising capacity. The value of intergovernmental aid to a voter, like the value of exported taxes, depends on the voter's tax share. The higher a voter's tax share, the greater the tax savings from a dollar of aid. Moreover, several studies have found that one dollar of aid, weighted by a voter's tax share, has a larger effect on spending than one dollar of income.[20]This result reflects the flypaper effect described earlier.

As is shown in table 10.1, both state aid and federal categorical aid have significant impacts on city spending—with a flypaper effect. For a city with general spending per capita, median income, and property export ratio equal to the 1982 average for our 86 cities, a $100 increase in state aid leads to a $32 increase in spending on general services, and a $100 increase in federal categorical aid leads to a $49 increase in this spending. The rest of these increases in aid goes to a cut in taxes—and hence an increase in spending on private goods—or to an increase in capital spending, which we do not examine. Federal revenue sharing has a similar impact on spending for general services, but it is not statistically significant. The flypaper effect implicit in these results is very large: $1 of state aid has 8 times the impact on spending of $1 of resident income; $1 of federal categorical aid has 13 times the impact of $1 of resident income.

As one would expect from the relatively low budget share of police services, federal categorical aid has a much smaller effect on police spending than on spending for general services; a $100 increase in this aid leads to a $2 increase in police spending. This result implies a modest flypaper effect: $1 of federal aid has 1.05 times the impact on police spending of $1 of resident income. Neither state aid nor federal general revenue sharing has a statistically significant impact on police spending.

The impact of federal categorical aid on fire spending is similar to its impact on police. To be specific, a $100 increase in this aid leads to a $1 increase in fire spending. Again, the flypaper effect is modest: $1 of this federal aid has 1.33 times the effect on fire spending of $1 of resident income. Although it does not affect police spending, state aid has a larger effect on fire spending than does federal categorical aid; a $100 increase in state aid boosts fire spending by $2. The flypaper effect here is fairly large: $1 of state aid has 2.7 times the effect on spending of $1 of resident income.

---

20. For a review of these studies, see Inman 1979b or Rubinfeld 1985. In the following calculations, the 1982 average property tax export ratio is used to calculate a tax share.

As in the case of police, federal general revenue sharing does not have a significant effect on fire spending.

These results provide strong support for the flypaper effect, namely that intergovernmental grants have a stronger effect on spending, and hence on service quality, than does an equivalent increase in resident income, after a voter's tax share is accounted for. This effect is particularly strong for general services. Because of data limitations, our analysis treats all grants as block grants even though some federal and state aid takes the form of matching grants. Unlike block grants, matching grants lower the price of public services and therefore have a larger effect on city spending than do block grants, even without a flypaper effect. Our results may reflect these price effects of matching grants and may therefore overstate the flypaper effect to some degree. Indeed, matching grants are the most common for general services, which may explain why the flypaper effect is higher for these services than for police or fire.[21]

A flypaper effect does not exist for federal general revenue sharing, however; the consistent insignificance of revenue sharing implies that cities use revenue-sharing grants to lower tax burdens or to build infrastructure, not to increase the quality of current city services.

Conclusions

Along with a variety of political and bureaucratic factors, the components of actual fiscal health, including resident income, exported taxes, public service costs, service responsibilities, and intergovernmental aid, are important determinants of spending decisions by city governments. City spending reflects the service quality selected by the city, the scope of its service responsibilities, and its public service costs. By accounting for all three of these factors, we find that the components of fiscal health also are important determinants of a city's service quality.

A city's restricted revenue-raising capacity depends primarily on the

---

21. The flypaper effect associated with exported taxes also is higher for general services than for police and fire services, even though exported taxes do not involve a matching rate. However, the magnitude of the difference across types of services is smaller with exported taxes than with grants. The federal aid flypaper effect for general services, for example, is over 10 times as great as for police and fire services, whereas the flypaper effect of the exported earnings tax for general services is less than 4 times as great as for police services; and the flypaper effect of the exported sales tax is only slightly larger for general services than for fire services.

income of its residents and on its ability to export taxes to nonresidents. Both of these components influence the quality of city services. Voters' demand for city services, like their demand for private goods, depends on their income. The higher residents' incomes, the higher their demand for city services, and the higher the quality of city services, particularly of police services. A city's ability to export its property tax burden is a key determinant of the tax price facing voters and hence of their demand for public services. The more property taxes a city can export to nonresidents, the lower residents' tax prices, the higher their demand for public services, and the higher the quality of city services.

Some cities have access to earnings or sales taxes, and a city's restricted revenue-raising capacity also reflects its ability to export the burden of these taxes to nonresidents. This component of fiscal health has a strong impact on city spending, and hence on service quality. The greater a city's ability to export earnings or sales tax burdens to nonresidents, the higher the quality of its public services. Moreover, exported tax burdens have a flypaper effect: that is, the impact on spending of one dollar of exported taxes is greater than the impact of one dollar of resident income.

Voters' tax prices, and hence the service quality they prefer, are influenced by a city's input costs and environmental characteristics, such as poverty and population density. Chapter 4 contains a detailed discussion of these input and environmental cost factors and a method for incorporating them into a public service cost index.

A city's service responsibilities strongly influence its spending; not surprisingly, the greater a city's service responsibilities, the more it spends on public services. City spending does not increase proportionately with responsibilities, however, either because extensive responsibilities impose a kind of fiscal overburden on cities or because they allow them to take advantage of economies of scope in the delivery of some types of service.

Categorical aid from its state or the federal government, but not federal general revenue sharing, also boosts a city's spending, and hence its service quality. In fact, categorical aid from either level of government has a strong flypaper effect; a one dollar increase in aid has a significantly larger impact on city spending than a one dollar increase in resident income. Federal general revenue sharing, on the other hand, serves to lower city tax burdens or to increase capital spending—not to increase current city service quality.

Appendix: The Determinants of Spending by Central Cities

This appendix presents our model of city spending, following the outline of chapter 10, and our empirical estimates of this model. These estimates are the basis of the cost indexes in chapter 4 as well as of the results in chapter 10. This appendix contains technical material; familiarity with economic models and regression techniques is assumed.

A Framework for Analyzing City Spending Decisions

The Basic Determinants of Citizens' Demand for Services

A voter's demand for city services is a function of her income and the price she must pay to obtain another unit of services (see Inman 1979b). In the standard case in which city services are financed entirely by a property tax and purchased at a constant cost per unit of service, the price a voter must pay for another unit of the service, which is called the tax price, TP, equals $(V/\overline{V})(C)$, where V is the market value of the voter's house, $\overline{V}$ is the value of all taxable property in the city divided by the number of voters, and C is the per voter cost of another unit of public services. Thus the demand function, in the well-known constant elasticity form, is:

$$(A10.1) \qquad S = kY^{\theta}(TP)^{\mu} = kY^{\theta}(V/\overline{V})^{\mu}(C)^{\mu},$$

where S is the level of local services per voter, Y is the voter's income, and k, θ, and μ are constants. Note that θ and μ (which is negative) are the income and price elasticitities of demand for public services.

A voter's desired public expenditure per voter, E, equals the desired level of service multiplied by the cost per unit of service or (S)(C). Hence the voter's desired public spending is equation (A10.1) multiplied by C; that is,

$$(A10.2) \qquad E = (S)(C) = kY^{\theta}(V/\overline{V})^{\mu}(C)^{\mu+1}$$

or, in logarithmic form,

$$(A10.3) \qquad \ln(E) = \ln(k) + \theta\ln(Y) + \mu\ln(V/\overline{V}) + (1+\mu)\ln(C).$$

Equation (A10.3) can be estimated with ordinary least squares.

Income and price elasticities and service costs (as well as other factors to be considered below) may differ from one type of public service to another, so we carry out separate analyses for three broad types of city services: police, fire, and general services.

The demand for public services varies from one citizen to the next. To estimate the impact of citizens' demand on actual spending decisions, one must employ a summary measure of the distribution of citizens' demands within the city. As we explained in the text, we obtain such a summary measure by inserting the median income and tax price into our citizen demand function, namely equation (A10.2).

Our model calls for the median of the income distribution for voters, whereas our data refer to the median of the income distribution for all residents. Let N stand for population, A for voters, and HH for households. In addition, let a subscript T indicate a city total and let a ^ indicate a median. Then we can rewrite equation (A10.2) as

$$E_T/A = k(\hat{Y}_A)^\theta [V/(V_T/A)]^\mu C^{1+\mu} \ .$$

Now assume that median income per person, $\hat{Y}_N$, equals median income per voter, $\hat{Y}_A$, multiplied by voters per household and divided by average household size. (This relationship is exactly true for mean incomes but may be only approximately true for median incomes.) It follows that:

(A10.4) $E_T/N = (E_T/A)(A/HH)(HH/N)$

$$= k[(A/HH)(HH/N)]^{1+\theta-\mu}[\hat{Y}_N]^\theta [V/(V_T/N)]^\mu C^{1+\mu} \ .$$

In short, multiplying equation (A10.2) by voters per household, (A/HH), and the inverse of household size, (HH/N), transforms the model from a per voter to per capita form and allows us to estimate it with available data. We assume that the number of voters is proportional to the adult population, and we measure the number of households by the number of occupied housing units.

One problem arises in implementing this transformation. We want to know the effect on city spending of income per voter, but equation (A10.4) estimates the effect on spending of income per person when one controls for (A/HH) and (HH/N). (The same problem applies to property tax base per person.) Therefore, we first regress (A/HH) and (HH/N) on the log of median income (and the log of per capita property tax base); then we include the residuals from this regression, that is, the proportions of (A/HH) and (HH/N) that are independent of median income (and per capita tax base) in our regressions. This procedure ensures that the coefficient of our income (or tax base) variable measures the impact on spending of an equal change in all three components of income (or tax base) per voter.

Also, we do not have data on median house value, so we assume that the demand for housing services, H, takes the following form, where P_H is the price of H:

(A10.5) $H = b'Y^\sigma P_H^v$.

The market value of a house, V, is the present value of the flow of housing services from that house or, approximately,

(A10.6) $V = P_H H / r = (b'/r) Y^\sigma P_H^{1+v} = bY^\sigma P_H^{1+v}$,

where r is the appropriate discount rate and $b = b'/r$. Substituting this expression into equation (A10.2) yields:

(A10.7) $E = [kb^v][(P_H^{\mu(1+v)}][Y^{\theta+\sigma\mu}]/[\bar V]^\mu$.

Thus the introduction of housing demand has three effects on equation (A10.3). First, it implies that the only property tax variable is $\bar V$. The coefficient of $\ln(\bar V)$ is $(-\mu)$. Second, it alters the interpretation of the coefficient of $\ln(Y)$, which is now θ plus $\sigma\mu$. Third, it leads to the addition of a housing price variable.

City Political Institutions

Political and bureaucratic institutions also influence city spending. We account for these institutions in four ways.

First, we employ a simple lagged adjustment assumption:

(A10.8) $(E_y)/(E_{y-1}) = [(E_y^*)/(E_{y-1})]^\lambda$

or

$$E_y = (E_y^*)^\lambda (E_{y-1})^{1-\lambda} ,$$

where E_y^* is the desired spending level in period y, as given by equation (A10.2). This equation implies that it takes $(1/\lambda)$ periods for actual spending to reach the desired growth for one period.

Substituting equation (A10.2) into equation (A10.8) and taking logarithms yields:

(A10.9) $\quad \ln(E_y) = \lambda\ln(k) + \lambda\theta\ln(Y) + \lambda\mu\ln(V/\overline{V})$

$$+ \lambda(1+\mu)\ln(C) + (1-\lambda)\ln(E_{y-1}) .$$

Thus a lagged adjustment assumption calls for the inclusion of the lagged dependent variable, $\ln(E_{y-1})$, in the spending regression. All the coefficients in this regression, including those of the additional variables in equations (A10.4) and (A10.7), reflect the adjustment parameter, λ, which equals 1 minus the coefficient of the lagged dependent variable.

Second, we include a dummy variable for cities with city managers. Third, we include a dummy variable for cities that face a severe property tax limit. Fourth, we include the share of the population in two key groups, homeowners and the elderly, that may influence spending decisions. (For more on the link between group preferences and spending, see Bergstrom and Goodman 1973; Inman 1978.) In addition, our regressions include one set of dummy variables for Census regions and another for years.

Fiscal Health and Spending

Two components of a city's fiscal health, resident income and the ability to export property taxes to nonresidents, appear in the basic model of city spending. Tax exporting, intergovernmental aid, public service costs, and service responsibilities also matter.

Tax Exporting and Intergovernmental Aid

In equation (A10.2), voters' demand for public services is a function of voters' income. Intergovernmental aid as well as income and sales taxes exported to nonresidents are like additions to resident income and therefore boost voters' demand for services. To account formally for nonproperty taxes and intergovernmental aid, let us define the export shares for property, income, and sales taxes as the nonresident tax base divided by the total tax base for each tax. In symbols, let e_p, e_y, and e_s be the export shares for the property, income, and sales taxes, respectively; let t_p, t_y, and t_s be the tax rates for these three taxes; let Z be consumption other than housing; and let A be per voter intergovernmental aid. Then the budget constraint for a single voter is:

(A10.10)		$Y(1-t_y) = Z(1+t_s) + P_H H + t_p V$,

and the budget constraint for a city government is

(A10.11)		$E = t_p \bar{V} + t_y \bar{Y} + t_s \bar{Z} + A$.

Substituting equation (A10.11) and the definitions of export shares into equation (A10.10) leads to the following combined budget constraint, where a subscript X identifies a nonresident share:

(A10.12)		$Y[1 + t_y(e_y-e_p)/(1-e_y) + t_s(1-e_p)Z_X/Y + (1-e_p)A/Y]$

$$= Z(1 + t_s e_p) + P_H H + (1-e_p)E .$$

The terms on the left side of equation (A10.12) measure resident income as augmented by exported income and sales taxes and by intergovernmental aid. Because nonresident income and sales tax bases and intergovernmental aid influence voters' demand for services, these variables, weighted by $(1-e_p)$, should be included in a spending regression. The coefficients of these variables reflect implicit tax rates on exported tax bases and flypaper effects.

Let Y^* be the sum of resident income, exported taxes, and aid. Then we want to substitute Y^* for Y in our estimating equation. But because Y^* is a sum, $\ln(Y^*)$ is nonlinear. Fortunately, the three terms in square brackets in equation (A10.12) usually sum to a small fraction, so we can make use of the approximation $\ln(1+a) \approx a$, which is accurate for small values of a, and write $\ln(Y^*)$ as:

(A10.13)		$\ln(Y^*) = \ln(Y) + t_y[(e_y-e_p)/(1-e_p)]$

$$+ t_s[(1-e_p)Z_X/Y] + [(1-e_p)A/Y] .$$

In sum, our log-linear estimating equation includes four resource variables: the log of median income, $\ln(Y)$, exportable income taxes, $[(e_y-e_p)/(1-e_y)]$; exportable sales taxes, $[(1-e_p)Z_X/Y]$; and intergovernmental aid, $[(1-e_p)A/Y]$. After correcting for our lagged adjustment assumption, the coefficient of $\ln(Y)$ is the income elasticity of demand for city services, θ, and the coefficient of each exportable tax base variable is θ multiplied by an implicit tax rate and, if it exists, a flypaper effect.

The Cost of Providing City Services

The cost of providing city services is a function of input prices and of environmental factors. Let I be an index of input prices, and let $\phi(C_1, \ldots, C_M)$ measure the impact of environmental factors, C_1 to C_M, on service costs. Under reasonable assumptions about the technology of public production, I has a multiplicative effect on spending (see Yinger 1986a). Thus, assuming a constant cost per unit of services, the cost function for city services is:

$$(A10.14) \qquad C = I\,[\phi(C_1, \ldots, C_M)\,]\,,$$

and

$$(A10.15) \qquad E = I\,[\phi(C_1, \ldots, C_M)]S\,.$$

To estimate the cost function for each type of service, we identify the relevant environmental cost variables and select an appropriate form for the φ function. On the basis of previous studies, especially Bradbury et al. (1984), and a priori reasoning, we selected the environmental cost variables discussed in chapter 4. Most of these are expressed as percentages, such as the percentage of the population below the poverty line. We assume that the harsher the environment, the greater the impact on service costs of a 1 percentage point increase in the harshness of the environment. For example, going from 20 to 21 percent poor residents will have a larger impact on service costs than going from 1 to 2 percent poor residents. An exponential function satisfies this assumption and enables us to include these percentages directly in our log-linear expenditure regressions. The coefficient of each cost variable (divided by $\lambda(1+\mu)$—see equation (A10.9)) indicates the percentage change in the cost of services for each percentage point increase in that cost variable.

A few cost variables receive special treatment. To account for the possibility of high service costs at both high and low population densities, we include both density and density squared in our regressions.

In addition, we hypothesize that service costs depend on the composition of a city's property. Suppose that the cost of providing services to property type i is c_i. Then, all else equal, total costs equal $\Sigma c_i P_i$, where P_i is the value of property of type i. Dividing all terms in this sum by $c_1 P_1$, where property type 1 is owner-occupied housing, we obtain $\Sigma c_1 P_1 [1 + (c_i/C_1)(P_i/P_1)]$. To incorporate this additive form into our log-linear regressions, we employ the approximation, valid for small a, that $\ln(1 + a) \approx a$; that is, the variable for property type i is the value of that property divided by the value of owner-occupied housing.

Finally, consider the role of city population. The link between spending on a public service and the service level depends on the "publicness" of that service. The usual formulation of this link (see Inman 1979b) is:

(A10.16) $S = (E)(N)/(N)^g = (E)(N)^{1-g}$.

That is, the per capita service level equals total spending divided by population raised to the power g, where g equals zero for a pure public good and one for a pure private good. A value of g greater than one implies diseconomies to population scale.

Solving equation (A10.16) for E yields $E = (S)(N)^{g-1}$. A comparison of this result with equation (A10.15) reveals that population can be considered a type of environmental cost variable. In the case of a pure public good, the provision of one unit of the service to one household automatically leads to the provision of one unit to all households—at no extra cost. In a relatively large community, therefore, the environment for producing a pure public good is relatively favorable and for producing a good with diseconomies to population scale is relatively harsh. In the case of a pure private good, the cost of increasing service quality cannot be shared among many people, and, all else equal, the per capita cost of a unit of service is the same in cities of all sizes. In the case of a good with diseconomies to population scale, larger cities have a higher per capita cost for public services; that is, larger cities have a relatively harsh environment for producing such a good. Thus the log of population appears in our log-linear expenditure regressions, and its coefficient is $\lambda(1+\mu)(g-1)$.

Service Responsibilities

The scope of city services is determined by a city's service responsibilities, whereas the quality of city services is determined by voters' demand and political institutions. More formally, the service level, S, is the product of service responsibilites, SR, and an index of service quality, SQ. Thus city spending for services of type L are:

(A10.17) $E_L = (S_L)(C_L) = (SR_L)(SQ_L)(C_L)$.

The left side of equation (A10.1) can now be more precisely defined as SQ, our service responsibility indexes measure SR_L, and our cost variables measure C_L. To account for the assignment of taxing authority, which accompanies the division of service responsibilities, we also multiply our income terms by (1-w), where w is taxes paid to overlying jurisdictions as a fraction of income.

Cities with higher service responsibilities may select a lower quality for the services they provide, so the coefficient of SR_L, say γ, need not be unity. Substituting (1-w), γ, and equation (A10.2) into equation (A10.17) yields:

$$(A10.18) \qquad E_L = [\,(k_L)(SR_L)\,]^{\gamma}\,[Y(1-w)]^{\theta}\,[V/\overline{V}\,]^{\mu}\,[\,C_L\,]^{1+\mu}$$

Thus $\ln(SR_L)$ and $\ln(1-w)$ must be added to equation (A10.9). We divide our total service responsibility index, which was derived in chapter 8, into five parts: police, fire, schools, hospitals, and everything else. The police and fire indexes appear in the police and fire equations. The "everything else" index appears in the general services equation.

Because responsibility for schools or hospitals is of the all-or-nothing sort, we account for it in a somewhat different way. Let $\overline{E}_{SCH}$ be the national average spending on schools and D_{SCH} be a dummy variable equal to one if a city has reponsibility for schools. Let $\overline{E}_{HOS}$ and D_{HOS} be the analogous variables for hospitals. Then the service responsibility index for general services, SRIG, is:

$$(A10.19) \qquad SRIG = SRIEE + \overline{E}_{SCH}D_{SCH} + \overline{E}_{HOS}D_{HOS}\,,$$

where SRIEE is the index for "everything else." The terms $\overline{E}_{SCH}$ and $\overline{E}_{HOS}$ are national averages, so they are constant across cities and we can estimate them. However, these terms enter SRIG additively, not multiplicatively, so we must use a (by now) familiar approximation:

$$SRIG = SRIEE(1 + \overline{E}_{SCH}\,D_{SCH}\,/SRIEE + \overline{E}_{HOS}\,D_{HOS}\,/SRIEE)$$

or

$$(A10.20) \qquad \ln(SRIG) \approx \ln(SRIEE) + \overline{E}_{SCH}\,(D_{SCH}\,/SRIEE)$$

$$+\,\overline{E}_{HOS}\,(D_{HOS}\,/SRIEE)\,.$$

Thus we include $D_{SCH}/SRIEE$ and $D_{HOS}/SRIEE$ as variables in our log-linear estimating equation and interpret their coefficients (divided by λ) as $\bar{E}_{SCH}$ and $\bar{E}_{HOS}$. Because the $\bar{E}$ terms change over time, we include school and hospital variables for each year in our sample.

Finally, the impact of a responsibility for schools depends on the number of children to be educated. Therefore, the term $\bar{E}_{SCH}$ can be written as $\bar{EK}_{SCH}$ (KIDS), where $\bar{EK}_{SCH}$ is national average spending per pupil and KIDS is children as a share of population. With this extension, the school variable is D_{SCH} (KIDS)/SRIEE, and its coefficient can be interpreted as $\bar{EK}_{SCH}$. To avoid possible simultaneity bias, we define KIDS on the basis of the number of children of school age in the city, not the number of pupils enrolled in the city's schools.

Empirical Results

Using multiple regression analysis, we estimated our model of city spending for the 86 major central cities in four years (1967, 1972, 1977, and 1982).

Variable Definitions

The variables included in our regression analysis are defined in table A10.1. Detailed algebraic definitions of the more complex variables, as derived earlier in this appendix, are given in table A10.2.

The Data

Many of the data for our regressions, including the variables for tax bases, export shares, property composition, and employment, were collected for earlier steps in our analysis and are described in the text or in previous appendixes. The rest of the data were obtained from a variety of sources, primarily the U.S. *Census of Governments* in various years (for expenditure data) and the 1970 and 1980 *Census of Population and Housing* (for environmental cost data). Specific sources are given in table A10.3.

Information was not available for every variable for every city for every year, and a variety of estimating techniques was used to fill in missing data. For example, data available only in 1970 and 1980 were trended to fill in 1972 and 1977 and were trended backward or forward to fill in 1967 and 1982. All filling in was carried out with as much information as possible. The ratio of city to national poverty rates, for example, was trended for each city, and this ratio was multiplied by the actual national poverty rate in each sample year to obtain an estimated city poverty rate. Data on median income do not exist for our sample years, so we estimated median income using an assumption about the form of the income distribution along with data on per capita income and on the percentage of the population in poverty. A detailed description of this estimating procedure is available from the authors.

A full description of the data sources and fill-in techniques is presented in tables A10.3 and A10.4.

Regression Results

The full set of regression results for the three services is given in table A10.5. The regression coefficients must be transformed into parameter estimates according to the functional forms derived above. Table 10.1 lists the estimated values of the key parameters.

As a form of sensitivity analysis, we tried an alternative formulation of the tax price based on the export ratio for the property tax and several alternative measures of resident income. These alternative approaches had little effect on our key results. In addition, we investigated the possibility of serial correlation in the error terms and found that it was not present. Finally, we considered, and rejected, the possibility that the property composition variables reflect property tax shifting (see Ladd 1975), not environmental costs. More information on this analysis is available from the authors.

Table A10.1
General Definitions of Variables

Variable	Definition
GENERAL	Log of per capita spending on general services
POLICE	Log of per capita spending on police services
FIRE	Log of per capita spending on fire services
YEARyy	Dummy for year 19yy
REGION-xx	Dummy for census region xx
ELDER	Percentage of population above 65 years old
OWNER	Percentage of housing units owner-occupied
HOMEPRICE	Log of housing price index
SRINET	Log of net service responsibility index (net of schools, hospitals, police, and fire)
SRIPOLICE	Log of police service responsibility index
SRIFIRE	Log of fire service responsibility index
SRISCHLyy	School responsibility varyiable for year 19yy[a]
SRIHOSPyy	Hospital responsibility variable for year 19yy[a]
CITYMAN	Dummy for city manager form of government[a]
TAXLIMIT	Dummy for severe property tax limit

Table A10.1 (Cont.)

Variable	Definition
INCOME	Log of median income[a]
HHSIZE	Log of household size[a]
VOTERS	Log of potential voters per household[a]
OVERTAX	Overlying tax take, as a percentage of income
PTAXBASE	Log of per capita property tax base
EXPEARN	Exportable income tax base variable[a]
EXPSALES	Exportable sales tax base variable[a]
FEDAID	Federal categorical aid variable[a]
FEDGRS	Federal general revenue sharing variable[a]
STATEAID	State aid variable[a]
LOGPOP	Log of city population
MANWAGE	Log of state manufacturing wage index[a]
LOGPRICE	Log of SMSA consumer price index (no housing, taxes)
DENSITY	Population density
DENSITY2	DENSITY squared
OLDHOUSE	Percentage of housing units over 20 years old
ONEHOUSE	Percentage of housing units in one-unit buildings
POVERTY	Percentage of population below poverty line
UNEMPLOY	City unemployment rate
RELPOP	City population as a percentage of SMSA population
EMPPRIVATE	Private employment in city as a percentage of city population
EMPGOV	Ratio of government to private employment
OWNSHARE	Property composition variable, owner-occupied housing[a]
PRORENTER	Property composition variable, rental housing[a]
PROTRADE	Property composition variable, trade property[a]
PROSERVICE	Property composition variable, service property[a]
PROINDUST	Property composition variable, industrial property[a]
PROVACANT	Property composition variable, other property[a]
GENERALL5	GENERAL lagged 5 years
POLICEL5	POLICE lagged 5 years
FIREL5	FIRE lagged 5 years

[a] Defined more fully in table A10.2.

Table A10.2
Detailed Definitions of Variables

Variable	Definition
Final variables	
SRISCHLyy	$(YEARyy)(DS)(KIDS)/SRINET^a$
SRIHOSPyy	$(YEARyy)(DH)/SRINET^a$
CITYMAN	Binary variable for cities with a city manager; includes 3 cities with commission form of government.
INCOME	Estimated median of income distribution per person[a]
HHSIZE	Variation in log of household size, LHHS, that is independent of INCOME and PTAXBASE; residuals of a regression of LHHS on these other two variables[a]
VOTERS	Variation in the log of potential voters per household, LHHV, that is independent of INCOME and PTAXBASE; residuals of a regression of LHHV on these other two variables; potential voters per household approximated by $(100\text{-}KIDS)/HHOLD^a$
EXPEARN	$(ERIPAY\text{-}ERPROP)/(1\text{-}ERIPAY)^a$
EXPSALES	$(1\text{-}ERPROP)(ERSALE)(PCTBSALE)/INCOME^a$
FEDAID	$(1\text{-}ERPROP)(PCFAID)/INCOME^a$
FEDGRS	$(1\text{-}ERPROP)(PCFGRS)/INCOME^a$
STATEAID	$(1\text{-}ERPROP)(PCSAID)/INCOME^a$
MANWAGE	Log of (SALDEF)(SMWAGE)
EMPGOV	PCEMPGOV/EMPPRIVATE
OWNSHARE	Log of PEROWN
PRORENTER	Value of rental housing as a percentage of property tax base, divided by $PEROWN^a$
PROTRADE	Value of trade (i.e., wholesale and retail) property as a percentage of property tax base, divided by PEROWN; value of trade property equals value of commercial property multiplied by $EMPTR/(EMPTR + EMPSR)^a$
PROSERVICE	Value of service (i.e., finance, insurance, real estate and derived services) property as a percentage of property tax base, divided by PEROWN; value of service property equals value of commercial property multiplied by $EMPSR/(EMPTR + EMPSR)^a$
PROINDUST	Value of industrial property as a percentage of property tax base, divided by $PEROWN^a$
PROVACANT	Value of vacant land and state-assessed property as a percentage of property tax base, divided by $PEROWN^a$
Variables used in defining final variables	
DS	Binary variable for cities with responsibility for schools
DH	Binary variable for cities with responsibility for hospitals
KIDS	School-aged children as percentage of city population
HHOLD	Number of households as measured by number of occupied housing units
ERIPAY	Export share for earnings tax base (nonresident/total)
ERPROP	Export share for property tax base (nonresident/total)
ERSALE	Export share for sales tax base (nonresident/total)
PCTBSALE	Actual per capita tax base for general sales tax

Table A10.2 (Cont.)

Variable	Definition
PCFAID	Federal aid (excluding revenue sharing) per capita
PCFGRS	Federal general revenue sharing per capita
PCSAID	State aid per capita
SALDEF	Implicit GNP deflator for state and local purchases (1967 = 1)
SMWAGE	Index of state manufacturing wage relative to U.S. average
PCEMPGOV	Employment in federal, state, and noncity local government as a percentage of city population
PEROWN	Value of owner-occupied property as a percentage of total property tax base
EMPTR	Employment in wholesale and retail trade
EMPSR	Employment in finance, insurance, real estate, and derived services

[a] Expression derived in the text of this appendix.

Table A10.3

Sources of Data for Variables in Regression Analysis

Variable	Source
GENERAL	CGF
POLICE	CGF
FIRE	CGF
ELDER	COP
OWNER	COP
HOMEPRICE	UFB
SRINET	Constructed by the authors (see chap. 8)
SRIPOLICE	Constructed by the authors (see chap. 8)
SRIFIRE	Constructed by the authors (see chap. 8)
SRISCHLyy	Constructed by the authors (see chap. 8)
SRIHOSPyy	Constructed by the authors (see chap. 8)
CITYMAN	CCDB
TAXLIMIT	Constructed by the authors from SFFF
INCOME	Constructed by the authors from CPS (see text)
HHSIZE	COP
VOTERS	COP
OVERTAX	Constructed by the authors (see chap. 7)
PTAXBASE	TPV
EXPEARN	Constructed by the authors (see text)
EXPSALES	Constructed by the authors (see text)
FEDAID	COG
FEDGRS	COG
STATEAID	COG
LOGPOP	CPS
MANWAGE	Browne and CEA
LOGPRICE	UFB
DENSITY	CCDB and CPS
OLDHOUSE	COP
ONEHOUSE	COP
POVERTY	COP and CEA
UNEMPLOY	BLS and COP
RELPOP	CPS
EMPPRIVATE	Constructed by the authors (see appendix to chap. 2)
EMPGOV	Constructed by the authors (see appendix to chap. 2)
OWNSHARE	TPV
PRORENTER	TPV
PROTRADE	TPV
PROSERVICE	TPV
PROINDUST	TPV
PROVACANT	TPV

Table A10.3 (Cont.)

Sources: BLS = U.S. Department of Labor, Bureau of Labor Statistics, *Employment and Unemployment in States and Local Areas, 1979* (Washington, D.C.: GPO, July 1981); *1982* (Washington, D.C.: GPO, July 1984).

Browne = Lynn Browne, "How Different are Regional Wages? A Second Look," *New England Economic Review*, March/April 1984, pp. 10-47.

CCDB = U.S. Department of Commerce, Bureau of the Census, *County and City Data Book, 1983* (Washington, D.C.: GPO, 1983).

CEA = "Annual Report of the Council of Economic Advisers," in *Economic Report of the President, 1984* (Washington, D.C.: GPO, 1984).

CGF = U.S. Department of Commerce, Bureau of the Census, *City Government Finances in 1966-67*, GF 67, no. 4 (Washington, D.C.: GPO, 1968); *in 1971-72*, GF 72, no. 4 (Washington, D.C.: GPO, 1973); *in 1976-77*, GF 57, no. 4 (Washington, D.C.: GPO, 1979); *in 1981-82*, GF 82, no. 4 (Washington, D.C.: GPO, 1983).

COP = U.S. Department of Commerce, Bureau of the Census, *Census of Population, 1980*, vol. 1, *Characteristics of the Population* (Washington, D.C.: GPO, 1983); *1970* (Washington, D.C: GPO, 1973).

CPS = U.S. Department of Commerce, Bureau of the Census *Current Population Reports*, P-25 series (Washington, D.C.: GPO, various years, 1969-82).

SFFF = Advisory Commission on Intergovernmental Relations, *Significant Features of Fiscal Federalism* (Washington D.C.: By the Author, various years, 1976/77-1983/84).

TPV = U.S. Department of Commerce, Bureau of the Census, *Census of Governments, 1967*, vol. 2, *Taxable Property Values* (Washington, D.C.: GPO, 1968); *1972* (Washington, D.C.: GPO, 1973); *1977* (Washington, D.C.: GPO, 1978); *1982* (Washington, D.C.: GPO, 1984).

UFB = U.S. Department of Labor, Bureau of Labor Statistics, "Autumn 1981 Urban Family Budgets and Comparative Indexes for Selected Urban Areas" (Washington, D.C.: By the Author, 1982).

Table A10.4
Methods Used to Fill In Missing Data

Variable	Method
GENERAL	N.A.
POLICE	N.A.
FIRE	N.A.
ELDER	Method 1
OWNER	Method 1
VOTERS	Method 1
HOMEPRICE	Method 3. Auxiliary regressions include LOGPOP, dummy for cities above 2 million, SMSA per capita income, OLDHSE, DENSITY, OWNER, percentage of housing units lacking complete plumbing, and regional dummies.
SRINET	N.A.
SRIPOLICE	N.A.
SRIFIRE	N.A.
SRISCHLyy	KIDS filled in by method 1
SRIHOSPyy	N.A.
CITYMAN	N.A.
TAXLIMIT	N.A.
INCOME	Estimated for all cities on the basis of per capita income (available for all cities) and POVERTY (see below).
OVERTAX	N.A.
PTAXBASE	Data missing for 43 observations (but exists for every city in at least one year); filled in by method 3. Auxiliary regressions explain the percentage change in the property tax base as a function of regional dummies, the percentage changes in population and in employment, and the shares of property value in each type of property.
EXPEARN	N.A.
EXPSALES	N.A.
FEDAID	N.A.
FEDGRS	N.A.
STATEAID	N.A.
LOGPOP	N.A.
MANWAGE	1967 SMWAGE filled in by method 1; 11 small states with no data filled in with average for their region.
DENSITY	N.A.
OLDHOUSE	Method 1
ONEHOUSE	Method 1
POVERTY	Method 2 using national poverty rate
UNEMPLOY	Data for 66 cities in 1967 filled in by method 2 using national unemployment rate.
RELPOP	N.A.
EMPPRIVATE	N.A.
OWNSHARE	Percentage residential filled in by method 2 using population; ratio of owner to renter filled in using method 1.
PRORENTER	Same as OWNSHARE
PROTRADE	Method 2 using trade employment

Table A10.4 (Cont.)

Variable	Method
PROSERVICE	Method 2 using service employment
PROINDUST	Method 2 using manufacturing employment
PROVACANT	Filled in as residual property category

Note: N.A.: Not applicable, no missing data. Method 1 was usually applied to variables with data from 1970 and 1980. A simple linear trend was used to fill in 1972 and 1977. Data were trended backward or forward at half the 1970-80 rate of change to fill in 1967 and 1982. Method 2 was usually applied to variables with data from 1970 and 1980 when some related variable was available for all four sample years. Ratio of variable to related variable was trended using method 1. Data were filled in for sample years by multiplying this trended ratio by the actual data for the related variable. Method 3 was used when data for a variable were missing for some cities in some years, and the variable was a function of several other variables, which were available for all cities in all years. An auxiliary regression was run on the subsample of cities with data, explaining the variable as a function of the other variables. On the basis of this regression, and the actual values of the explanatory variables, the variable was predicted for the rest of the cities.

Table A10.5
Results of Regressions to Explain City Spending

Variable	General		Police		Fire	
	Coefficient	t-Statistic	Coefficient	t-Statistic	Coefficient	t-Statistic
Year and region dummies						
Constant	-4.7681	-1.034	-10.0295	-2.399	-10.1621	-2.365
YEAR72	-0.0051	-0.030	-0.0111	-0.064	-0.1288	-0.814
YEAR77	-0.1513	-0.368	-0.3536	-0.897	-0.6425	-1.606
YEAR82	-0.5946	-0.853	-0.9741	-1.492	-1.4177	-2.057
REGION-NE	0.1509	1.409	0.0122	0.123	0.0770	0.984
REGION-MA	0.0807	1.133	0.0637	0.847	0.0698	1.126
REGION-ENC	0.0264	0.475	-0.0282	-0.509	0.0043	0.079
REGION-WNC	0.1118	1.677	-0.0276	-0.422	-0.0231	-0.390
REGION-SA	0.1555	1.669	0.0834	0.940	-0.0596	-0.945
REGION-ESC	0.0139	0.165	-0.0316	-0.383	-0.0393	-0.586
REGION-WSC	-0.1065	-1.461	-0.1281	-1.769	-0.0804	-1.325
REGION-MT	0.0022	0.044	0.0175	0.354	-0.0230	-0.476
Institutional, preference, and other control variables						
Lagged Dependent Variable	0.4432	11.623	0.5438	26.077	0.5950	25.923
ELDER	-0.0141	2.295	0.0053	0.904	0.0011	0.207
OWNER	0.0041	1.818	0.0032	0.946	0.0013	0.417
CITYMAN	-0.0474	1.735	-0.0217	0.865	-0.0026	0.111
TAXLIMIT	-0.0921	1.880	-0.0251	0.581	-0.0728	1.789
HHSIZE	-0.1169	0.379	0.2904	1.054	-0.0243	0.094
VOTERS	0.4798	3.577	-0.0843	0.693	-0.0423	0.366
HOMEPRICE	0.0299	0.347	0.0184	0.239	-0.0294	0.381
OVERTAX	0.0926	0.112	-0.4532	0.576	0.2531	0.397

Table A10.5 (Cont.)

Variable	General		Police		Fire	
	Coefficient	t-Statistic	Coefficient	t-Statistic	Coefficient	t-Statistic
Basic demand variables, exported taxes, and intergovernmental aid						
INCOME	0.2517	0.445	0.8756	1.739	0.5812	1.234
PTAXBASE	0.0874	2.496	0.0442	1.398	0.0464	1.549
EXPEARN	0.0932	1.492	0.0911	1.657	- 0.1013	0.247
EXPSALES	0.0093	0.557	0.1476	0.942	0.2058	1.393
FEDAID	4.8279	3.988	1.4056	1.319	1.1833	1.245
FEDGRS	2.9513	0.180	-17.7029	-1.228	-19.2460	1.396
STATEAID	3.1721	2.650	0.1535	0.199	2.3685	3.184
Service responsibilities						
SRINET	0.3560	6.217				
SRIPOLICE			0.0819	1.071		
SRIFIRE					0.1229	1.822
SRISCHL67	0.9274	9.247				
SRISCHL72	1.2328	7.133				
SRISCHL77	1.3030	4.778				
SRISCHL82	2.5139	5.073				
SRIHOSP67	10.6236	2.303				
SRIHOSP72	14.8200	1.788				
SRIHOSP77	24.0682	3.043				
SRIHOSP82	25.2596	1.671				
Input and environmental costs						
MANWAGE	0.4855	1.643	0.4495	1.686	1.2182	2.845
LOGPRICE	0.0639	2.928	0.0852	4.012	- 0.0149	-0.761
LOGPOP						
DENSITY	-0.33E-4	-2.983	- 0.34E-5	-0.342	- 0.11E-5	-0.113
DENSITY2	0.10E-8	2.077	- 0.24E-10	-0.054	- 0.29E-9	-0.682

Table A10.5 (Cont.)

Variable	General		Police		Fire	
	Coefficient	t-Statistic	Coefficient	t-Statistic	Coefficient	t-Statistic
OLDHOUSE	0.0027	2.176	0.0002	0.196	0.0025	2.280
ONEHOUSE			- 0.0031	-1.552	- 0.0010	-0.510
POVERTY	0.0086	0.687	0.0226	2.001	0.0152	1.434
UNEMPLOY			0.0008	0.118		
RELPOP	-0.0022	-2.455	- 0.0026	-3.153	- 0.0009	-1.176
EMPPRIVATE	0.1371	2.422	0.1616	-2.993	0.1431	2.734
EMPGOV	0.0347	0.594	0.0914	-1.688	0.0486	0.905
PRORENTER	-0.0052	-0.159	0.0398	-1.330	0.0471	1.657
PROTRADE	-0.0265	-0.461	- 0.0402	-0.794	0.0637	1.309
PROSERVICE	0.0314	0.680	- 0.0089	-0.223	- 0.0735	-1.940
PROINDUST	-0.0446	-1.066	- 0.0137	-0.360	- 0.0698	-1.957
PROVACANT	0.0429	1.684	0.0190	0.821	0.0348	1.589
Summary statistics						
R-Squared	0.9648		0.9517		0.9475	
F-Statistic	158.5644		132.11		122.52	
Observations	340		340		336	

Note: Hartford is excluded from all regressions. Garden Grove, CA, which did not have a fire department in all years, is excluded from the fire regression.

11

State and Federal Assistance to Central Cities

Between 1939 and 1971, 15 major central cities received from their states the authority to tax both resident and nonresident earnings in the city. In 1985, Massachusetts passed a new program of intergovernmental aid designed to compensate cities in which revenue-raising capacity was low or public service costs were high. The federal general revenue sharing program for local governments, which was enacted in 1972 and rescinded in 1986, provided revenue to cities with few strings attached. These actions illustrate the crucial role states and the federal government play in city finances. The state determines many of a city's key fiscal institutions and provides it with intergovernmental grants, and the federal government supports cities through a variety of grant programs.

In this chapter we examine state and federal assistance to central cities. What types of cities—large or small, rich or poor—receive the most assistance? To what extent is state and federal assistance directed toward the cities in the poorest fiscal health? Do states that provide generous intergovernmental grants tend to provide less assistance through institutions? Do states cut back assistance, through either institutions or grants, when a city receives more federal aid? After looking closely at these questions here, we present in chapter 12 recommendations for reforming state and federal assistance to cities.

Measuring State Assistance to Cities

Our standardized fiscal health index measures each city's fiscal health with the same set of fiscal institutions. Our actual fiscal health index incorporates each city's actual availability and form of taxes, the taxes collected by overlying jurisdictions, the city's service responsibilities, and state intergovernmental aid. These fiscal institutions and grants are determined by states, not by cities. States decide which taxes and tax bases a city may employ, which other local governments will overlap with cities, which services each city is responsible for providing, and how much in intergovernmental grants each city will receive. It follows that the difference between these two indexes measures the net effect of state-determined fiscal institutions and state grants on city finances. Consequently we calculate the overall state role for a city simply by subtracting its standardized fiscal health index from its actual fiscal health index. Because both indexes have an average value of zero in 1972, the state role also has an average value of zero in 1972. Thus our measure of the state role, like our measures of fiscal health, is relative, not absolute; it reflects both differences in state assistance across cities in 1982 and changes in state assistance to cities between 1972 and 1982.[1]

Many discussions of state assistance to cities focus exclusively on state intergovernmental grants. This focus is misleading. As we pointed out in chapter 9, state grants and state-imposed fiscal institutions come as a package. Some cities may receive relatively high levels of intergovernmental grants from their state because the state assigns extensive service responsibilities to them. Similarly, some states may allow a city to levy an earnings tax on commuters, and thereby share some of its tax burden with suburbanites, instead of giving that city more intergovernmental aid. Our approach is unique because it allows us to calculate the net effect of interrelated state actions, not just the effect of the most visible action, namely intergovernmental grants.

Because it reflects institutional factors as well as intergovernmental grants, state assistance to cities, as we use the term, is not a simple state budgetary outcome for a single year. It reflects the consequences for city fiscal health of state policy decisions, such as a decision to allow a city to tax commuter earnings or a decision to assume responsibility for welfare spending, that may have been made far in the past. If the number of commuters into a city grows over time, for example, then the fiscal consequences of denying that city access to a tax on commuter earnings also grows over time. Moreover, our measure of state assistance reflects institutional

---

1. Remember that the standardized health index does not depend on the selected tax burden for which it is calculated. With our method one would obtain exactly the same standardized fiscal health as a percentage of revenue-raising capacity with a 3 percent tax burden or with a 10 percent tax burden. The actual fiscal health index does not have this property; selecting a tax burden other than the typical one we selected would alter the index. To make the bases of the two indexes comparable, all one has to do is assume that the tax burden in the standardized index is set to generate the average restricted revenue-raising capacity. In other words, the base of the difference—that is, of the state role— is restricted revenue-raising capacity.

and grant factors that are determined predominantly by state actions, but it is not, strictly speaking, completely insulated from the influence of the federal or city governments. In fact, a "pure" measure of state assistance to cities is not logically possible because federal, state, and city decisions all influence one another. Nevertheless, our measures of state assistance concentrate on aspects of fiscal institutions and of state intergovernmental grants over which state governments have final control. States, not cities, are the constitutional units in the United States. Cities ultimately derive all their powers from their state. Over time, of course, cities have become key actors in their own right, and they often influence state decisions. A skillful lobbying campaign by a city government, for example, may persuade a state to let the city tax commuter earnings. But even in this case, the final decision must be made by the state government.[2]

Table 11.1 shows net state assistance to 10 selected cities. This table combines one column from table 9.1, on actual fiscal health, and one from table 5.1, on standardized fiscal health. As we noted in chapter 9, the changes in fiscal institutions and state aid are responsible for a large drop in the fiscal health of Atlanta and Santa Ana, California, and for a large improvement in the fiscal health of Baltimore, Detroit, and Newark, New Jersey.

Overall state assistance to a city can be broken down into state assistance through institutions and through grants. As we show in a later section, assistance through institutions and assistance through grants have somewhat different determinants but are related; states that give more assistance through one channel tend to give less through the other. Among the cities

---

2. An even more complex simultaneity involves federal welfare aid that is passed through the states to the cities. A few cities in our sample still have responsibility for welfare spending. The federal government provides a matching grant to help state and local governments pay for Aid to Families with Dependent Children, the main welfare program. If the state provides welfare, this grant goes to the state; if the city provides welfare, it goes to the city; and because it is a matching grant, the greater the spending on welfare, the greater the amount of the grant. The state government decides whether cities are responsible for welfare and sets the benefit and eligibility rules that determine welfare spending. As a result, the state government determines how much welfare aid each city will receive, given the characteristics of the federal matching grant. Although some welfare aid to cities comes out of the federal budget, in other words, all variation in this aid across cities and over time is determined by state actions, and it is appropriate to include this so-called pass-through aid as part of state assistance through grants. Another form of federal pass-through aid, namely school aid for cities with dependent school districts, is not influenced by state actions, so we treat it as federal categorical aid to those cities. We are grateful to Seymour Sacks for suggestions about the data to account for federal pass-through aid.

Table 11.1
Calculating State Assistance to Cities
(Illustrative Cities)

	(1) Standardized Fiscal Health (%)	(2) Actual Fiscal Health (%)	(3) State Assistance (%)
Atlanta, GA	- 26.9	-65.9	-39.0
Baltimore, MD	- 45.7	6.8	52.6
Boston, MA	- 11.9	2.3	14.2
Denver, CO	5.0	- 4.9	- 9.8
Detroit, MI	- 91.9	-30.8	61.1
Ft. Lauderdale, FL	44.7	44.5	- 0.2
Kansas City, MO	- 33.6	8.6	42.2
Newark, NJ	-109.7	-21.5	88.2
Santa Ana, CA	23.8	-17.2	-41.0
Virginia Beach, VA	27.1	16.3	-10.8

Note: Column 1 is from table 5.1; column 2 is from table 9.1; and column 3 equals column 2 minus column 1.

in table 11.1, Atlanta, Santa Ana, Baltimore, and Detroit all receive negative institutional assistance from their state; that is, the tax burden they can export through the taxes they are allowed to use does not compensate them for the loss of revenue-raising capacity due to taxes collected by overlying jurisdictions or the high expenditure need associated with extensive service responsibilities. This negative institutional assistance is magnified by relatively low state grants in Atlanta and Santa Ana but is more than offset by relatively generous grants in Baltimore and Detroit. Newark receives a positive boost to its actual fiscal health both from fiscal institutions and from generous state aid.

To carry out a formal breakdown of state assistance into its institutional and grant components, we first set state intergovernmental grants equal to zero in every city and calculate actual fiscal health using the method explained in chapter 9. This method ensures that no-grants actual fiscal health equals zero in the average city in 1972. State assistance through institutions equals this no-grants actual fiscal health minus standardized fiscal health. In other words, state assistance through institutions, which can be negative, summarizes the effects of actual access to taxes, taxes collected by overlying jurisdictions, and the assignment of service responsibilities on a city's fiscal health.

State assistance through grants equals actual fiscal health minus no-grants fiscal health. This measure of state assistance through grants also can be negative. To understand why this is true, remember that the existence of state intergovernmental grants raises the service quality that the average city could afford in 1972, which is the baseline service quality, and therefore raises expenditure need in all cities. For any particular city, actual state grants may not be sufficient to finance this increase in expenditure need; if not, the impact of state grants on our measure of fiscal health is negative. In other words, our measures of state assistance through institutions and through grants, like our measures of fiscal health, are relative to the average city in 1972. Even though grants themselves are always positive, grant assistance relative to the 1972 average can be negative.[3]

State Assistance to Cities, 1982

State assistance to cities comes in many different forms. On the institutional side, states provide some cities with access to taxes with high export ratios and limit the service responsibilities of other cities. On the grant side, some states dispense unrestricted grants to cities, others collect certain taxes and share the proceeds with local governments, and all furnish grants to pay for a large share of the cost of local education and welfare expenditures (see Aaronson and Hilley 1986, chap. 4). Because of all this variety, state assistance to central cities does not take the same form in every state or even in every city within a state.

Overall state assistance to various categories of city, along with its breakdown into assistance through institutions and through grants, is presented in table 11.2. In the average city, state actions led to an improvement in 1982 fiscal health equal to 6 percent of restricted revenue-raising capacity. This state assistance is divided fairly evenly between institutions and grants. Remember that 1982 fiscal health is relative to 1972; it follows that changes in state institutional and grant assistance to cities between 1972 and 1982 were equivalent to the provision of outside resources equal to 6 percent of capacity. Fiscal health without state assistance—that is, stand-

---

3. This breakdown is exact in the sense that state assistance through institutions plus state assistance through grants exactly equals overall state assistance. Note that no-grant actual fiscal health, like standardized fiscal health, is invariant with respect to the selected tax burden. For comparability, therefore, all fiscal health measures and all measures of state assistance should be interpreted as a percentage of restricted revenue-raising capacity including grants.

ardized fiscal health—declined 11 percentage points in the average city between 1972 and 1982; state assistance therefore cut the 1972-82 decline in fiscal health in the average city approximately in half.

The standard deviation of state assistance is fairly large relative to its average, which suggests wide variation in state assistance across states and across cities within states. State assistance is positive, that is, it boosts fiscal health, in 39 of the 70 cities with complete data; it exceeds 25 percent of capacity in 16 cities and is below -25 percent of capacity in 11 others. State assistance through institutions and through grants both have large standard deviations. Moreover, these two forms of assistance are negatively correlated; cities with high assistance through institutions tend to have low or negative assistance through grants, and vice versa.[4]

State assistance is strongly linked to city size, as measured by population. State assistance is negative in the two smallest population classes of central cities and equals 25 percent of capacity in cities with more than 1 million people. As a result, state assistance leads to a substantial improvement in the fiscal health of the larger cities relative to the smaller ones. Most of the relatively high assistance for large cities comes in the form of grants; indeed, state aid through institutions tends to be somewhat smaller for larger cities.

Cities with the poorest residents receive the most state assistance; in fact, fiscal institutions increase the fiscal health index of these cities by 33 percentage points. This assistance, which comes through both institutions and grants, greatly reduces the fiscal disadvantage of these cities relative to cities with richer residents. State assistance has a modest negative effect on the fiscal health of cities in three of the four other resident income quintiles.[5]

In contrast, state assistance does not appear to be closely linked to city economic health. Cities with the best economic health receive negative assistance from their states, whereas cities in other economic health categories receive positive assistance between 5 and 12 percent of capacity. Overall, state assistance appears to be aimed toward cities with the poorest residents and away from cities with strong economic health.

As we discussed in chapter 7, the fiscal structure of a city falls into one

---

4. The correlation coefficient between the two forms of state assistance is -0.73.
5. Note that state assistance through institutions is negative in the second and fourth quintiles, and state assistance through grants is negative in the fifth quintile. Overall, state assistance through grants tends to be lower in cities with richer residents whereas state assistance through institutions does not show any clear relationship with resident income.

Table 11.2
State and Federal Assistance to Central Cities, 1982
(71 Cities)

	Number of Cities	State Assistance			Federal Assistance		
		Total	Fiscal Institutions	Grants	Total	Categorical Aid	GRS[a]
All Cities	70	6.0	2.7	3.4	7.0	2.1	4.9
Standard deviation	70	26.2	35.4	36.4	13.7	13.1	2.5
City population in thousands							
Less than 100	6	- 1.8	8.7	-10.5	- 3.9	- 8.5	4.6
100-250	19	- 2.7	5.8	- 8.5	4.2	0.0	4.2
250-500	26	4.5	4.6	- 0.0	10.1	4.3	5.8
500-1,000	14	17.4	- 7.6	25.0	7.0	3.0	4.0
Greater than 1,000	5	24.6	2.5	22.1	15.1	9.1	6.0
Resident income per capita							
Quintile 1	11	33.3	10.4	22.9	12.8	8.5	4.3
Quintile 2	17	- 4.5	- 5.6	1.1	2.9	- 2.2	5.2
Quintile 3	15	19.2	14.6	4.7	12.6	7.4	5.2
Quintile 4	14	- 5.1	- 8.6	3.4	5.4	- 0.2	5.6
Quintile 5	13	- 6.5	5.3	-11.8	2.9	- 1.0	3.9
City economic health[b]							
Quintile 1	13	5.7	4.7	1.0	8.3	3.4	4.9
Quintile 2	14	11.2	- 1.3	12.5	7.2	2.6	4.6
Quintile 3	14	6.9	- 1.0	7.9	6.3	1.8	4.5
Quintile 4	14	11.8	19.7	- 7.8	8.1	2.2	5.9
Quintile 5	15	- 4.8	- 7.8	3.1	5.5	1.0	4.5

Table 11.2 (Cont.)

City type	Number of Cities	State Assistance			Federal Assistance		
		Total	Fiscal Institutions	Grants	Total	Categorical Aid	GRS[a]
City type							
Separate city, uniform state	25	14.0	8.0	5.9	11.9	6.2	5.7
Separate City, mixed state	25	-7.7	-5.3	-2.4	5.8	0.6	5.2
City-county, uniform state	13	11.7	2.7	9.1	3.9	0.4	3.5
City-county, mixed state	7	16.2	12.2	4.1	-0.0	-3.4	3.4
Washington, D.C.[c]	1	-49.3	-49.3	0.0	45.8	45.0	0.8

Note: State and federal assistance are expressed as percentages of a city's 1982 restricted revenue-raising capacity. Each entry is an average for the indicated category of city.

[a]General revenue sharing.

[b]City economic health is private employment in the city divided by city population.

[c]Federal assistance to Washington, D.C. through institutions is entered under state assistance through institutions.

of four broad classes. Some cities are city-counties, with responsibility for both city and county functions, whereas other cities coexist with legally separate counties, which have their own service responsibilities. In addition, some states have uniform systems in which all cities are either city-counties or separate cities, whereas other states have mixed systems with some cities of each type. These two distinctions lead to a four-way classification: separate cities and city-counties in uniform and mixed systems.

Table 11.2 reveals that states with mixed systems are not generous to separate cities. State actions lower the fiscal health of these cities by 8 percentage points, with negative assistance through both institutions and grants. This result suggests that when some city-counties are present, states prefer to channel assistance to counties, leaving separate cities in the lurch. This preference does not harm separate cities when no city-counties exist in their state, and it obviously does not harm city-counties. Indeed, these three fiscal structure classes all receive positive state assistance between 12 and 16 percent of capacity, with contributions from both institutions and grants.

Another way to summarize state assistance is to ask whether it is directed toward the cities that need it the most. In other words, do cities with poor fiscal health before state assistance receive more help—or at least less harm—from state actions? We can answer this question by comparing our standardized fiscal health index, which measures fiscal health before state actions, with the net amount of state assistance, which is the difference between the actual and standardized fiscal health indexes. This relationship is illustrated in figure 11.1, which plots standardized fiscal health and the state role for the 70 central cities with complete data. The answer to the question is clearly affirmative: States do tend to provide more assistance to cities in poor standardized fiscal health than to those in good standarized fiscal health.

One can be more precise about this relationship. As is shown by the line drawn in figure 11.1, a city with standardized fiscal index that is 1 percentage point below average will receive state assistance that is 0.48 percentage points above average. If the standardized fiscal health of city A is 10 percentage points below that of city B, therefore, one can expect almost one-half of this difference, or 4.8 percentage points, to be offset by state assistance. To put it another way, state assistance is directed toward the cities

Figure 11.1
Standardized Fiscal Health and State Assistance, 1982
(70 cities; as Proportions of Restricted Capacity)

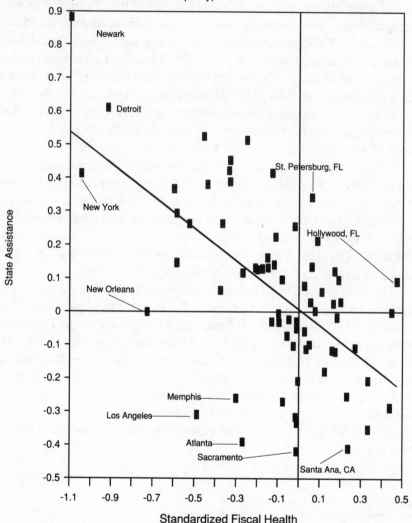

that need it the most. This relationship is highly significant statistically; that is, it is very unlikely to have arisen by chance.[6]

Yet another way to summarize state assistance is to see how it varies across states. Table 11.3 presents state average fiscal health and state assistance for the 29 states into which falls at least one of the 70 major cities with complete data. These states are ranked by state role, in decreasing order.

Table 11.3 reveals that the intrastate average standardized fiscal health varies widely across states. The 6 cities in Florida have an average standardized fiscal health of +17 percent, whereas the 4 cities in New York and the 6 in Ohio have an average fiscal health below -33 percent, and the single major cities in Michigan, Illinois, and Louisiana have fiscal health indexes below -50 percent. In effect, the cost of bringing major cities up to a given level of fiscal health varies widely from one state to another.[7]

The level of state assistance also varies widely. Nineteen states make a positive overall contribution to the fiscal health of their central cities, five make a contribution above 50 percent of capacity, and four make a contribution below -10 percent of capacity. Michigan is the most generous state: its actions raise the fiscal health of its one major city by over 60 percentage points. Georgia is the least generous state: its actions lower the fiscal health of its one major city by almost 40 percentage points.

Insights into the link between average standardized fiscal health and the state role also emerge from table 11.3. The seven most generous states all have cities with standardized fiscal health far below average. Two of the three least generous state, California and Utah, have cities with fiscal health far above average. Nevertheless, the link between standardized fiscal health and the state role is not uniform. Florida is relatively generous to its cities despite their relatively high standardized fiscal health, and Louisiana, Tennessee, and Georgia provide relatively little assistance to their major cities despite the fact that these cities have far-below-average standardized fiscal health.

---

6. These results are based on a descriptive regression of state assistance, SROLE, on standardized fiscal health, SFH. The coefficient of SFH is -0.48, and its t-statistic is -6.1.
7. The results in table 11.3 are not a direct measure of this cost to the state. Our fiscal health index expresses the per capita difference between capacity and need as a percentage of capacity. To translate this index into state costs, therefore, one must multiply it by city population and by city revenue-raising capacity, and sum over all cities in the state.

Table 11.3
State-wide Average Assistance to Central Cities, 1982
(70 Cities)

	Number of Cities	As a Percentage of 1982 Capacity			1972-82 Percentage Point Change		
		Standardized Fiscal Health	Actual Fiscal Health	State Assistance	Standardized Fiscal Health	Actual Fiscal Health	State Assistance
Michigan	1	-91.86	-30.76	61.10	-41.24	-12.76	28.48
Maryland	1	-45.74	6.84	52.58	-31.53	0.90	32.43
Indiana	1	-24.99	26.46	51.45	1.75	65.39	63.64
New Jersey	2	-49.35	- 2.24	47.11	-49.11	-21.05	28.06
Wisconsin	1	-33.09	12.31	45.40	-16.83	- 9.99	6.84
Ohio	6	-34.98	- 8.57	26.41	-20.76	- 2.58	18.18
Missouri	2	-35.66	-11.36	24.30	-17.86	17.98	35.85
Arizona	2	- 2.50	15.56	18.05	- 8.44	2.35	10.79
New York	4	-37.19	-20.10	17.09	-13.10	8.93	22.02
Florida	6	16.79	33.25	16.46	- 4.17	6.06	10.23
Connecticut	1	-14.98	1.25	16.23	-21.95	- 2.22	19.73
Illinois	1	-58.53	-43.84	14.69	-20.57	-28.13	- 7.56
Massachusetts	1	-11.87	2.30	14.17	- 6.78	31.07	37.85
Minnesota	2	-14.78	- 1.54	13.24	-15.08	3.90	18.98
Hawaii	1	-20.91	- 7.79	13.12	2.17	-24.13	-26.30
Kentucky	1	-26.89	-15.26	11.63	-19.69	5.93	25.62
Oklahoma	2	12.36	18.57	6.21	7.98	22.48	14.49
Pennsylvania	2	-33.84	-28.90	4.94	-11.05	-24.43	-13.38
Rhode Island	3	13.08	17.79	4.70	- 1.03	18.85	19.89
Louisiana	1	-72.73	-72.77	- 0.04	- 8.96	-30.79	-21.83
Oregon	1	- 9.76	-10.19	- 0.43	- 8.62	0.41	9.03

Table 11.3 (Cont.)

	Number of Cities	As a Percentage of 1982 Capacity			1972-82 Percentage Point Change		
		Standardized Fiscal Health	Actual Fiscal Health	State Assistance	Standardized Fiscal Health	Actual Fiscal Health	State Assistance
Virginia	4	4.16	1.91	- 2.25	-12.11	- 9.58	2.54
North Carolina	4	14.03	9.70	- 4.33	- 3.68	- 5.70	-2.01
Nebraska	1	- 5.69	-12.90	- 7.21	- 6.70	-23.27	-16.57
Colorado	1	4.98	- 4.86	- 9.84	0.78	- 3.57	-4.35
Tennessee	2	-19.87	-34.38	-14.52	8.14	- 5.65	2.48
California	13	6.60	-11.80	-18.41	- 7.42	-17.06	-9.64
Utah	2	5.64	-19.96	-25.60	- 2.27	-23.64	-21.37
Georgia	1	-26.91	-65.87	-38.96	-29.03	-66.06	-37.03

Note: For both 1982 levels and 1972-82 changes, state assistance equals actual fiscal health minus standardized fiscal health.

Changes in State Assistance to Cities, 1972-1982

Changes in state assistance to cities are described in table 11.4. Because the average values of both standardized fiscal health and actual fiscal health are set to zero in 1972, the state role in 1972, which is the difference between these two indexes, also equals zero. As a result, the average change in the state role between 1972 and 1982, which is in the first row of column 2, is the same as the average state role in 1982, namely 6 percent. The changes in many cities diverge widely from this average: 43 experienced an increase in state assistance over this period, 12 experienced an increase in state assistance greater than 20 percentage points, and 7 experienced a decrease in state assistance greater than 20 percentage points.

Changes in overall state assistance exhibit no apparent pattern across cities grouped by population. Larger cities tended to experience smaller increases or even declines in state assistance through institutions and larger increases through grants. These two tendencies roughly offset each other, so that the top, middle, and bottom population classes of city all experienced increases in state assistance of between 6 and 9 percent of capacity.

Changes in state assistance were particularly favorable for cities with low levels of and low or moderate growth in resident income. Cities with low and stable resident incomes received large increases in state assistance through grants, and those with low and moderately growing resident income received large increases in state assistance through institutions. All other income growth categories of city received below-average increases in state assistance. In other words, changes in state assistance improved the relative fiscal health of the poorest cities.

Table 11.4 suggests a weak link between changes in a city's economic health and changes in its state assistance. Thanks largely to changes in state assistance through grants, cities with low growth in economic health experienced increases in state assistance whereas those with high growth in economic health experienced declines in state assistance.

Finally, changes in state assistance had a negative impact on the fiscal health of separate cities in mixed fiscal systems. This negative impact reflects a large decline in assistance through grants, which was only partially offset by an increase in assistance through institutions. Average state assistance increased for cities in all other fiscal structure classes. This increase was particularly large for city-counties.

One might also ask whether changes in state assistance are related to changes in standardized fiscal health. The answer to this question is affirmative. On average, a 1 percentage point decrease in a city's standardized fis-

Table 11.4
Changes in State and Federal Assistance to Central Cities, 1972-1982
(71 Cities)

(1)	(2)	(3)	(4)		(5)	(6)	(7)
		Percentage Point Change in:					
	Number of Cities	State Assistance			Federal Assistance		
		Total	Fiscal Institutions	Grants	Total	Categorical Aid	GRS[a]
All cities	70	6.0	2.7	3.4	7.0	2.1	4.9
City population in thousands							
Less than 100	6	8.6	6.9	1.7	2.0	-2.6	4.6
100-250	19	0.1	4.1	-4.1	5.4	1.2	4.2
250-500	26	7.0	2.9	4.1	6.2	0.4	5.8
500-1,000	14	11.1	0.5	10.6	10.6	6.5	4.0
Greater than 1,000	5	6.4	-3.2	9.6	13.9	8.0	6.0
Below-average income in 1971							
Low growth	18	12.1	1.4	10.7	7.1	2.1	5.0
Medium growth	10	14.6	18.2	-3.6	11.8	7.4	4.4
High growth	6	-6.4	-4.7	-1.8	2.9	-3.3	6.2
Above-average income in 1971							
Low growth	7	4.2	10.8	-6.6	11.6	7.2	4.4
Medium growth	17	3.9	-2.3	6.2	5.8	0.8	5.0
High growth	12	0.1	-2.4	2.5	4.1	-0.5	4.6

Table 11.4 (Cont.)

	(2)	(3)	(4)		(5)	(6)	(7)
(1)		Percentage Point Change in:					
	Number of Cities	State Assistance			Federal Assistance		
		Total	Fiscal		Total	Categorical Aid	GRS[a]
			Institutions	Grants			
Below-average economic health in 1972							
Low growth	11	5.1	2.3	2.8	12.1	7.3	4.7
Medium growth	9	-0.1	2.9	-3.1	12.5	7.8	4.7
High growth	15	-2.0	2.3	-4.3	3.9	-1.1	5.0
Above-average economic health in 1972							
Low growth	15	9.8	-3.2	13.0	10.8	6.2	4.6
Medium growth	13	22.3	12.4	9.9	6.0	1.3	4.7
High growth	7	-5.5	-1.6	-3.9	-7.1	-13.3	6.2
City type							
Separate city, uniform state	25	7.5	-5.6	13.2	10.1	4.3	5.7
Separate city, mixed state	25	-3.0	2.7	-5.8	3.5	-1.7	5.2
City-county, uniform state	13	13.5	7.5	6.0	8.2	4.7	3.5
City-county, mixed state	7	19.1	23.2	-4.1	6.6	3.2	3.4
Washington, D.C.[b]	1	1.3	1.3	0.0	11.2	10.4	0.8

Note: City categories for income change and economic health change are defined in tables 3.4 and 2.2 respectively. The change in each type of assistance equals 1982 assistance as a percentage of 1982 restricted revenue-raising capacity minus 1972 assistance as a percentage of 1972 restricted revenue-raising capacity. Each entry is an average change for the indicated category of city.

[a] General revenue sharing.

[b] The change in federal assistance to Washington, D.C. through institutions is listed in the column describing state assistance through institutions.

cal health leads to a 0.51 percent increase in state assistance. In other words, about one-half of a decline in standardized fiscal health is offset by state actions. This relationship is highly significant statistically.[8]

Changes in state assistance by state are given in table 11.3. Thanks to expanded grants, which more than offset a decline in state assistance through institutions, Indiana had the largest increase in state assistance to its major city; Georgia had the largest decrease in state assistance. State assistance increased in five states, decreased by 0 to 20 percent in eleven, and decreased by more than 20 percent in thirteen. State assistance increased in some states with large declines in city standardized fiscal health, such as Maryland, New Jersey, and Missouri, but it decreased in some other states with such declines, such as Illinois, Kentucky, and Georgia.

Federal Assistance to Central Cities, 1982

Aid from the federal government is an important source of revenue for large cities. In 1982, total federal aid equaled about $116 per capita in the average major central city, of which almost one-fifth was general revenue sharing. Federal aid to cities increased dramatically between 1972 and 1978 and declined between 1978 and 1982. On average, federal aid to major cities grew about 4 percent per year over the 1972-82 decade, measured in constant dollars.

Federal aid first became an important source of aid for cities in the late 1960s, when Great Society initiatives provided cities with grants to support manpower training, elementary and secondary education, and community development. Many of these programs continued to grow during the 1970s, and they were supplemented by general revenue sharing and a series of countercyclical grant programs passed in response to the 1974-75 recession. General revenue sharing, which was implemented in 1974, provided unrestricted funds to all general purpose local governments.[9] The countercyclical programs, which were designed to help stabilize the national economy and to offset some of the fiscal pressures on state and local governments resulting from a recession, included Anti-Recession Fiscal Assistance, additional grants for public works, and support for public service jobs

---

8. This result is based on a descriptive regression of the change in SROLE, or DSROLE, on the change in SFH, or DSFH. The coefficient of DSFH is -0.51, and its t-statistic is -2.8.
9. General revenue sharing also provided funds to state governments. This portion of the program was rescinded in 1980.

under the Comprehensive Employment and Training Act (CETA).

As is illustrated in figure 11.2, which plots direct federal aid to cities between 1965 and 1984 as a percentage of their general revenue from own sources, these programs resulted in a striking increase in federal aid.[10] By 1978 direct federal aid equaled over 25 percent of cities' own-source revenues. Moreover, the contribution of federal aid exceeded 50 percent of own-source revenue in a few cities, including Buffalo and Detroit. The period of growth in federal aid to cities ended in 1978 with the elimination of the countercyclical programs and the leveling off of other programs. The election of President Reagan in 1980 accelerated this turnaround. By 1982 federal aid to cities had declined to 18.4 percent of own-source revenues, its level in the early 1970s; by 1984 it had declined still further, to 14.5 percent; and in 1986 federal general revenue sharing to cities was eliminated.[11]

As we explained earlier, our actual fiscal health index is designed to highlight the role of state assistance to cities and therefore does not reflect federal grants. In this section we complete our analysis by incorporating federal categorical grants and federal general revenue sharing into our measure of city fiscal health. In chapter 12 we consider the implications of our findings for federal grant policy. The case of Washington, D.C., is unique in that there is no state government and all outside assistance comes from the federal government. Washington also has unique, and with our data unmeasurable, responsibilities associated with being the nation's capital. As a result, the federal role there is considered in a separate section.

Our objective is not to determine federal assistance to cities in some absolute sense but instead to determine how it varies across cities and over time. In fact, federal grants enter our analysis in the same way as state intergovernmental grants; that is, federal grants add directly to a city's revenue-raising capacity, but they also increase the service quality in the average city. The baseline service quality with federal grants is the service quality that could be obtained in 1972 by a city with average restricted revenue-raising capacity, including federal grants, and with average actual expenditure need. A city's fiscal health with federal grants reflects its restricted capacity including grants and this baseline service quality with grants. Federal assistance to a city is the difference between its actual fis-

---

10. This figure reflects direct aid only. It does not include aid passed through the states to cities.
11. For a good discussion of the forces behind the expansion in federal aid and of the seeds of its destruction, see Reischauer 1986.

Figure 11.2
Direct Federal Aid to Cities, 1965-86
(As a Percentage of Own-Source Revenue)

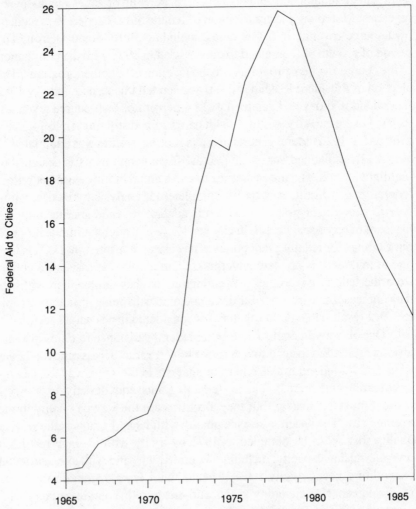

Source: U.S. Bureau of the Census, <u>City Government Finances</u>, various years.

cal health with and without federal grants. Because it is a relative measure, federal assistance through categorical grants can be negative. General revenue sharing did not exist in 1972, however, so that it adds to a city's restricted revenue-raising capacity in 1982 without affecting the baseline service quality; as a result, our measure of federal assistance through general revenue sharing is positive in every city.[12]

Federal assistance to cities in 1982 is summarized in the last three columns of table 11.2. In the average city federal grants raise fiscal health by 7.0 percent of capacity. About two-thirds of this assistance arrives in the form of general revenue sharing. The variation in federal assistance, particularly in general revenue sharing, is noticeably smaller than the variation in state assistance. The one standard deviation range in total federal assistance, into which most cities fall, is -6.7 percent to +20.7 percent of capacity.

Federal grants narrow the difference in fiscal health between large and small central cities. In cities with populations below 100,000, the revenue received from federal grants is not great enough to finance the increase in the baseline service quality that federal grants allow; as a result the ability of these cities to provide baseline service quality actually declines because of federal grants. On the other hand, federal grants increase the fiscal health of the largest class of city by 15 percentage points. Federal grants therefore close the fiscal health gap between the largest and smallest cities by 19 percentage points. The narrowing of this gap is accomplished almost entirely through federal categorical grants; all population classes of city receive federal assistance from general revenue sharing between 4 and 6 percent of capacity.

Federal grants also provide a significant boost, 13 percentage points, to the fiscal health of cities with the poorest residents. Cities in the third quintile of resident income receive almost as much federal assistance. Those in the other quintiles receive small positive assistance from federal grants, entirely through general revenue sharing; on average, cities in these other quintiles receive negative assistance through federal categorical grants.

Federal assistance is slightly higher for cities in poor economic health than for those in good economic health, although the difference is only about 3 percent of capacity. Most of this relatively large assistance to cities in poor economic health comes through categorical grants; as with other city clas-

---

12. Because general revenue sharing does not affect the baseline service quality, its impact on a city's fiscal health is simply the city's revenue sharing grant divided by its 1982 restricted revenue-raising capacity including federal grants.

sifications, the average city in each economic health category receives about the same assistance through general revenue sharing.

Finally, table 11.2 reveals that federal grants are particularly beneficial for separate cities in states with a uniform fiscal system. Separate cities in states with a mixed fiscal system, which receive large negative assistance from their states, receive the second most federal assistance. These results reflect the fact that some federal aid programs furnish approximately the same per capita amount to all city governments, regardless of their service responsibilities. Separate cities tend to have lower responsibilities and lower restricted revenue-raising capacity than city-counties. As a result a given amount of aid per capita represents a relatively large share of their restricted capacity, and the boost in baseline service quality made possible by federal categorical grants has a relatively small impact on their actual expenditure need. The net effect is that constant per capita grants provide relatively high assistance, as we measure it, to separate cities.

Another key question is whether federal assistance, like state assistance, is directed toward the cities with the poorest fiscal health. To answer this question, we focus on the relationship between federal aid and city fiscal health measured in dollars per capita rather than as a percentage of capacity.[13] In dollar terms a city's standardized fiscal health is measured by its *standardized need-capacity gap*, which we define as the difference between its standardized expenditure need and its revenue-raising capacity, both expressed in per capita terms.[14] The question then is how a city's federal assistance per capita is linked to the three components of its actual fiscal health per capita, namely its standardized need-capacity gap, its state grants per capita, and its state institutional assistance per capita.

Using data for 1982, we find that both federal categorical grants and general revenue sharing are positively related to a city's standardized need-capacity gap; that is, both forms of federal aid are directed toward cities in poorer standardized fiscal health. If the standardized gap is $1.00 higher in city A than in city B, then city A can expect to receive $0.11 more than city B in federal categorical grants and could expect to receive $0.01 more than

---

13. In table 11.2 federal aid to a city is expressed as a percentage of the city's restricted revenue-raising capacity, which by definition includes state assistance. Actual fiscal health also incorporates state assistance, so federal aid and actual fiscal health are correlated by definition. We address the question in the text in terms of dollars per capita to avoid this definitional link.

14. A city's standardized need-capacity gap also equals its fiscal health multiplied by -1 and by its revenue-raising capacity. This gap by category of city is presented in the column 4 of table 5.2.

city B in federal revenue sharing. Although the magnitude of the second impact is very small, largely because general revenue sharing did not differ very much across cities, both these relationships are highly significant statistically.[15]

Somewhat surprisingly, both forms of federal aid also are positively related to state grants; after the standardized need-capacity gap is controlled for, cities that receive relatively high state grants also receive relatively high federal grants. In contrast, state institutional assistance is negatively related to federal categorical aid and positively related to federal general revenue sharing. On average, cities with favorable fiscal institutions receive less federal categorical aid and more federal general revenue sharing than cities with unfavorable fiscal institutions.

Changes in Federal Assistance to Cities, 1972-1982

As we reported earlier, federal assistance led to a 7.0 percentage point increase in the average fiscal health of major cities between 1972 and 1982. This impact reflects both the introduction of general revenue sharing and growth in federal categorical grants. Increases in federal aid to cities over this period were slightly greater than increases in state assistance. As we noted earlier, however, federal grants to cities started declining in 1978, and this positive contribution of federal grants to the fiscal health of the average central city may have disappeared by 1984—with further declines still ahead.[16]

---

15. The results in this paragraph and the next are based on two simple descriptive regressions. The first estimates federal categorical aid per capita, FCAT, as a function of the standardized need-capacity gap, SGAP, state aid per capita, SAID, and state institutional aid per capita, SINST, which is the index of state institutional assistance described in the text multiplied by revenue-raising capacity. In this regression the coefficient (t-statistic) for SGAP is 0.106 (3.86), for SAID is 0.177 (3.93), and for SINST is -0.030 (-1.78). The first two coefficients are significant at the 1 percent level, and the third is significant at the 10 percent level. The second regression estimates federal general revenue sharing per capita, FGRS, as a function of SGAP, SAID, and SINST. The coefficient (t-statistic) for SGAP is 0.012 (4.03), for SAID is 0.011 (2.39), and for SINST is 0.004 (2.36). The first coefficient is significant at the 1 percent level, and the last two are significant at the 5 percent level.

16. Our measure of the change in federal assistance to cities roughly corresponds to the drop in federal aid to cities as a percentage of their own-source revenue. This percentage went from 10.8 percent in 1972 to 18.4 percent in 1982—a 7.6 percentage point increase. By 1984 this percentage was down to 14.5. See figure 11.2.

Changes in federal assistance for various categories of city are described in table 11.4. Changes in federal grants had the largest positive impact, 14 percentage points, on the fiscal health of the largest cities, and the smallest positive impact, 2 percentage points, on the smallest cities. These changes narrowed the fiscal health gap between these two classes of city. In general, cities with larger populations tended to receive larger increases in assistance through categorical aid. Because general revenue sharing did not exist in 1972, the level of and change in assistance through revenue sharing are the same, so that, as we noted earlier, all population classes of city receive about the same level of (change in) revenue sharing assistance.

Increases in federal assistance through categorical aid tended to be greater for cities with slowly growing resident incomes or slowly growing economic health. Because general revenue sharing does not vary much by category of city, these patterns also appear in total federal assistance.

Finally, we find that changes in federal categorical grants and the level of general revenue sharing, all of which represents a change from 1972, are positively related to changes in a city's standardized need-capacity gap. In other words, cities with deteriorating standardized fiscal health experienced growing assistance from the federal government. However, this link is small and not statistically significant for categorical grants and is no longer relevant for general revenue sharing.[17]

Federal Assistance to Washington, D.C.

In Washington, D.C., the "state" role is played by the federal government; that is, the federal government decides on the availability and form of city taxes, on the role of overlying jurisdictions, and the city's service responsibilities. The federal government also provides intergovernmental grants to Washington, as it does to other cities. In this section we examine the net effect of fiscal institutions and federal grants on the fiscal health of the nation's capital.

---

17. The results in the test are based on the two simple descriptive regressions in footnote 14 expressed in change form. Let a first letter D indicate a change between 1972 and 1982. Then the first regression estimates DFCAT as a function of DSGAP, DSAID, and DSINST. The coefficient (t-statistic) of DSGAP is 0.070 (1.03), of DSAID is 0.230 (2.16), and of DSINST is 0.014 (0.54). The dependent variable in the second regression is DFGRS, and the coefficient of DSGAP is 0.017 (2.57), of DSAID is 0.012 (1.11), and of DSINST is 0.006 (2.36).

Tables 11.2 and 11.4, like tables 5.2, 5.3, 9.2, and 9.3, contain separate rows for Washington, D.C. The last row of table 5.2 reveals that the 1982 standardized fiscal health index for the District of Columbia is 14.3 percent, which is considerably better than that of the average city. Although Washington has relatively high costs, and therefore relatively high standardized expenditure need, its revenue-raising capacity is even higher relative to other cities, largely because it is situated in a large, relatively wealthy metropolitan area.

The District of Columbia's actual fiscal health is reported in the last row of table 9.2. Not surprisingly, its actual expenditure need and restricted revenue-raising capacity are much higher than those of other cities: it has responsibility for all state and local services, it does not need to compete with a state or a county for taxable resources, and it receives relatively many grants from the federal government. After accounting for all these factors, we find that Washington's actual fiscal health index is 10.0 percent; adding general revenue sharing brings the index up to 10.8 percent. The fiscal health of the average city after federal grants equals average actual fiscal health without federal grants plus the average assistance provided by federal grants, or (-4.9 + 7.0) = 2.1 percent. Thus the actual fiscal health of the nation's capital after federal grants is better than that of the average city after federal grants.

The impact of federally determined institutions and grants on Washington, D.C.'s fiscal health is presented in the last row of table 11.2. Federally determined institutions have a large negative impact on Washington's fiscal health; its access to taxes is not sufficient to finance its extensive service responsibilities. Federal grants, on the other hand, particularly categorical grants, have a large positive effect on its fiscal health. The effect of institutions is slightly larger than the effect of grants, so that the net impact of federal actions is to lower the District of Columbia's fiscal health by (49.3 - 45.8) = 3.5 percentage points.[18] Net federal assistance to Washington is almost 10 percentage points below state assistance in the average central city and almost 17 percentage points below combined state and federal assistance in the average city. As is shown in table 11.3, only seven of the twenty-nine states with major central cities (and complete data) are less generous to their average city than the federal government is to

---

18. The breakdown of federal aid between assistance through institutions and assistance through grants is identical to that carried out for state assistance. Assistance through institutions equals actual fiscal health with zero grants minus standardized fiscal health; assistance through grants equals actual fiscal health with actual grants minus actual fiscal health with zero grants.

Washington. Thus the net effect of state and federal assistance is to improve the health of the average city relative to the nation's capital.

These calculations do not constitute a complete analysis of the federal role in Washington, D.C. They do not reflect spending requirements placed on the city government because it is the nation's capital, nor do they reflect services provided directly to city residents by the federal government. We make no attempt to determine the net impact on the District of Columbia's fiscal health of the fiscal flows associated with being the nation's capital. Our results therefore should be interpreted as a measure of the city's fiscal health before these special fiscal flows. With this interpretation in mind, we find that the federal government's contribution to Washington's fiscal health is very negative, even compared to the contributions of states to their major cities.

Federal assistance to Washington, D.C., increased considerably between 1972 and 1982. As is shown in table 11.4, federal assistance through institutions increased by 1.3 percentage points, and federal assistance through grants increased by 11.2 percentage points. The net result was an increase in federal assistance equal to 12.5 percent of the District of Columbia's revenue-raising capacity.[19] This increase in overall federal assistance is almost exactly equal to the 13 percentage point increase in state plus federal assistance in the average major city. These results indicate that, subject to the above interpretation, the federal government's assistance to Washington has improved relative to the assistance provided by the average state to its major cities, but it has not improved relative to state plus federal assistance to the average city, and it still remains far less generous than the average state's assistance to its cities.

The Determinants of State Assistance to Cities

So far we have described the state and federal assistance received by various categories of city. In this section we go beyond description to ask the following questions: To what extent do state policy makers consider state aid through institutions and through grants to be substitutes for each other? Do states attempt to compensate cities with poor fiscal health? Does

---

19. These results also indicate that in 1972 federal assistance to Washington, D.C., was negative; to be precise, it was 1982 net assistance, 4 percent, minus the increase in assistance, 20 percent, or -16 percent of capacity. This result confirms, with a much more complete methodology, the conclusion reached by one of the authors in 1971. See Yinger and Meyers 1971.

a state's own fiscal health influence the amount of assistance it provides to its cities? Does a state cut back assistance to a city when either the city or the state receives more aid from the federal government?

Our measures of state and federal assistance to cities, namely state assistance through institutions and grants and federal assistance in the form of categorical aid and general revenue sharing, allow us to examine state assistance through institutions and grants as functions of each other, of standardized fiscal health, of both types of federal aid, and of other relevant factors. By answering the questions in the preceding paragraph, this analysis provides insight into the behavior of state policy makers in 1982 and, as is explored in chapter 12, provides guidance for future state and federal policy. The technical details of our analysis are presented in Yinger and Ladd (1988).

The variables in our behavioral model of state assistance to cities are expressed in terms of dollars per capita. Thus, for example, a city's fiscal condition is measured by its standardized need-capacity gap, that is, its standardized expenditure need minus its potential revenue-raising capacity. Four principal conclusions emerge from our analysis.

First, we find that a focus on either state intergovernmental grants or fiscal institutions alone can provide a highly misleading picture of a state's assistance to its cities. States that are relatively generous with one of these two forms of assistance tend to be relatively parsimonious with the other. Moreover, relatively high grants to cities tend to be more than offset by relatively low institutional assistance, so that the states with the most generous intergovernmental grants tend to be the ones that provide the least overall assistance to their cities.

We arrive at this conclusion in two steps. In step one we examine state policy makers' behavior. We find that they view assistance to cities through institutions and through grants as imperfect substitutes for each other. State policy makers act as if they believe that cities benefit from assistance through both institutions and grants, but that $1 of grants makes a larger contribution to a city's fiscal health than $1 of assistance through institutions. This finding suggests that, dollar for dollar, state policymakers place a higher value on the city services that are supported by grants than on the general support for city finances that is provided by exported tax burdens or lower service responsibilities.

In step two we recognize that the two forms of state assistance are simultaneously determined. Suppose, for example, that for some economic or political reason, state A gives $1 more grants per capital to its major city, city A, than state B gives to its city, city B. This higher level of state grants will lead to a lower level of state assistance through institutions to city A, which will lead, in turn, to a still higher level of state grants, and so on. In comparing these two cities, therefore, one cannot determine the ultimate relationship between the two forms of state assistance without accounting for these feedback effects. Although we examine state assistance at one point in time, namely 1982, we believe that this form of feedback also occurs over time, at least in the long run. On average, an exogenous increase in either form of state assistance to a particular city initiates a simultaneous set of adjustments in both forms of assistance.

Accounting for both state policy makers' behavior and the feedback between the two types of state assistance, we find that the ultimate impact of grants starting $1.00 higher in city A than in city B for some economic or political reason is a $2.38 disadvantage in state institutional assistance for city A and an additional $0.76 advantage in state grants, or a $0.62 net disadvantage for city A in total state assistance. Similarly, a $1.00 advantage in state assistance through institutions that is caused by some economic or political factor leads to a $0.57 disadvantage in state grants, which leads, in turn, to an additional $0.76 advantage in assistance through institutions. In this case city A's original $1.00 advantage in institutional assistance becomes a net advantage of $1.19. All these figures are expressed in per capita terms.

Second, states act, on average, as if they are attempting to compensate cities in relatively poor fiscal health. In other words, states direct more assistance to cities in poor fiscal health (before state assistance) than to those in good fiscal health. The net impact of this equalizing behavior by state policy makers is quite striking. We find that if the standardized need-capacity gap is $1.00 higher in city A than in city B, then city A can expect to receive $0.10 more in state grants and $0.55 more in state assistance through institutions. When other factors are controlled for, state assistance eliminates almost two-thirds of the differences across cities in standardized need-capacity gaps. This behavioral link between state assistance and city fiscal condition is stronger than the descriptive link presented earlier in this chapter, which is calculated without controlling for the other determinants of state assistance.

These findings do not imply that state governments actually measure standardized need-capacity gaps and use them in making state policy. Apparently, however, states are aware of the principal components of standardized fiscal health, such as the per capita income of city residents or the concentration of poverty in the city, and account for these components in their assistance decisions.

Although most discussions of the equalizing impact of state policy focus on grants, we find that most of the compensation for relatively low fiscal health is accomplished through fiscal institutions. On average, states do over five times as much to improve the relative position of fiscally troubled cities by giving them access to taxes with export potential and by divesting them of service responsibilities than by giving them above-average grants per capita. Decisions about fiscal institutions are not made, of course, as part of an annual budgetary process, and indeed a given city's fiscal institutions may not change for decades. Nevertheless, states tend to provide favorable institutional settings for cities that are continually hard pressed by economic and social circumstances. For example, 5 of the 6 cities with the poorest standardized fiscal health and 11 of the 20 least healthy cities are allowed to tax the earnings of nonresident commuters.

This conclusion, like the first, involves two logical steps. First, we find that state policy makers design grants and institutional assistance to be higher for cities in relatively poor fiscal health. Second, we account for the simultaneity between state grants and state assistance through institutions. States that give extensive grants to cities in poor fiscal health, for example, are likely to provide relatively little institutional assistance to those cities, and this low level of institutional assistance, in turn, influences the generosity of state grants. The final link between state assistance and city fiscal health, which is stated above, reflects both of these steps.

Third, the better a state's own fiscal health, the more assistance it gives to its central cities. Although we do not attempt a complete analysis of state fiscal health, we do have information on one of its key determinants, namely state income per capita. When one follows the approach in chapter 3, a state's revenue-raising capacity equals its per capita income plus its ability to export taxes to nonresidents. We find that if income per capita is $100.00 higher in state A than in state B, cities in state A will receive $0.35 more per capita in grants and $0.11 more per capita in assistance through institutions than the cities in state B.[20]

Once again, this conclusion reflects both the behavior of state policy makers and the feedback effects between the two forms of state assistance. State policy makers respond to the preferences of their constituents. In the case of assistance through grants, this conclusion reflects the fact that state

---

20. A state's fiscal health also depends on its costs for providing assistance to cities. This cost depends on the number of people in cities that need assistance, which we measure by the share of state population that lives in a central city. We find, as expected, that states with a high share of their population in cities give less assistance through grants, but this link is not statistically significant.

income is a key determinant of a state voters' ability and willingness to provide public services, including services supported by grants to cities. In the case of assistance through institutions, this conclusion implies that voters in states with higher incomes typically are more willing than those in states with lower incomes to shift some of the burden of providing city services into noncity residents. The link between state income and state assistance to cities is important because it shows that the level of state assistance depends not only on state policy makers' attitudes toward cities but also on a state's revenue-raising capacity, which is largely outside the state's control.

Finally, we find that, on average, state governments do not cut back their assistance to cities in response to federal grants—either to the cities or to the states. Cities with relatively high federal grants, either categorical grants or general revenue sharing, do not receive relatively low assistance from their state. And cities in states that receive relatively high federal grants do not receive more state assistance than other cities. These results lead to two conclusions that prove useful in chapter 12. First, changes in federal grants to cities are unlikely to result in significant changes in state assistance to cities. Second, the federal government should not expect state governments to be its agents in assisting troubled cities; that is, the federal government should not expect an increase in federal aid to a state to result in more state assistance for cities in that state.

Conclusions

State actions improved the 1982 fiscal health of the average central city, with approximately equal contributions from assistance through institutions and through grants. These actions also helped alleviate the fiscal disadvantages of certain classes of city, such as very large ones and those with very poor residents. To put it another way, cities with poorer standardized fiscal health tend to receive more assistance from their state, both through institutions and through grants.

Thanks to state assistance provided through institutions and grants, the 1972-82 decline in city fiscal health caused by economic and social factors was cut approximately in half. Changes in state assistance through grants, and to a lesser extent through institutions, were more favorable for cities that experienced greater declines in fiscal health.

State policy makers regard assistance through institutions and through grants as substitutes for each other; an increase in assistance through one route will be offset to some degree by a decrease in assistance through the other. Moreover, we find that state policy makers design state assistance programs to focus on the neediest cities. After controlling for other determinants of state assistance, we find that grants and fiscal institutions combined eliminate almost two-thirds of the differences in fiscal health across cities. About four-fifths of this equalizing is accomplished through institutional assistance.

State assistance to cities is affected by state fiscal health; states with higher revenue-raising capacity tend to provide more assistance to their cities. In addition, states do not cut back their assistance to cities that receive relatively high assistance from the federal government, nor do states that receive relatively high federal aid themselves provide relatively high assistance to their cities.

Federal grants also improved the 1982 fiscal health of the average city. Both types of federal assistance are to some degree directed toward cities with lower standardized fiscal health, although the magnitude of this link is quite small for general revenue sharing. Federal assistance to cities increased between 1972 and 1982, largely because of the introduction of general revenue sharing. Federal categorical grants also increased rapidly between 1972 and 1978, but they declined thereafter, so that federal assistance to cities through categorical grants increased modestly over the 1972-82 period.

The federal government plays a unique role in Washington, D.C. It provides generous grants to Washington but also has established fiscal institutions that greatly undercut the ability of the city to provide services to its residents. The second effect is slightly stronger, so that net federal assistance to the nation's capital is negative. Federal assistance to Washington also is considerably less generous than state plus federal assistance in the average city and less generous than state assistance in all but seven states. Between 1972 and 1982, federal institutional and grant assistance to the District of Columbia increased substantially, but not by enough to reverse the federal government's relative lack of generosity to the nation's capital.

Appendix: Calculating State Assistance to Central Cities

A key step in our analysis is the measurement of state assistance through institutions and grants. In this appendix we describe our state assistance calculations and present our 1972 and 1982 results for the 71 central cities with complete data.

Our calculations begin with each city's standardized fiscal health, as calculated in the appendix to chapter 5, and each city's actual fiscal health, as calculated in the appendix to chapter 9. These two indexes differ because actual fiscal health, unlike standardized fiscal health, accounts for a city's access to taxes, the taxes collected by overlying jurisdictions, the city's service responsibilities, and state intergovernmental grants. Thus total state assistance to a city is defined to be the difference between these two indexes.

To divide total state assistance into assistance through institutions and grants, we define a no-grants actual health index for each city on the assumption that it does not receive any state grants. This step follows the procedure in the appendix to chapter 9 and therefore ensures that the average value of this no-grants actual fiscal health index is zero in 1972. (As before, the average across all cities excluding Washington, D.C., equals zero.)

A city's assistance through institutions is defined to be the difference between its no-grants actual fiscal health index and its standardized fiscal health index. A city's assistance through grants is defined to be the difference between its actual fiscal health index and its no-grants actual fiscal health index. Because all three fiscal health indexes in these calculations equal zero for the average city in 1972, the differences between them, namely the two state assistance measures, also equal zero in the average city in 1972. It follows that negative state assistance to a city (through either institutions or grants, in either 1972 or 1982) corresponds to assistance that is below the 1972 average.

Total state assistance to 71 major cities in 1972 and 1982, along with state assistance through grants and institutions, is presented in table A11.1.

Table A11.1
State Assistance Through Grants and Institutions, 1972 and 1982
(71 Cities)

	1972			1982		
	Institutions (%)	Grants (%)	Total (%)	Institutions (%)	Grants (%)	Total (%)
Akron, OH	36.3	-13.9	22.5	34.7	-21.8	12.9
Albany, NY	-11.1	4.8	- 6.3	14.0	7.3	21.3
Anaheim, CA	-11.9	-11.6	-23.5	-12.4	-22.9	-35.2
Atlanta, GA	8.4	-10.4	- 1.9	-15.4	-23.6	-39.0
Baltimore, MD	-43.3	63.4	20.1	-14.7	67.3	52.6
Boston, MA	4.5	-28.1	-23.7	9.2	5.0	14.2
Buffalo, NY	-72.7	79.4	6.7	-47.1	73.5	26.4
Charlotte, NC	1.3	- 2.6	- 1.3	- 2.6	- 8.7	-11.3
Chicago, IL	37.2	-14.9	22.3	20.5	- 5.8	14.7
Cincinnati, OH	-27.6	-24.6	-52.2	44.7	- 5.7	39.0
Cleveland, OH	36.3	-18.6	17.7	50.0	-20.5	29.4
Clifton, NJ	16.3	-17.7	- 1.4	17.9	-11.9	6.0
Columbus, OH	33.8	-12.8	21.0	43.3	-16.9	26.5
Dayton, OH	35.6	-11.2	24.4	54.3	-16.2	38.1
Denver, CO	-31.4	25.9	- 5.5	- 3.4	- 6.5	- 9.9
Detroit, MI	14.3	18.3	32.6	-41.8	102.9	61.1
Ft. Lauderdale, FL	12.5	-15.8	- 3.3	11.1	-11.3	- 0.2
Garden Grove, CA	- 9.1	- 3.7	-12.9	- 9.7	-19.0	-28.7
Greensboro, NC	3.7	- 5.7	- 2.0	-10.6	13.6	3.0
High Point, NC	8.3	- 7.1	1.1	- 8.8	- 2.8	-11.7
Hollywood, FL	17.4	-14.2	3.2	17.4	- 8.2	9.2
Honolulu, HI	57.7	-18.3	39.4	43.3	-30.2	13.1
Indianapolis, IN	- 2.2	-10.0	-12.2	-49.2	100.6	51.4
Jacksonville, FL	48.8	-17.4	31.4	47.2	- 5.6	41.6
Kansas City, MO	49.5	-22.2	27.4	63.1	-20.9	42.2

Table A11.1 (Cont.)

	1972			1982		
	Institutions (%)	Grants (%)	Total (%)	Institutions (%)	Grants (%)	Total (%)
Hartford, CT	11.2	-14.7	- 3.5	9.6	6.7	16.2
Long Beach, CA	- 2.6	- 5.8	- 8.5	- 1.6	- 0.7	- 2.3
Los Angeles, CA	4.0	- 9.2	- 5.2	2.1	-32.9	-30.9
Louisville, KY	15.6	-29.6	-14.0	34.0	-22.4	11.6
Memphis, TN	206.2	195.2	-11.0	188.7	162.8	-25.9
Miami, FL	0.6	-29.0	-28.4	- 3.6	- 8.3	-11.9
Milwaukee, WI	26.4	12.2	38.6	- 6.9	52.3	45.4
Minneapolis, MN	-28.8	23.0	- 5.7	-69.9	83.1	13.2
Nashville-Davidson, TN	-18.0	- 5.1	-23.0	10.3	-13.5	- 3.1
Newark, NJ	24.4	15.1	39.5	18.6	69.6	88.2
New Orleans, LA	30.0	- 8.2	21.8	15.0	-15.0	- 0.0
New York, NY	-61.4	71.7	10.4	6.9	34.5	41.4
Norfolk, VA	-15.3	22.2	6.8	1.0	8.7	9.7
Oakland, CA	- 9.2	- 3.1	-12.3	-11.8	-19.9	-31.6
Ogden, UT	23.1	-30.0	- 6.9	12.3	-30.2	-17.9
Oklahoma City, OK	17.4	-27.5	-10.1	30.2	-27.4	2.8
Omaha, NB	16.2	- 6.8	9.4	4.5	-11.7	- 7.2
Ontario, CA	- 1.1	- 5.2	- 6.3	- 6.9	-18.4	-25.3
Pawtucket, RI	8.3	- 9.4	- 1.1	23.0	-10.8	12.2
Philadelphia, PA	34.3	- 3.1	31.3	24.9	12.0	36.9
Phoenix, AZ	7.1	- 4.4	2.6	2.6	19.9	22.5
Pittsburgh, PA	- 6.9	12.3	5.4	-30.0	3.1	-27.0
Portland, OR	3.8	-13.2	- 9.5	9.5	- 9.9	- 0.4
Portsmouth, VA	-39.0	40.6	1.6	-13.1	10.3	- 2.8
Providence, RI	15.1	-12.0	3.1	34.1	-11.6	22.5
Richmond, VA	-25.7	22.6	- 3.0	- 5.6	0.6	- 5.1

Table A11.1 (Cont.)

	1972			1982		
	Institutions (%)	Grants (%)	Total (%)	Institutions (%)	Grants (%)	Total (%)
Riverside, CA	9.2	- 9.3	- 0.1	14.6	- 6.8	7.8
Rochester, NY	-84.7	54.2	-30.5	-46.2	25.5	-20.7
Sacramento, CA	- 1.7	- 4.0	- 5.7	-12.2	-29.6	-41.8
St. Louis, MO	-15.3	-35.1	-50.4	29.6	-23.2	6.4
St. Paul, MN	-22.3	27.9	5.6	-63.8	53.6	-10.2
St. Petersburg, FL	34.8	-21.6	13.3	39.3	- 4.9	34.4
Salt Lake City, UT	25.6	-27.1	- 1.5	4.2	-37.5	-33.3
San Bernardino, CA	10.4	-13.6	- 3.2	18.7	-24.6	- 5.9
San Diego, CA	10.6	- 8.8	1.9	9.9	-12.9	- 3.0
San Francisco, CA	-34.5	20.2	-14.3	-30.4	30.6	0.3
San Jose, CA	6.2	- 6.6	- 0.4	9.1	-10.8	- 1.7
Santa Ana, CA	-10.4	-13.1	-23.5	-16.8	-24.2	-41.0
Tampa, FL	46.3	-25.1	21.2	35.5	- 9.8	25.7
Toledo, OH	26.3	-10.3	16.0	25.3	-12.7	12.6
Tucson, AZ	9.2	2.7	11.9	9.1	4.5	13.6
Tulsa, OK	15.6	-22.1	- 6.5	29.3	-19.7	9.6
Virginia Beach, VA	-29.7	5.0	-24.6	-11.5	0.7	-10.8
Warwick, RI	-34.2	-13.4	-47.5	- 6.2	-14.4	-20.7
Winston-Salem, NC	2.8	- 9.9	- 7.2	- 5.8	8.3	2.6
Washington, DC	-50.6	34.6	-16.0	-49.3	45.0	-4.3
Average	0.0	0.0	0.0	2.7	3.4	6.0

Note: Each entry is expressed as a percentage of a city's restricted revenue-raising capacity. The entries for Washington, D.C. measure assistance from the federal government. The averages in the last row exclude Washington, D.C.

12
Rethinking State and Federal Policy Toward Central Cities

The following quotations illustrate the important debate now taking place about the future of U.S. federalism:

> I am proposing a major effort to restore American federalism.
>
> The key to this program is that the States and localities make the critical choices.... A major sorting out of Federal, state and local responsibilities will occur, and the Federal presence and intervention in State and local affairs will gradually diminish. (President Ronald Reagan, 1983 budget message.)

> We believe that a fair and balanced budget policy as it affects the nation's cities and towns is essential to the ability of our country to be economically strong and to raise the standard of living.
>
> Proposals to make further cuts in key municipal programs and to impose new federal taxes on essential services are counterproductive. With more than 80 percent of the nation's economies built upon our cities and towns, any proposals to weaken our partnership do not make sense. (Pam Plumb, Vice President of the National League of Cities, testimony before the Budget Committee of the U.S. House of Representatives, February 1987.)

A key issue in this debate is whether central cities need outside help. Are major cities in serious fiscal trouble? Can cities, particularly those in poor fiscal health, help themselves, or do they require new assistance from higher levels of government? To the extent that additional assistance for cities is needed, how much of it should come from the states? What are the most appropriate forms of state assistance? Should the Reagan administration's policy of cutting federal aid to cities be continued, or should past cuts be restored and federal aid to cities increased? How should federal aid to cities be designed? These questions are of vital interest to the future of our federal system. In this chapter we search for answers.

Trends in City Fiscal Health

National economic and social trends have taken their toll on the fiscal health of cities. Between 1972 and 1982, gradual growth in the incomes of city residents and expanding possibilities in many cities for exporting tax burdens to nonresidents increased revenue-raising capacity in the average central city by 8.6 percent. But this increase in capacity did not keep up with increases in expenditure need: a higher concentration of poverty in cities and unfavorable changes in other environmental factors boosted standardized expenditure need in the average city by 19.2 percent. In 1982 the average central city, if it were to provide the same service quality at the same tax burden as in 1972, needed additional revenue from outside sources equal to 11 percent of its 1982 revenue-raising capacity. Stated differently, the average city experienced an 11 percentage-point decline in its standardized fiscal health between 1972 and 1982.

This tightening of the fiscal constraints on cities contrasts with an increase in real income, that is, in income adjusted for inflation, over the same period. The real per capita income of U.S. citizens is a rough measure of their command over all goods and services, including those provided by the public sector. Real per capita disposable income is a rough measure of their command over private goods and services. Between 1972 and 1982 per capita real income in the nation grew by 6.5 percent, and per capita real disposable income by 5.4 percent. During this period, therefore, the constraints on consumption in general were loosening, while the economic constraints on city finances were becoming more restrictive.

State assistance to cities, broadly defined to include assistance through institutional arrangements as well as through intergovernmental grants, partially offset the adverse effects of economic and social trends. But even with rising state assistance, the average city experienced a decline of 5 percentage points in its actual fiscal health, which is its fiscal health after state assistance, between 1972 and 1982. In other words, after one accounts for the growth in both forms of state assistance during the period, the typical city needed additional revenue from outside sources equal to 5 percent of its 1982 actual revenue-raising capacity in order to provide the same service level at the same tax burden as in 1972.

The nationwide tax revolt complicates the interpretation of the state role. The decline of 5 percentage points in average actual city fiscal health reflects the shifts in taxing authority and service responsibilities associated with the tax revolt in individual states, but it does not reflect the nationwide reduction in total state and local tax burdens during the 1972-82 period. This reduction, caused by voters' preference for lower tax burdens, can be interpreted as an additional constraint on the ability of cities to provide public services.[1] The impact of the tax revolt was large: after accounting for this additional constraint, we find that the average central city experienced a decline of 14 percentage points in its actual fiscal health between 1972 and 1982.

Increases in federal aid during this decade provided approximately the amount of assistance needed to prevent a decline in the fiscal health of the average central city—excluding the effects of the nationwide tax revolt. That is, the large negative impact of national economic and social trends was offset by a combination of increased state and federal assistance. But if we interpret the tax revolt as an additional constraint on city finances, then increases in federal aid were only enough to cut in half the decline in fiscal health of the average central city from 1972 to 1982.

We make no attempt to forecast formally the fiscal condition of cities in the years ahead. However, the economic and social trends that have undercut city fiscal health, such as limited growth in incomes, suburbanization, and the concentration of poverty in central cities, show no signs of abating.[2] For example, the poverty rate in central cities in 1986 was 18 percent, which is high by historical standards and identical to the rate in 1981. We believe that the outlook is for continued decline in the standardized fiscal health of the average central city. In other words, economic and social trends will continue to make it more difficult for cities to maintain service quality without increasing tax burdens.

We also foresee a continuing, but smaller, decline in the actual fiscal health of cities, that is, in their fiscal health after state assistance. States are likely to continue helping their troubled cities, but this future assistance, like that in the past, is unlikely to counter fully the adverse fiscal effects of economic and social trends. Moreover, the continuing tax limitation movement puts pressure on state governments to cut expenditures, including in-

---

1. Recall from chapter 9 that an alternative interpretation is that the tax revolt induced management improvements—and thereby did not constrain cities. No study of which we are aware measures the extent of these induced improvements in management, but we believe that they were relatively modest.
2. We are not alone in expecting these trends to continue. For example, a recent report by the National Research Council concludes, "The most troublesome trend identified by this committee is the growing concentration of poor people in central cities" (National Research Council 1988, 11).

tergovernmental grants; and our analysis of state behavior in chapter 11 provides no evidence to support the conclusion that states will increase their assistance to cities in response to cuts in federal aid to cities.

Diversity in City Fiscal Health

Throughout this book we have focused on diversity among cities grouped along three dimensions: population, resident income, and city economic health as measured by the number of private sector jobs per city resident. We find that the fiscal health of cities varies substantially along two of these three dimensions.

The greatest variation in fiscal health appears when we group cities by population. On average, central cities with populations over 1 million are much worse off than smaller ones in terms of both their revenue-raising capacity and their standardized expenditure need. Average capacity is 25 percentage points lower, and average standardized need is 53 percentage points higher, for the largest cities than for the smallest ones (those with populations below 100,000). These patterns produce a standardized fiscal health of -72 percent in the largest and +16 percent in the smallest cities. Thus the largest cities would need assistance equal to 72 percent of their 1982 revenue-raising capacity to raise their 1982 fiscal health to the average level of all cities in 1972. The positive fiscal health of the smaller cities means that they have the ability to increase their service levels or to reduce their tax burdens relative to the 1972 average for all cities.

States are relatively generous to larger cities. Net state assistance to the largest cities amounted to 25 percent of their 1982 revenue-raising capacity, in contrast to net negative assistance for the smallest cities. But even with high state assistance, the largest cities are in relatively poor fiscal health: their 1982 average actual fiscal health index is -48 percent. Even with their low state assistance, the smallest cities have a 1982 average fiscal health index of +7 percent. The largest cities also receive relatively high federal aid, but this aid is by no means enough to raise their fiscal health to the average.

The patterns are equally clear, although the disparities are not as large, for cities grouped by the income of residents. Among the five resident income classes, central cities with the poorest residents have the poorest fiscal health in 1982. This result arises because low resident income leads, all else equal, to low revenue-raising capacity and because low resident income is highly correlated with the presence of poverty and other factors that contribute to a harsher environment for providing public services—that is, to a higher expenditure need. In fact, compared to the cities with the richest residents, those with the poorest residents have a revenue-raising capacity that is 21 percentage points lower and a standardized need that is 40 percentage points higher. The average standardized fiscal health index of the cities with the poorest residents is -46 percent. Relatively generous state assistance to this group of cities boosted their 1982 actual fiscal health index to -13 percent, which is still far below average. Relatively generous federal grants raised the fiscal health of these cities almost to the national average in1982.

The third way of grouping cities, by economic health as measured by the number of private jobs relative to city population, is not a good predictor of fiscal health. Cities with strong private economies tend to have higher revenue-raising capacity than those with few jobs per capita, but they also have higher standardized expenditure need. These results come from the mixed fiscal blessing of commuters, who add to a city's revenue-raising capacity but also to its costs for providing public service.

Diversity across cities also is the hallmark of changes in fiscal health between 1972 and 1982. The largest cities and those with the smallest growth in resident income experienced disproportionately large declines in standardized fiscal health over this period. These declines reflect the rapid growth of their standardized expenditure need. In the case of cities with low-income residents, however, the decline in fiscal health was mainly due to relatively slow growth in their revenue-raising capacity combined with average growth in their standardized need.

Cities with the fastest-growing private economies experienced above-average increases in both revenue-raising capacity and standardized expenditure need. The latter increases were somewhat larger on average. Thus even cities with growing private economies are not immune to declines in fiscal health. Nevertheless, standardized fiscal health fell 10-15 percentage points, on average, in central cities with relatively little growth in the number of private jobs per capita, whereas it fell by only 1-6 percentage points, on average, in those with rapid growth in their economies. Although rapid growth in the private economy does not assure improving fiscal health, the evidence suggests that a growing private economy is more conducive to fiscal recovery than is a declining one.

One surprising finding is that structural change in a city's economy, as measured by a shift from manufacturing to service employment, does not appear to have a substantial effect on either the city's revenue-raising capacity or its public service costs and therefore does not have a significant effect on its standardized fiscal health.

In our judgment this diversity is not likely to disappear. Resident income, the ability to export tax burdens, and the harshness of the city environment for providing public services will continue to differ across cities and, as these factors are altered by national economic and social trends, to change more rapidly in some cities than in others. Moreover, some central cities may be caught in a vicious circle of fiscal and economic decline. Deteriorating city fiscal health forces service cuts or tax increases, which may drive away high-income taxpayers. The loss of high-income taxpayers undercuts revenue-raising capacity and boosts service costs, thereby causing yet further declines in city fiscal health (for a clear discussion see Bradbury, Downs, and Small 1982). We expect that state and perhaps federal aid will offset the resulting fiscal disparities to some degree, but even on average they will not offset them completely, and they will fall far short of eliminating the fiscal advantages or disadvantages faced by some cities.

Implications for Intergovernmental Assistance to Cities

Two broad conclusions emerge from our analysis: First, national economic and social trends have caused, and are likely to continue to cause, a deterioration in the fiscal health of the average major central city. And second, residents in some types of city, particularly very large ones and those with relatively poor residents, are faced with unfavorable and deteriorating fiscal circumstances.

Are these conclusions a cause for concern to state and federal policy makers? Could not city governments themselves solve these fiscal problems? Could not the residents of fiscally troubled cities simply pack up and move to jurisdictions in better fiscal health? Even if city actions and the mobility of residents cannot eliminate cities' fiscal difficulties, what social objectives would be served by additional assistance from state or federal governments?

The Limited Ability of Cities to Help Themselves

As we measure it, a city's fiscal health, standardized or actual, depends on economic, social, and institutional factors that are largely outside the city's control. Poor fiscal health is not caused by poor management, corruption, or profligate spending, and a city government's ability to alter the city's fiscal health is severely limited. Moreover, poor fiscal health implies that a city must accept a higher-than-average tax burden to provide average quality services or, alternatively, it must accept lower-than-average service quality to have an average tax burden.

We do not mean to imply that city officials should give up. On the contrary, they can improve the quality of public services without raising the tax burden on residents by taking advantage of the fiscal options available to them, implementing improvements in management, eliminating corruption, and designing policies to facilitate their city's economic growth. Nevertheless, the policy tools available to city officials are weak compared to the impact on city finances of national economic, social, and fiscal trends.

We showed in chapter 6 that many cities take advantage of the fiscal options available to them. For example, some use property tax exemptions and explicit or de facto property tax classification to shift the tax burden toward business property, which allows for greater exporting of tax burdens to nonresidents, and some of the cities that are allowed to levy an earnings tax on commuters have increased their reliance on that tax over time. These strategies are not available to most cities, however, and they have limited potential for overcoming fiscal difficulties. Even when revenue-raising capacity is measured with actual tax bases, for example, 20 out of 71 cities experienced a decline in capacity between 1972 and 1982.

Better management clearly improves fiscal options, but we believe that the scope for improvement through this route is limited. Although we have not made a detailed examination of city management practices, our analysis of city spending decisions provides some support for this belief. Suppose, for example, that one-half of the expenditure cuts associated with the city manager form of government and a severe property tax limitation represent not cuts in service quality but improvements in management. Even with this strong assumption, the results presented in chapter 10 indicate that these improvements would save only about 4 percent of a typical city's budget.[3]

In principle, cities also may be able to influence the constraints imposed on them by economic, social, and fiscal factors. For example, they can attempt to promote the growth of their economic base. An evaluation of alternative city economic development policies is beyond the scope of this book, but the extensive literature on this subject indicates that the policy

---

3. According to our estimates, cities with city managers spend 5 percent less on general services (but no less on police and fire services) than those with mayors, and cities with severe property tax limitations spend 9 percent less on general services and 7 percent less on fire services (but no less on police) than those without these limitations. General services constitute about one-half of a typical city's budget, and fire services about 20 percent. So if one-half of these spending differences are caused by greater managerial efficiency, the total potential savings from better management through these two routes is 50 percent of $[.5 \cdot (.05+.09)+.2 \cdot (.07)]$ or 4 percent. Management reforms also might increase revenue-raising capacity—but only if they succeeded in increasing the tax burden imposed on nonresidents.

tools available to cities are limited and are unlikely to have much effect on the location decisions of businesses.[4] Cities should take whatever cost-effective steps they can to protect their current economic base and to help make this base grow, but national trends affecting city economies, such as suburbanization, interregional migration, and the shift from manufacturing to services, are considerably more powerful than the economic development policies within the fiscal reach of cities.

Finally, cities are partners, albeit junior ones, in the design of the fiscal institutions in their state. Skillful negotiating with state and county officials may loosen the fiscal constraints imposed on a city. But the power of cities in negotiations with states appears to be limited. For example, despite the dramatic contribution that an earnings tax applied to commuters can make to the fiscal health of a city, only 15 of the 86 major central cities are allowed to levy such a tax, and no city has been granted the authority to levy an earnings tax since 1972.

The Limited Mobility of City Residents

A second possibility is that households can escape cities in poor fiscal health by moving away. No household would stay in a fiscally disadvantaged city, this argument goes, unless it received some nonfiscal compensation, such as high wages or low housing prices, for the relatively high tax burden or low quality of services. We do not accept this argument. Poor, elderly, and handicapped people, as well as blacks and Hispanics, all of whom are disproportionately represented in central cities, face formidable barriers to mobility, barriers that limit their ability to improve their fiscal options.

Moving is expensive, and people with few resources often cannot afford to move in response to a deterioration in the fiscal condition of their city. Many city residents also may not be able to afford the housing in a jurisdiction with better fiscal health. Moving may be particularly disruptive or even physically difficult for elderly or handicapped city residents. Members of racial and ethnic minorities, particularly blacks and Hispanics, con-

---

4. See, for example, Schmenner 1982 or Wasylenko 1986. In our view most of the economic development policies undertaken by cities are counterproductive; they give away scarce resources to businesses that would have located in the city even without a financial inducement from the city treasury. These policies may actually lower revenue-raising capacity by shifting the tax burden away from the high-export portion of the base. Moreover, to the extent that better public services or lower tax rates do attract businesses, cities in poor fiscal health are, by definition, at a competitive disadvantage.

tinue to face discrimination in housing and employment that restricts their access to the suburbs.[5] Finally, unanticipated increases in city taxes or declines in public service quality are likely to cause a decline in the market value of city housing (see Yinger et al. 1988, with references). If so, current city homeowners cannot fully escape these fiscal events by moving, because they will realize a capital loss when they sell their house.

Besides these costs to individuals, from the point of view of society at large, mobility may be a relatively costly way to deal with fiscal disparities across cities. Moving consumes real resources that could be devoted to other activities. Moreover, extensive moving imposes two forms of social cost. First, the movement of a higher-income person out of a city may lead to a decline in revenue-raising capacity and possibly to a higher per capita cost of services, thereby imposing real costs on the remaining residents.[6] These conclusions follow directly from our analysis in chapters 3 and 4. A drop in average income lowers a city's revenue-raising capacity, and an increase in the poverty rate raises its public service costs. In addition, any loss of population through moving, whether or not the movers have high incomes, may lead to an underutilization of existing infrastructure. Closing a school in one city and building a new one in another is not, in general, a gain to society. Second, extensive moving in response to fiscal conditions may fundamentally alter the social character of a city.[7] For example, the growing concentration of poor people, elderly, and minorities in cities may, to a certain extent, be the product of mobility; many higher-income people may have moved away in response to the deterioration of fiscal conditions in cities. The costs of these social changes are difficult to measure, but we believe they are cause for concern.

Overall, mobility clearly is an important feature of our federal system, but it cannot be relied upon to alleviate completely the burden on city residents of a poor or deteriorating fiscal situation. Moreover, direct intervention by higher levels of government to offset deteriorating fiscal health may prove to be less costly to society than relying on mobility as an adjustment mechanism.

---

5. Recent strong evidence documents the continuing power of racial and ethnic discrimination. For evidence on discrimination in housing, see Yinger 1986b, 1987; in mortgage lending, Schafer and Ladd 1981; and in employment, Ehrenberg and Smith 1985.
6. For an extended discussion of the efficency losses from excess mobility with a somewhat different focus, see Boadway and Wildasin 1984, chap. 15.
7. The social character of cities was of concern to several analysts in the recent debate on federal income tax deductions for state and local taxes. See Gramlich 1985a; Chernick and Reschovsky 1987.

The Case for More Intergovernmental Assistance

Thus, despite the efforts of city governments and the mobility of city residents, national economic and social trends will continue to cause a gradual decline in the fiscal health of the average central city, and some cities, such as those with relatively large populations or poor residents, will continue to have much poorer fiscal health than others. Additional assistance from higher levels of government to cities in poor or deteriorating fiscal health would contribute to three important social objectives: to help poor and disadvantaged citizens, to help citizens make transitions forced by national economic and social trends, and to ensure that all residents of a metropolitan area are treated fairly.

Many U.S. citizens and policy makers believe that governments have an obligation to assist poor people, who are disproportionately represented in cities. The most direct way to help poor people is through income transfer programs for individuals. However, such programs are unlikely to ensure levels of city services that reflect the preferences of the poor; because of their limited political power, the poor have relatively little say in decisions about the quality of public services.[8] In addition, many people make the categorical equity judgment that all citizens should have access to an adequate level of certain key services, including education and police protection. According to this judgment, it would be unfair for children to be denied a good education or for poor families to be denied police and fire protection services simply because they live in a city with a low revenue-raising capacity or a harsh environment for providing public services. Thus a concern for poor people implies that higher levels of government should, to some degree, offset the low fiscal health of some cities.[9]

---

8. Another way to put this is that in some circumstances, poor people themselves might place a higher value on additional assistance to cities than on additional transfer payments. A fascinating example of this possibility recently was debated in Los Angeles. The city councillor for a very poor neighborhood proposed a special tax levy on that neighborhood to pay for more police there. Although the proposal was defeated at the polls, it received considerable support; that is, many neighborhood residents placed a higher value on more police services than on personal consumption. Moreover, the support for this proposal may greatly understate residents' desire for more police services because, as many residents no doubt realized, the proposal could not guarantee that the additional tax money would be added to, instead of substituted for, the money already spent on police in the neighborhood. For more information on this proposal, see Cummings 1987 and Stevenson 1987.

9. One recent book (Paul Peterson et al. 1986) argues that the federal government should assist people but not places. For the reasons outlined in the text, we strongly disagree with the conclusion that assistance to places is not needed.

The second social objective is to help people make transitions imposed on them by national trends that are outside their control, such as inter-regional migration, the suburbanization of employment, and the increase in urban poverty. Additional assistance to some cities can be justified as one way to aid people who are hard hit by national economic and social trends.[10] The case for such assistance is greater where the adverse effects of the na-tional trends are the greatest, that is, in large cities and in those with low and declining resident incomes.

The third social objective is to promote the fair treatment of all resi-dents in a metropolitan area. A central city is not an isolated entity but part of a metropolitan system. Policies to account for interconnections among the jurisdictions in this system, and their effects on fairness, can be carried out only by a higher level of government.

Two types of interconnection are particularly important. First, some city services provide benefits to suburban residents.[11] Commuters and visitors benefit from police protection and highway maintenance, for ex-ample. To encourage city governments to provid[11]rvices and to compen-sate them for doing so, higher levels of government must provide matching grants or access to taxes with export potential.[12]

Second, the economies and fiscal rules of the jurisdictions in a metropolitan area are heavily intertwined, so it is appropriate to evaluate

---

10. Assistance to city governments is not, of course, the only way to aid these people. Governments also can provide job training and other programs to less-en the costs of transition. Programs to counteract the economic trends and their effects, such as urban economic development programs, could be provided to cities with declining economic health. Some of these programs are discussed briefly in a later section.
11. These benefit spillovers, which have both equity and efficiency consequences, are extensively discussed in the literature. See Oates 1972, Neenen 1981, and Gordon 1983.
12. As we reported in chapter 10, we find that a $1.00 increase in exported earn-ings taxes leads to a $0.19 increase in spending on general services and a $0.03 increase in spending on police services; and a $1.00 increase in exported sales taxes leads to a $0.03 increase in spending for fire services. Exported sales taxes have a larger, but statistically insignificant, effect on general services. A precise measurement of spillover benefits is difficult. See, for example, Neenan 1981. Nevertheless, we believe that, precisely because of its centrality, a central city typically provides many services, including highways and traffic regulation, parks, and libraries, that benefit suburbanites and justify extensive exporting on both equity and efficiency grounds.

the metropolitan tax system—not simply the taxes employed by each jurisdiction separately. Through no fault of its own, the central city is often the jurisdiction with the poorest taxpayers and the harshest environment for providing public services, and hence with the highest tax rates.[13] Thus a metropolitan tax system that restricts each jurisdiction to the taxable resources of its own residents can be highly regressive. Policies to increase the exporting of city tax burdens, such as property tax classification or an earnings tax on nonresidents, or increases in intergovernmental aid financed by more progressive revenue systems at either the state or federal level, can be justified on the grounds that they moderate the regressiveness of the metropolitan tax system.

We showed in chapter 11 that state and federal assistance to cities increased between 1972 and 1982 and that relatively high assistance is given to cities in relatively poor fiscal health. However, the increases in and targeting of this intergovernmental assistance are not sufficient to offset the severe fiscal disadvantages of some cities, such as very large ones. In addition, the national economic and social trends that are the fundamental source of cities' fiscal difficulties have continued, and federal aid has been cut back substantially since 1982. These three social objectives cannot be met in the future without increases in intergovernmental assistance.

In sum, powerful economic and social trends have led and will continue to lead to a deterioration in the fiscal condition of the average central city and to a large and growing fiscal disadvantage for many cities, such as those with large populations or with low and falling resident income. Additional assistance to needy cities is justified to avoid the large social costs associated with excessive moving, to help the poor and disadvantaged residents who are concentrated in central cities, to help people make transitions caused by national trends outside their control, and to account for the interconnections among jurisdictions in a metropolitan area. Different people will place different weights on each of these objectives, but we believe that the objectives are important and that they cannot be achieved without more intergovernmental assistance to cities that are in poor fiscal health.

---

13. A study by the ACIR (1984) finds that among the 85 largest metropolitan areas in 1981, the ratio of central city taxes per capita to suburban taxes per capita was 1.37. The same source indicates that per capita central city income is 89 percent of per capita suburban income, on average. It follows that the ratio of city tax burden, which is taxes divided by income, to suburban tax burden is $1.37/.89 = 1.54$; on average, the city tax burden exceeds the suburban tax burden by over 50 percent. There is, of course, enormous variation around this average. In some metropolitan areas, including Atlanta, Nashville, Pittsburgh, and Washington, D.C., the central city tax burden is more than twice as great as the suburban tax burden.

The Role of State Governments

We have shown that states provide a great deal of assistance to their cities, especially to those in poor fiscal health. On average, between 1972 and 1982, increases in state assistance offset about one-half of the decline in central cities' standardized fiscal health. Furthermore, states provide substantially more assistance to cities that are in poor fiscal health, including those with low-income residents or with large populations, than to cities in good fiscal health. States dispense this assistance both through institutions and through intergovernmental grants. Some states allow their cities to levy taxes with high export potential, others have taken over welfare or other service responsibilities, and still others distribute more grants to cities in poorer fiscal health.

Even after all this state assistance, however, actual fiscal health declined in the average city between 1972 and 1982, and some cities have much poorer actual fiscal health than others. We have argued that some cities should receive more assistance from higher levels of government. The question here is: Should that additional assistance come from the states?

The Case for More State Assistance

States have one enormous advantage over the federal government in providing assistance to cities: they control the fiscal rules under which cities operate. As a result, states inevitably have detailed knowledge about the fiscal constraints that confront each of their cities and have access to a wide variety of policy instruments for helping cities that are in fiscal trouble. This knowledge and flexibility enable states to design assistance packages that fit the circumstances of each city. As a result, states can make important contributions to achieving the objectives described earlier: avoiding the costs of excess moving, assisting the poor, easing certain transitions, and accounting for metropolitan interconnections.

In many cases assistance to central cities involves complex negotiations among officials of the state, the city, and other local jurisdictions. The decision to allow a central city to levy an earnings tax on commuters, for example, has a direct bearing on the fiscal health of the suburbs. Weighing the role of the city in the metropolitan economy, the spillovers of city services to suburban residents, and other factors relevant to this decision can be done only at the state level.

Reliance on state governments to provide assistance to cities also has the advantage of promoting diversity and policy innovation.[14] Different states are likely to try different approaches to direct city assistance. As a result, citizens have more choice in deciding where to live, and policy makers have the opportunity to compare alternative approaches and thereby determine the best way to help cities in various situations.

We conclude that states must continue to be, as they have been in the past, key providers of assistance to cities. Assistance provided through fiscal institutions inevitably must be designed and implemented at the state level. And states are in a unique position to identify and account for the specific circumstances of individual cities and their metropolitan areas.

Forms of State Assistance

The most direct way for states to assist cities that are in poor fiscal health is through an equalizing grant program. As was shown in chapter 11, state grant programs, on average, give somewhat more money to cities that are in poorer fiscal health. Apparently, factors that are correlated with city fiscal health are incorporated into grant programs. One clear example is the widespread policy of providing more school aid to school districts (including some cities) with a smaller equalized property tax base. Although cost factors are rarely considered in state aid formulas, at least one state, Massachusetts, gives general purpose state grants designed to compensate cities with low revenue-raising capacity and high public service costs (see Bradbury et al. 1984). Using the concepts we have developed in this book, all states could design grant programs that would target aid more accurately toward cities that are in poor fiscal health.

Our results in chapter 11 indicate that states do even more through institutions than through grants to improve the relative position of the cities with poorest fiscal health. Two forms of state assistance through fiscal institutions appear to have particular potential for improving the fiscal health of many cities. First, states can allow cities to levy an earnings tax that applies to the earnings of commuters; and second, states can take over the provision of certain services currently financed by the cities. These actions

---

14. These advantages have been emphasized by the Reagan administration. See for example, the 1983 Report of the Council of Economic Advisers, pp. 90-91, in *Economic Report of the President, 1983* (Washington, D.C.: GPO, 1983).

would not provide the same benefit to every city, but they would provide significant assistance in many cases.

As we have documented in chapter 3, an earnings tax that applies to both residents and commuters would enable most cities to export a relatively high share of their tax burdens to nonresidents. Allowing a city to use such a tax therefore tends to give a large boost to its revenue-raising capacity. It appears that cities with poor standardized fiscal health are more likely to receive the authority for this type of tax; as we noted earlier, 5 of the 6 least healthy cities (and 11 of the 20 least healthy cities) levy an earnings tax that applies, to some degree, to commuters. Among the 10 least healthy cities, however, New Orleans, Chicago, Buffalo, and Los Angeles do not have an earnings tax, and Baltimore has one that is restricted to its residents. In all of these cities, the potential for exporting tax burdens to nonresidents is greater with an earnings tax than with any tax the cities actually employ. Overall, many fiscally troubled cities would benefit greatly from receiving the authority for an earnings tax on commuters.[15]

In our view one of the appealing features of a tax on all earnings in a city is that it recognizes the city's connections with its suburbs. Placing some of the tax burden on suburbanites accounts for the benefits they receive from city services, and it lowers the regressiveness of the metropolitan tax system, to which both city and suburbs belong. An earnings tax that cannot be applied to commuters does not add to a city's revenue-raising capacity and indeed may undercut this capacity by encouraging residents to move to the suburbs.

Some states also may be able to contribute significantly to the fiscal health of their cities by assuming responsibility for certain services the cities currently provide. The most obvious example is welfare; states are in a better position than are cities to finance welfare services because higher taxes to pay for the services may drive higher-income people out of a city. In fact, most states already have taken over welfare services; only about 10 major cities (and only one, New York, among those with the poorest actual fiscal health) spent a significant amount on welfare in 1982. Nevertheless, state takeover of welfare would greatly aid New York and a few other cities, including Denver, San Francisco, and Richmond, Virginia, with approximately average actual fiscal health. In some cases a city provides services, such

---

15. A commuter tax does not encourage people to move out of a city, because they must pay the tax wherever they live. If the tax is shifted to firms, and if the location decisions of firms are sensitive to small differences in tax rates, however, a commuter tax could cause some firms to leave the city. Bradbury and Ladd 1987 find some evidence to support this conclusion.

as courts or corrections, to the people in an area that extends beyond its boundaries. State takeover of these services can be a sensible way to spread the burden for financing these services across all the people who benefit from them.

Cities with poor fiscal health must select relatively low-quality public services or relatively high tax burdens or both. Any policy that improves their fiscal health compensates them to some degree for these fiscal disadvantages. However, some policy interventions encourage cities to improve their service quality, and others encourage them to lower their tax burden. Among grant policies, matching grants are the best way to promote higher quality of services (and categorical matching grants are the best way to do this for a particular service), and revenue-sharing grants are the best way to lower city tax burdens. These conclusions are widely recognized in the literature and also emerge from our analysis of city spending decisions in chapter 10.[16] Among institutional policies, which have received little attention in previous studies, state takeover of general services and the granting of access to exportable taxes lead both to improved service quality and to lower local taxes. The impact of these policies on the quality of services is higher than that of general revenue sharing but lower than that of other forms of intergovernmental grants.

The Role of the Federal Government

The federal government also provides substantial assistance to cities, although this assistance is shrinking. In the average central city between 1972 and 1982, increases in federal aid offset the decline in actual fiscal health, which incorporates state aid but not federal aid. Moreover, our analysis in chapter 11 shows that federal aid is, to some degree, directed toward cities that are in poor standardized fiscal health.

The years since 1982 have witnessed large cuts in federal aid to cities, including the elimination, in 1986, of general revenue sharing. The question here is whether these cuts are a step in the right direction. Should additional assistance to needy cities be left up to the states, or should the federal government, as well as the states, provide more aid? To the extent that new federal aid is provided, should it take the same form as existing programs or should the form be changed?

---

16. For a review of the literature, see Inman 1979b or Rubinfeld 1985. Remember that our analysis in chapter 10 cannot rule out the possibility that general revenue sharing promotes capital spending.

The Case for More Federal Assistance

The important role of state governments notwithstanding, a strong case can be made for more direct federal assistance to cities. As we have already emphasized, the actual fiscal health of major central cities would have declined by 5 percentage points, on average, between 1972 and 1982 had there been no increase in federal aid to cities.[17] Thus one argument for maintaining federal assistance is simply that it is necessary to maintain the average fiscal health of U.S. cities. But even without a decline in average actual fiscal health, three considerations support the case for more federal assistance to particular cities.

First, states differ in their own fiscal health. Some states have higher revenue-raising capacity and lower costs of providing public services than do others (see Barro 1984). Following our definition of city revenue-raising capacity, one could say that a state's revenue-raising capacity depends on its per capita income and its ability to export taxes to nonresidents. State public service costs depend on the service being considered. In the case of assistance to cities, one key cost factor is the number of cities that need assistance; a state in which one-half of the population lives in fiscally troubled cities must spend more to bring its cities up to a given level of fiscal health than a state in which only one small city, with, say, 5 percent of the state's population, needs help.

As we reported in chapter 11, our study of states' behavior (Yinger and Ladd 1988) provides an estimate of the link between state fiscal health and state assistance to cities. We find that the higher a state's per capita income, the higher its assistance to cities, through both institutions and grants. A state with per capita income one standard deviation above the mean provides over $40 per capita (or 50 percent) more assistance through grants and about $14 per capita more in assistance through institutions, after city fiscal health and other factors are controlled for, than does a state with average income.

It follows that the federal government has a role to play even if all states are equally committed to assisting their fiscally troubled cities. Because of relatively low state revenue-raising capacity or relatively many unhealthy cities, some states are less able than others to offset fiscal disparities among their cities. Through no fault of their own or of their state, the residents of unhealthy cities in these states receive lower-quality services or pay higher taxes than residents of equally troubled cities in other states. Equal treatment of city residents in all states requires federal intervention.

---

17. If the nationwide tax revolt is included, average actual fiscal health declined 14 percentage points.

Second, the federal government has a unique role to play in assuring minimum standards of living for poor and disadvantaged households (see Ladd and Doolittle 1982; Brown and Oates 1985; or Gramlich 1985b). To a large extent poverty and disadvantage are national problems, so that the benefits from alleviating them are not limited to residents of the state in which people are being helped. Anyone who cares about helping the poor benefits from a reduction in poverty, no matter where it occurs. Thus the benefit principle of tax equity, which says that it is fair for the beneficiaries of a service to pay for it, implies that taxpayers throughout the nation should bear the burden of assisting poor and disadvantaged households. To the extent that poverty is outside the control of state and local officials, it is unfair for the residents of some states to bear a relatively high burden for reducing poverty while the burden on the residents of other states is relatively small. Moreover, the possible interstate mobility of wealthy taxpayers or of potential beneficiaries of assistance programs may induce some state governments to provide less assistance than is acceptable from the national point of view. (For further analysis, see Gramlich 1985b; Brown and Oates 1985.)

It follows that assistance to poor and disadvantaged citizens, including that provided through city services, should be a national, not just a state or city, responsibility. Federal assistance should be highest for cities that are in the poorest fiscal health; in these cities, after all, poor and disadvantaged people receive the lowest-quality public services, and service quality is low in part because of a concentration of poor and disadvantaged citizens.

Third, the federal government is in a much better position than state governments to respond to national trends in employment and population, such as suburbanization and interregional migration, and to the impact of these trends on the fiscal health of cities. Only the federal government can implement a policy that treats fairly the residents of different states. To the extent, therefore, that policy makers' objectives in assisting cities include compensating people who are hurt by national trends or minimizing wasteful moving caused by these trends, the federal government has a key role to play.

In sum, federal assistance to cities is needed to ensure fair treatment of city residents in states with different fiscal health, to help poor and disadvantaged city residents, and to offset the fiscal consequences for cities of national economic and social trends. Achieving these objectives does not require more federal aid to all cities, but it does require an increase in federal aid to cities with poor or deteriorating fiscal health. In this era of high federal deficits and a widespread consensus about the need to hold down federal spending, it is worth emphasizing that these objectives can be achieved without restoring recent federal aid cuts in all cities. Although a federal aid program that is focused on those cities that need help the most is likely to face several political obstacles (Paul Peterson et al. 1986), such a program is the most cost-effective way to ensure the fair treatment of city residents in different states, to help poor and disadvantaged city residents, and to offset the fiscal consequences of national trends.

Forms of Federal Assistance

In 1982 federal aid to cities was less focused on cities with poor or deteriorating fiscal health than was state assistance. This conclusion is particularly true for general revenue sharing, which was constrained by a relatively small budget and the political need to give positive grants to a large number of local governments. Although more directed toward cities with poor fiscal health than revenue sharing, federal categorical grants were also less tilted toward unhealthy cities than was state assistance through either institutions or grants.

The question then is how to design a federal aid program to assist the cities that need help the most. Presumably the ultimate objectives of federal assistance to cities are to improve the quality of services or to lower the tax burden on residents or both. Given these objectives, it might seem that federal aid should be directed toward cities with relatively poor actual fiscal health, that is, relatively poor fiscal health after state assistance is accounted for. However, distributing federal aid to cities inversely with their actual fiscal health would have the undesirable consequence of rewarding states that are not generous to their cities.

We believe that the best way to avoid this problem is to direct federal aid toward cities with poor *standardized* fiscal health—instead of those with poor *actual* fiscal health. This approach aids cities that are hit hard by national economic and social trends, which are largely outside both state and city control. It is especially appropriate if a major objective of federal assistance is to offset the adverse effects of these trends.

To identify cities with poor standardized fiscal health, federal policy makers need not calculate our specific measure. Instead they can use more readily available city characteristics that are good predictors of standardized fiscal health. As we show in chapter 5, these characteristics include a city's population, resident income, and poverty rate. A standardized fiscal health measure that is a weighted average of these three characteristics alone can explain over 60 percent of the variation in our more complete measure (see table 5.4).

If aid is given solely on the basis of a city's standardized fiscal health, one might argue that residents of cities receiving minimal state assistance are not treated fairly. Through no fault of their own, these residents would receive lower-quality services or pay higher taxes than residents of cities with comparable standardized fiscal health but more state assistance. A possible solution to this problem is to adjust the amount of federal aid given to a city according to the fiscal health of its state, which could be approximated by the state's per capita income. According to this approach the federal government would give more aid, all else equal, to a city whose state, through no fault of its own, is in poor fiscal health than to one whose state is in good fiscal health. This approach would compensate a city that receives relatively low state assistance, but only to the extent that this low assistance is due to the state's poor fiscal health and not to its limited concern for its cities.[18]

Federal aid also should recognize the role of overlying jurisdictions. Suppose a separate city and a city-county have the same standardized fiscal health. If the federal government gives the same amount of aid per capita to each city, the city-county will be short-changed because it has more responsibilities. To put it another way, the county that shares territory with the separate city will be short-changed unless it, too, receives aid. Note that our measure of standardized fiscal health (unlike our measure of actual fiscal health) simply reflects the characteristics of the location defined by city boundaries—not of the legal entity defined by the city government. In effect it measures the fiscal constraints facing the set of jurisdictions that provide services in that location. Thus federal aid tied to standardized fiscal health should be divided among all the jurisdictions with major service responsibilities within the city's boundaries.

Although an exact division would be complicated to design, we believe that a reasonable division could be achieved if the share of aid for each type of jurisdiction were linked to the share of local spending in that state as-

---

18. From estimates described in chapter 11, we know the average impact of state fiscal health on state assistance to cities. In our view a reasonable approach would be for the federal government to give enough aid to cities in fiscally unhealthy states to offset this average impact. This approach ensures that all cities receive the aid they would receive if their state had average fiscal health.

sociated with that type of jurisdiction.[19] Suppose, for example, that in a particular state cities carry out 75 percent of the local spending, and counties that overlap with the cities carry out the other 25 percent. Then 75 percent of the aid based on fiscal health to any "city" in that state should go to the city government and the rest should go to the county.

Finally, different forms of federal aid, like different forms of state aid, have different effects on city behavior. We find that federal categorical grants, some of which have matching rates, have a larger effect on city operating spending than does federal general revenue sharing, which leads to reduced city tax burdens and perhaps to increased capital spending. This finding is consistent with the results of many previous studies. To the extent that they want to improve the quality of city services in general, or of particular city services such as police, federal policy makers should employ matching instead of revenue-sharing grants.

Thus we conclude that the form of federal aid needs to be changed. To be cost-effective, it should be more sharply focused than past federal aid programs on cities with poor standardized fiscal health, that is, on cities whose ability to deliver adequate public services at reasonable tax rates has been undercut by economic and social trends. Moreover, to promote the fair treatment of cities in different circumstances, we believe that cities with poor standardized fiscal health should receive more aid if they are located in a state that has poor fiscal health and that the aid given within a city's boundaries should be divided among the local governments that provide services there. One of the key objectives of federal policy is to ensure adequate levels of important public services, including education and police and fire protection, for poor and disadvantaged city residents. To the extent that federal policy makers want to achieve this objective, they should give new categorical matching grants, not revenue sharing, to the neediest cities. Such grants would encourage these cities to raise the quality of these public services instead of cutting city taxes.

---

19. The main technical complication is that the cost of public services varies from one service to the next, so that different jurisdictions in the same location may face different costs. Dividing aid according to expenditure shares accounts roughly, but only roughly, for these cost differences. Another technical problem is that jurisdiction boundaries often do not coincide. An adjustment based on population could roughly account for differences in boundaries. A third problem is that some states take major responsibility for some "city" services, such as welfare and other social services.

cutback in grants is likely to be relatively small. Hence this type of federal program could induce states to boost their overall assistance to cities.

Another question of concern for federal policy makers is how state governments respond to federal assistance to cities. Do state governments provide less assistance to cities that receive more federal aid? Does state assistance to cities increase when federal aid to cities is cut? State government responses to recent reductions in federal aid might shed light on this question, but the evidence to date is unclear (see George Peterson 1984; Nathan, Doolittle, and Associates 1983; Ladd 1984; and Peterson and Lewis 1986).

In 1981 the federal government ended all funding for public service jobs through CETA; under President Reagan's new federalism initiatives in the 1980s, many narrowly defined federal programs of aid to local governments were consolidated into block grants to states at reduced funding levels; and in 1986 general revenue sharing to local governments was eliminated. The available evidence indicates that neither the states nor the cities acted to offset the federal cuts in CETA. Evidence about the states' response to the grant consolidation is not so clear. To some degree the federal government mitigated the short-run impact on cities of the shift to state block grants by imposing pass-through requirements; however, the evidence suggests some shifting of total aid away from larger cities to rural areas and smaller communities. According to one study (Nathan, Doolittle, and Associates 1983, chap. 4), this spreading of aid funds is most clear for the health block grants and in some states for community services grants. (For predictions based on a behavioral model, see Craig and Imman 1986.) Early evidence suggested that states did little to replace cutbacks in federal grants, but subsequent evidence suggests relatively complete replacement in some states (see the Urban Institute study described in George Peterson 1984; also Nathan, Doolittle, and Associates 1983; and Ladd 1984). Because this replacement spending includes new spending by local governments as well as by state governments, however, even full replacement does not prove that state governments are responsible for counteracting the federal aid reduction.

This discussion reveals that existing studies do not focus directly on the main question here: Do states offset cuts in federal aid to cities by providing more state assistance to cities? These studies do not control for determinants of state grants other than changes in federal aid, and they do not consider changes in state institutional assistance. Thus they cannot sort out the effects on state grant programs of federal aid cuts from the effects of other events, and they cannot determine the impact of federal aid changes on total state assistance to cities.

The Interaction Between Federal and State Assistance

So far, we have focused on direct federal aid to cities. In light of t widespread opinion that states can and should play a larger role in our sy tem of federalism, federal policy makers might consider an alternative ap proach, namely encouraging state governments to provide more assistanc to their cities by giving the states more aid. Our statistical analysis (Yinger and Ladd 1988) leads us to reject this indirect approach.[20] Higher federal aid to a state does not induce it to give more assistance to cities—through either institutions or grants.

A variant on this theme is for the federal government to encourage states to help their cities by implementing new federal aid programs explicitly designed to reward states that provide relatively generous intergovernmental assistance. This approach faces a difficult practical problem: how to measure the generosity of state assistance. A comprehensive measure of state assistance through both institutions and grants is difficult to obtain, and the use of a partial measure could lead to unintended behavioral responses by the state government.

Suppose, for example, that a federal aid program rewarded states for giving relatively high intergovernmental grants. Then according to our analysis of state behavior, states would be encouraged to cut back on institutional assistance and to increase their grants. As we explained in chapter 11, we find that state policy makers view grants as more "powerful" in assisting cities than assistance through institutions; that is, $1 of grants is perceived to provide the same help as $2 of institutional aid. As a result, the cutback in assistance through institutions could exceed the increase in grants, at least in the long run, and the federal policy could actually make cities worse off.

A more promising approach is for the federal government to reward states that provide institutional assistance to cities. For example, it could reward states that allow cities to use taxes with export potential, such as commuter taxes, or that have taken over the responsibility for welfare or other services provided by cities but with benefits that extend beyond city boundaries. A federal program of this type would encourage states to substitute institutional assistance for grants to some degree, but because state policy makers appear to view institutional assistance as less powerful, the

---

20. The federal government may want to provide aid to states for other purposes; for example, it may want to compensate those with poor fiscal health. The point here is that the federal government should not try to aid cities by giving more aid to states.

Our analysis of state behavior in chapter 11 finds no evidence to support the view that states respond to federal aid to cities. In particular we find no support for the view that states give less assistance, through either institutions or grants, to cities that receive larger amounts of federal aid. This finding implies that federal policy makers cannot rely on state governments to offset reductions in federal aid to cities. In addition it implies that federal policy makers need not be concerned that additional federal assistance to cities will be offset by lower state assistance.

Policies with Indirect Effects on City Finances

Although outside the purview of this book, several state and federal policies with indirect effects on city finances also should be mentioned. Of particular interest are policies that encourage the growth of city economies and policies that reduce the harshness of the city environment for providing public services.

As was summarized earlier, a growing private economy promotes city fiscal recovery, but it does not guarantee an improvement in city fiscal health, because of the growth in expenditure need that accompanies a growth in private jobs. Moreover, city governments have limited tools for promoting the development of their economies. State and federal governments have far more resources and are better able to respond to the national trends that are the primary determinants of changes in a city's economic base. Job training programs help city residents learn the skills that are needed to keep up with changing patterns of employment. The federal tax exemption of interest on industrial development bonds helps finance urban economic development projects. State and federal contributions to urban enterprise zones would help make such zones attractive to new businesses.

We have reservations, however, about several of these specific programs. Widespread use of industrial development bonds, for example, raises the cost to cities of borrowing for basic infrastructure needs, and a large share of the subsidy they involve goes to high-income bondholders— not to economic development projects. The cutback in these bonds in the 1986 federal income tax reform was appropriate (see John Peterson 1987). In addition, the available evidence indicates that business incentives in urban enterprise zones, namely tax breaks and the lifting of regulations, are unlikely to entice many outside businesses into the central city (although they may entice businesses from across town). Indeed, these incentives may have less impact on the location decisions of businesses than does the quality of city services (for a thorough discussion see Jacobs and Wasylenko 1981).

Training programs for individuals and aid provided directly to cities therefore appear to be more cost-effective ways to promote urban economic development than either industrial development bonds or urban enterprise zones.

State and federal procurement and employment policies also affect the economic development of cities. Money that flows into a city from a higher level of government tends to expand economic activity in the city and therefore to raise the income of its residents and its revenue-raising capacity. In our judgment these policies should not be based primarily on economic development considerations; for the most part, government purchases should be made from the highest-quality producer at a given price, and government jobs should be located where they are needed and effective. On the other hand, these policies sometimes can help to further economic development goals without raising costs significantly or placing jobs in inappropriate locations. Massachusetts provides a case in point: a policy to locate state government jobs in central cities has contributed to the revitalization of many central cities in the state (see Ferguson and Ladd 1988).

Numerous state and federal policies also influence the harshness of the environment for providing services in cities. The results we report in chapter 4 demonstrate, for example, that the cost of providing city services, particularly police services, is higher in cities with more poor residents or more old housing. Federal and state income transfer programs assist poor people and therefore moderate the harshness of the environment, but in recent years these programs have not kept up with the growth of poverty in cities (for an excellent overview of federal poverty programs, see Danziger and Weinberg 1986). During the 1970s the federal government also built or subsidized the construction of thousands of housing units in cities. Most analysts agree that this construction allowed the most deteriorated housing to be demolished and therefore improved the quality of the housing stock and the environment for providing city services (see Downs 1983). These programs have been virtually eliminated, however, and some recent evidence suggests that the number of deteriorated housing units has grown rapidly during the 1980s (see Apgar 1984; Brown and Yinger 1986). Lowering the cost of city services is not and should not be the primary goal of federal and state income transfer and housing programs, but nonetheless, these programs do contribute to city fiscal health.

Conclusions

Our detailed investigation into the fiscal health of central cities has provided answers to the questions posed at the beginning of this chapter. We conclude by summarizing these answers.

Are Central Cities in Serious Fiscal Trouble?

Several national economic and social trends, including suburbanization and the concentration of poverty in cities, have undercut the ability of U.S. central cities to deliver adequate public services at reasonable tax rates. Indeed, these trends caused a significant decline in the fiscal health of the average city between 1972 and 1982. The trends do not affect all cities to the same degree; the largest cities and those whose residents have relatively low incomes are in particularly poor fiscal health. Increased assistance from state governments, through both fiscal institutions and intergovernmental grants, offset about one-half of the decline in city fiscal health between 1972 and 1982 and boosted the relative position of large cities, those with poor residents, and others in relatively poor fiscal condition. Nevertheless, even after state assistance, cities differ widely in their 1982 fiscal health. Cities also benefit from federal aid, but in 1982 this aid was less directed toward the neediest cities than was state assistance.

After both state and federal assistance, the average city's fiscal health was about as high in 1982 as in 1972, but federal aid has been cut substantially since 1982, and national economic and social trends continue to place pressure on city finances. More importantly, the range in fiscal health across cities is striking, and, through no fault of their own, many cities with relatively large populations or with relatively poor residents find themselves in serious fiscal trouble.

Do Cities Need More Assistance?

Public officials can make a modest contribution to the fiscal health of their city by taking advantage of the fiscal options that are available to them, implementing managerial reforms, and designing cost-effective economic development policies. Economic and social trends, however, are largely outside the control of city officials and are more powerful than the policy tools to which they have access.

Some residents of fiscally troubled cities may be able to move to cities with higher-quality services or lower taxes. Other residents cannot move, however, because of high moving costs, a lack of affordable housing, or racial discrimination. Moreover, extensive moving may impose unacceptable costs on society, in the form of wasted resources and changes in the social character of cities.

Thus state and federal officials cannot count on actions by city governments and residents to eliminate the problems caused by poor city fiscal health. Assistance to cities from higher levels of government is needed to achieve several important social objectives, namely to assist the poor and disadvantaged people who are concentrated in central cities, to help people cope with transitions caused by economic and social trends outside their control, and to account for the linkages among the jurisdictions in a metropolitan area. Although transfer programs for individuals are the most direct way to assist the poor, assistance to cities also helps the poor because it boosts the quality of vital city services, on which the poor depend but over which they have little control.

What Role Should States Play?

States determine the fiscal rules under which cities operate, and they have detailed knowledge about the fiscal and economic circumstances of their cities. As a result, states have many policy tools with which to help cities and can design assistance packages that fit each city's particular situation. Moreover, a reliance on state instead of federal actions encourages diversity and policy innovation because different states will try different forms of assistance. In addition to intergovernmental grants directed toward cities that are in poor fiscal health, states could provide substantial assistance to many cities by allowing them to tax all income earned in the city or by taking over welfare and services, such as courts, whose benefits extend beyond the city limits.

Is More Federal Assistance Needed?

Federal assistance to cities can complement state assistance in several ways. The federal government is in a unique position to offset differences in fiscal health across states (and the consequences of such differences for state assistance to cities), to provide aid to poor and disadvantaged citizens, and to moderate the consequences of national economic and social trends. To avoid rewarding states that are not generous to their cities, the federal government should direct aid toward cities that are in poor fiscal health because of economic and social trends—not toward those that suffer because of restrictive fiscal institutions or meager state grants. The federal government should not expect to help cities by giving more aid to state governments; states that receive more federal aid themselves do not appear to provide more assistance to their cities.

In short, a federal aid program that is focused on cities in relatively poor fiscal health can make a cost-effective contribution to achieving several important social objectives. In this era of federal budget stringency, the challenge is to find a political strategy that makes it possible to direct federal aid to the cities that need it the most.

References

Advisory Commission on Intergovernmental Relations (ACIR). Various years 1976/77-1983/84. *Significant Features of Fiscal Federalism*. Washington, D.C.: By the Author.

————. 1981. *Measuring the Fiscal Capacity and Effort of State and Local Areas*. Washington, D.C.: By the Author.

————. 1982. *State and Local Roles in the Federal System*. Washington, D.C.: By the Author.

————. 1984. Fiscal Disparities: Central Cities and Suburbs, 1981. Washington, D.C.: By the Author.

————. 1986. *Measuring State Fiscal Capacity: Alternative Measures and Their Uses*. Washington, D.C.: By the Author.

Apgar, William C., Jr. 1985. "Recent Trends in Housing Quality and Affordability: A Reassessment." Working Paper No. W85-5. Cambridge, Mass.: MIT-Harvard Joint Center for Housing Studies.

Aronson, J. Richard, and John L. Hilley. 1986. *Financing State and Local Governments*, 4th ed. Washington, D.C.: Brookings Institution.

Aronson, J. Richard, and Arthur E. King. 1978. "Is There a Fiscal Crisis Outside of New York?" *National Tax Journal* 31 (June): 135-55.

Bahl, Roy. 1984. *Financing State and Local Government in the 1980s*. New York: Oxford University Press.

Bahl, Roy, and David Greytak. 1976. "The Response of City Government Revenues to Changes in Employment Structure." *Land Economics* 52 (November): 415-34.

Barro, Stephen M. 1985. *State Fiscal Capacity: An Assessment of Measurement Methods*. Final report to the U.S. Department of Housing and Urban Development. Washington, D.C.: SMB Economic Research.

————. 1986. "State Fiscal Capacity Measures: A Theoretical Critique." In Clyde Reeves, ed., *Measuring Fiscal Capacity*, pp. 51-86. Boston: Oelgeschlager, Gunn, and Hain.

Bergstrom, Theodore C., and Robert P. Goodman. 1973. "Private Demands for Public Goods." *American Economic Review* 63 (June): 280-96.

Black, J. Thomas. 1980. "The Changing Economic Role of Central Cities and Suburbs." In A. Solomon, ed., *The Prospective City*, pp. 80-123. Cambridge, Mass.: MIT Press.

Boadway, Robin W., and David E. Wildasin. 1984. *Public Sector Economics*, 2d ed. Boston: Little, Brown and Co.

Bradbury, Katharine L. 1982. "Fiscal Distress in Large U.S. Cities." *New England Economic Review* (January/February): 33-44.

————. 1983. "Structural Fiscal Distress in Cities—Causes and Consequences." *New England Economic Review* (January/February): 32-43.

————. 1984. "Urban Decline and Distress: An Update." *New England Economic Review* (July/August): 39-57.

Bradbury, Katharine L., Anthony Downs, and Kenneth A. Small. 1982. *Urban Decline and the Future of American Cities*. Washington, D.C.: Brookings Institution.

Bradbury, Katharine L., and Helen F. Ladd. 1982a. "Proposition 2 1/2: Initial Impacts, Part I." *New England Economic Review* (January/February): 13-24.

————. 1982b. "Proposition 2 1/2: Initial Impacts, Part II." *New England Economic Review* (March/April): 48-62.

————. 1985. "Changes in the Revenue-Raising Capacity of U.S. Cities, 1970-1982." *New England Economic Review* (March/April): 20-37.

————. 1987. "City Property Taxes: The Effects of Economic Change and Competitive Pressures." *New England Economic Review* (July-August): 22-36.

Bradbury, Katharine L., Helen F. Ladd, Mark Perrault, Andrew Reschovsky, and John Yinger. 1984. "State Aid to Offset Fiscal Disparities across Communities." *National Tax Journal* 37 (June): 151-70.

Bradbury, Katharine L., and John Yinger. 1984. "Making Ends Meet: Boston's Budget in the 1980s." *New England Economic Review* (March/April): 18-28.

Bradford, David F., R. A. Malt, and Wallace E. Oates. 1969. "The Rising Cost of Local Public Services: Some Evidence and Reflections." *National Tax Journal* 22 (June): 185-202.

Brazer, Harvey, and Ann Anderson. 1975. "A Cost Adjusted Index for Michigan School Districts." In *Selected Papers in School Finance, 1975*, pp. 23-81. Washington, D.C.: U.S. Department of Health, Education, and Welfare.

Brown, Charles C., and Wallace E. Oates. 1985. "Assistance to the Poor in a Federal System." Sloan Working Paper 11-85. College Park, Md: Department of Economics, University of Maryland.

Brown, H. James, Robyn Swaim Phillips, and Avis Vidal. 1983. "The Growth and Restructuring of Metropolitan Economies: Decentralization and Industrial Change during the 1970s." Final Report to the U.S. Department of Housing and Urban Development. Cambridge, Mass.: Department of City and Regional Planning, Harvard University.

Brown, H. James, and John Yinger. 1986. "Homeownership and Housing Affordability in the United States: The 1986 Report." Cambridge, Mass.: MIT-Harvard Joint Center for Housing Studies.

Browne, Lynn. 1984. "How Different Are Regional Wages? A Second Look." *New England Economic Review* (March/April): 40-47.

Brueckner, Jan K. 1981. "Congested Public Goods: The Case of Fire Protection." *Journal of Public Economics* 15 (February): 45-58.

Bunce, Harold L., and Robert L. Goldberg. 1979. *City Need and Community Development Funding.* Washington, D.C.: U.S. Department of Housing and Urban Development.

Bunce, Harold L., and Sue G. Neal. 1984. "Trends in City Conditions during the 1970s: A Survey of Demographic and Socioeconomic Changes." *Publius: The Journal of Federalism* 14 (Spring): 7-19.

Burchell, Robert W., James H. Carr, Richard L. Florida, James Nemeth, Michael Pawlik, and Felix R. Barreto. 1984. *The New Reality of Municipal Finance: The Rise and Fall of the Intergovernmental City.* New Brunwsick, N.J.: Center for Urban Policy Research, Rutgers University.

Chambers, Jay G. 1978. "Education Cost Differentials and the Allocation of State Aid for Elementary/Secondary Education." *Journal of Human Resources* 13 (Fall): 459-81.

Chernick, Howard, and Andrew Reschovsky. 1987. "The Deductability of State and Local Taxes." *National Tax Journal* 40 (March): 95-102.

Clark, Terry Nichols, and Lorna Crowley Ferguson. 1983. *City Money: Political Processes, Fiscal Strain and Retrenchment.* New York: Columbia University Press.

Craig, Stephen G. 1987. "The Deterrent Impact of Police: An Examination of a Locally Provided Service." *Journal of Urban Economics* 21 (May): 298-311.

Craig, Stephen G., and Robert P. Inman. 1986. "Education, Welfare, and the 'New' Federalism: State Budgeting in a Federal Public Economy." In H. S. Rosen, ed., *Studies in State and Local Public Finance,* pp. 187-222. Chicago: University of Chicago Press.

Cuciti, Peggy. 1978. "City Need and the Responsiveness of Federal Grant Programs." Washington, D.C.: Congressional Budget Office.

Cummings, Judith. 1987. "Voters Decline to Pay for Police in Inner-City Area of Los Angeles." *The New York Times*, 4 June, p. A24, col. 1.

Danziger, Sheldon H., and Daniel H. Weinberg, 1986. *Fighting Poverty: What Works and What Doesn't.* Cambridge, Mass.: Harvard University Press.

Dearborn, Philip M. 1988. "Fiscal Conditions in Large American Cities, 1971-1984." In M.G.H. McGeary and L.E. Lynn, Jr., eds., *Urban Change and Poverty*, pp. 255-83. Washington, D.C.: National Academy Press.

Downs, Anthony. 1983. *Rental Housing in the 1980s.* Washington, D.C.: Brookings Institution.

Economic Report of the President. 1984. Washington, D.C.: GPO, 1984.

Ehrenberg, Ronald G., and Robert S. Smith. 1985. *Modern Labor Economics.* Glenview, Ill.: Scott Foresman and Co.

Estrich, Susan. 1984. "Crime and the Poor." In M. Carballo and M. J. Bane, eds., *The State and the Poor in the 1980s*, pp. 207-32. Boston: Auburn House.

Ferguson, Ronald, and Helen F. Ladd. 1986. "Measuring the Fiscal Capacity of U.S. Cities." In Clyde Reeves, ed., *Measuring Fiscal Capacity*, pp. 141-68. Boston: Oelgeschlager, Gunn, and Hain.

————. 1988. "State Economic Renaissance," and "Pioneering State Economic Strategy." In R. S. Fosler, ed., *The New Economic Role of American States: Strategies and Institutions for a Competitive World*, pp. 19-87. New York: Oxford University Press.

Ganz, Alexander, and Thomas O'Brien. 1973. "The City: Sandbox, Reservation, or Dynamo?" *Public Policy* 21 (Winter): 107-23.

Garn, Harvey A., and Larry Clinton Ledebur. 1980. "The Economic Performance and Prospects of Cities." In A. Solomon, ed., *The Prospective City*, pp. 204-51. Cambridge, Mass.: MIT Press.

Gold, Steven D. 1982. "Local Sales and Income Taxes: How Much Are They Used? Should They Be More Widespread?" National Conference of State Legislatures, Legislative Finance Paper No. 24 (July).

Gordon, Roger H. 1983. "An Optimal Taxation Approach to Fiscal Federalism." *Quarterly Journal of Economics* (November): 567-86.

Gramlich, Edward N. 1976. "The New York Fiscal Crisis: What Happened and What Is to Be Done?" *American Economic Review* 66 (May): 415-29.

————. 1985a. "The Deductibility of State and Local Taxes." *National Tax Journal* 38 (December): 447-66.

————. 1985b. "Reforming U.S. Federal Arrangements." In J. M. Quigley and Daniel L. Rubinfeld, eds., *American Domestic Priorities: An Economic Appraisal*, pp. 34-69. Berkeley and Los Angeles: University of California Press.

Hamilton, Bruce. 1983. "The Flypaper Effect and Other Anomalies." *Journal of Public Economics* 22 (December): 347-62.

Howell, James M., and Charles F. Stamm. 1979. *Urban Fiscal Stress*. Boston: First National Bank of Boston and Touche Ross.

Inman, Robert P. 1978. "Testing Political Economy's ' As If ' Proposition: Is the Median Voter Really Decisive?" *Public Choice* (Winter): 45-65.

―――. 1979a. "Dissecting the Urban Crisis: Facts and Counterfacts." *National Tax Journal* 32 (June): 127-42.

―――. 1979b. "The Fiscal Performance of Local Governments: An Interpretive Review." In P. Mieszkowski and M. Straszheim, eds., *Current Issues in Urban Economics*, pp. 270-321. Baltimore: Johns Hopkins University Press.

―――. 1981. "The Local Decision to Tax." Paper presented at Taxation, Resources and Economic Development (TRED) Conference at the Lincoln Institute of Land Policy Research, Cambridge, Mass. (September).

Jacobs, Susan S., and Michael Wasylenko. 1981. "Government Policy to Stimulate Economic Development: Enterprise Zones." In N. Walzer and D. L. Chicoine, eds., *Financing State and Local Governments in the 1980s*, pp. 175-201. Cambridge, Mass.: Oegelschlager, Gunn, and Hain.

Kendrick, John. 1973. *Postwar Productivity Trends in the United States, 1948-1969*. New York: Columbia University Press.

Kramer, Pearl M. 1982. *Urban Public Finance: A Case Study of 38 Cities*. Albany: State University of New York Press.

Ladd, Helen F. 1975. "Local Education Expenditures, Fiscal Capacity, and the Composition of the Property Tax Base." *National Tax Journal* 28 (June): 145-58.

―――. 1984. "Federal Aid to State and Local Governments." In J. L. Palmer and G. Mills, eds., *Federal Budget Policy in the 1980s*, pp. 165-202. Washington, D.C.: Urban Institute Press.

Ladd, Helen F., and Frederick C. Doolittle. 1982. "Which Level of Government Should Assist Poor People?" *National Tax Journal* 35 (September): 323-36.

McLure, Charles E., Jr. 1967. "The Interstate Exporting of State and Local Taxes: Estimates for 1962." *Natonal Tax Journal* 20 (March): 49-77.

―――. 1970. "Taxation, Substitution, and Industrial Location." *Journal of Political Economy* 78 (January/February): 112-32.

―――. 1977. "The 'New View' of the Property Tax: A Caveat." *National Tax Journal* 30 (March): 69-75.

Mieszkowski, Peter. 1972. "The Property Tax: An Excise Tax or a Profits Tax?" *Journal of Public Economics* 1: 73-96.

Nathan, Richard P., and Charles Adams. 1976. "Understanding Central City Hardship." *Political Science Quarterly* 91 (Spring): 47-62.

Nathan, Richard P., Frederick C. Doolittle, and Associates. 1983. *The Consequences of Cuts: The Effects of the Reagan Domestic Program on State and Local Governments.* Princeton, N.J.: Princeton Urban and Regional Research Center.

Nathan, Richard P., and James W. Fossett. 1978. "Urban Conditions: The Future of the Federal Role." *Proceedings of the 71st Annual Convention of the National Tax Association-Tax Institute of America*, pp. 30-41. Columbus, Ohio: National Tax Association.

National Research Council. Committee on National Urban Policy. 1988. In M.H.G. McGeary and L. E. Lynn, Jr., Eds., *Urban Change and Poverty*, pp. 3-64. Washington, D.C.: National Academy Press.

Neenan, William B. 1981. *Urban Public Economics.* Belmont, Calif.: Wadsworth.

Noyelle, Thierry J., and Thomas M. Stanback, Jr. 1983. *Economic Transformation of American Cities.* Totowa, N.J.: Rowman and Allanheld.

Oates, Wallace E. 1972. *Fiscal Federalism.* New York: Harcourt, Brace, Jovanovich.

Peterson, George E. 1976. "Finance." In W. Gorham and N. Glazer, eds., *The Urban Predicament*, pp. 35-118. Washington, D.C.: Urban Institute Press.

————. 1984. "Federalism and the States: An Experiment in Decentralization." In J. L. Palmer and I. V. Sawhill, eds., *The Reagan Record*, chap. 7. Cambridge, Mass.: Ballinger Publishing Company.

Peterson, George E., and Carol W. Lewis. 1986. *Reagan and the Cities.* Washington, D.C.: Urban Institute Press.

Peterson, John E. 1987. "Examining the Impacts of the 1986 Tax Reform Act on the Municipal Securities Market." *National Tax Journal* 40 (September): 393-402.

Peterson, Paul E., ed. 1985. *The New Urban Reality.* Washington, D.C.: Brookings Institution.

Peterson, Paul E., Barry G. Rabe, and Kenneth K. Wong. 1986. *When Federalism Works.* Washington, D.C.: Brookings Institution.

Phares, Donald. 1980. *Who Pays State and Local Taxes?* Cambridge, Mass.: Oelgeschlager, Gunn, and Hain.

Reeves, Clyde, ed. 1986. *Measuring Fiscal Capacity.* Boston: Oelgeschlager, Gunn, and Hain.

Reischauer, Robert D. 1986. "The Rise and Fall of National Urban Policy: The Fiscal Dimension." Paper presented at the National Urban Policy Conference, Denver, Colo. (June).

Rubinfeld, Daniel L. 1985. "The Economics of the Local Public Sector." In A. Auerbach and M. Feldstein, eds., *Handbook of Public Economics*, pp. 87-161. Amsterdam: North-Holland.

Schafer, Robert, and Helen F. Ladd. 1981. *Discrimination in Mortgage Lending*. Cambridge, Mass.: MIT Press.

Schmenner, Roger. 1982. "Industrial Location and Urban Public Management." In A. Solomon, ed., *The Prospective City*, 446-68. Cambridge, Mass.: MIT Press.

Stevenson, Richard W. 1987. "Los Angeles District to Vote on Hiring More Police." *The New York Times*, 25 February, p. A14, col. 3.

Survey of Buying Power. 1982. Special issue of *Sales and Marketing Management*.

U.S. Department of Commerce. Bureau of the Census. 1968. *Census of Governments 1967*. Vol. 2. *Taxable Property Values and Assessment-Sales Ratios*. Washington, D.C.: GPO.

————. 1973. *Census of Governments, 1972*. Vol. 2. *Taxable Property Values and Assessment-Sales Ratios*. Washington, D.C.: GPO.

————. 1978. *Census of Governments, 1977.*. Vol. 2. *Taxable Property Values and Assessment-Sales Ratios*. Washington, D.C.: GPO.

————. 1984. *Census of Governments, 1982*. Vol. 2. *Taxable Property Values and Assessment-Sales Ratios*. Washington, D.C.: GPO.

————. 1974. *Census of Governments, 1972*. Vol. 3. *Public Employment*. Washington, D.C.: GPO.

————. 1979. *Census of Governments, 1977*. Vol. 3. *Public Employment*. Washington, D.C.: GPO.

————. 1984. *Census of Governments, 1982*. Vol. 3. *Government Employment*. Washington, D.C.: GPO.

————. 1975. *Census of Governments, 1972*. Vol. 5. *Local Governments in Metropolitan Areas*. Washington, D.C.: GPO.

————. 1980. *Census of Governments, 1977*. Vol. 5. *Local Governments in Metropolitan Areas*. Washington, D.C.: GPO.

————. 1985. *Census of Governments, 1982*. Vol. 5. *Local Governments in Metropolitan Areas*. Washington, D.C.: GPO.

————. 1984. *Census of Housing and Population, 1980*. Vol. 2. *Subject Reports: Place of Work*. Washington, D.C.: GPO.

————. 1976. *Census of Manufactures, 1972*. Washington, D.C.: GPO.

————. 1981. *Census of Manufactures, 1977*. Washington, D.C.: GPO.

————. 1985. *Census of Manufactures, 1982*. Washington, D.C.: GPO.

————. 1973. *Census of Population, 1970.* Vol. 1. *Characteristics of the Population.* Washington, D.C.: GPO.

————. 1983. *Census of Population, 1980.* Vol. 1. *Characteristics of the Population,* chap. A, p. 1. Washington, D.C.: GPO.

————. 1984. *Census of Population, 1980.* Vol. 2. *Subject Reports: Journey to Work.* Washington, D.C.: GPO.

————. 1973. *Census of Population, 1970.* Vol. 2. *Subject Reports: Journey to Work.* Washington, D.C.: GPO.

————. 1976. *Census of Retail Trade, 1972.* Washington, D.C.: GPO.

————. 1980. *Census of Retail Trade, 1977.* Washington, D.C.: GPO.

————. 1984. *Census of Retail Trade, 1982.* Washington, D.C.: GPO.

————. 1976. *Census of Selected Services, 1972.* Washington, D.C.: GPO.

————. 1981. *Census of Service Industries, 1977.* Washington, D.C.: GPO.

————. 1984. *Census of Service Industries, 1982.* Washington, D.C.: GPO.

————. 1976. *Census of Wholesale Trade, 1972.* Washington, D.C.: GPO.

————. 1981. *Census of Wholesale Trade, 1977.* Washington, D.C.: GPO.

————. 1984. *Census of Wholesale Trade, 1982.* Washington, D.C.: GPO.

————. 1968. *City Government Finances in 1966-67.* GF 67, no. 4. Washington, D.C.: GPO.

————. 1973. *City Government Finances in 1971-72.* GF 72, no. 4. Washington, D.C.: GPO.

————. 1979. *City Government Finances in 1976-77.* GF 77, no. 4. Washington, D.C.: GPO.

————. 1983. *City Government Finances in 1981-82.* GF 82, no. 4. Washington, D.C.: GPO.

————. 1978. *County and City Data Book, 1977.* Washington, D.C.: GPO.

————. 1983. *County and City Data Book, 1982.* Washington, D.C.: GPO.

————. 1973. *County Business Patterns, 1972.* Washington, D.C.: GPO.

————. 1979. *County Business Patterns, 1977.* Washington, D.C.: GPO.

————. 1984. *County Business Patterns, 1982.* Washington, D.C.: GPO.

————. Various years 1969-82. *Current Population Reports.* P-25 series. Washington, D.C.: GPO.

————. 1982. *Current Population Reports.* P-26 series. Washington, D.C.: GPO.

————. 1988. *Current Population Reports.* P-60 series. *Money Income and Poverty Status of Families and Persons in the U.S.* Washington, D.C.: GPO.

U.S. Department of Labor. Bureau of Labor Statistics. 1982. Autumn 1981 Urban Family Budgets and Comparative Indexes for Selected Urban Areas." Washington, D.C.: By the Author.

————. 1981. *Employment and Unemployment in States and Local Areas, 1979.* Washington, D.C.: GPO.

————. 1984. *Employment and Unemployment in States and Local Areas, 1982.* Washington, D.C.: GPO.

U.S. Department of the Treasury. Office of State and Local Finance. 1978. "Report on the Fiscal Impact of the Economic Stimulus Package on 48 Large Urban Governments." Washington, D.C.: By the Author.

U.S. Office of Personnel Management. Selected years 1972-82. *Report of Employment by Geographic Area.* Washington, D.C.: GPO.

Wasylenko, Michael. 1986. "The Effects of Business Climate on Employment Growth: A Review of the Evidence." In N. Walzer and D.L. Chicoine, eds., *Financing Economic Development in the 1980s: Issues and Trends*, pp. 34-54. New York: Praeger.

Wendling, Wayne. 1981. "The Cost of Education Index: Measurement of Price Differences of Education Personnel among New York State School Districts." *Journal of Education Finance* 6 (Spring): 485-504.

Yinger, John. 1986a. "On Fiscal Disparities across Cities." *Journal of Urban Economics* 19 (May): 316-37.

————. 1986b. "Measuring Discrimination with Fair Housing Audits: Caught in the Act." *American Economic Review* 76 (December): 881-93.

————. 1987. "The Racial Dimension of Urban Housing Markets in the 1980s." In G. A. Tobin, ed., *Divided Neighborhoods: Changing Patterns of Racial Segregation*, pp. 43-67. Newbury Park, Calif.: Sage Publications.

Yinger, John, Howard S. Bloom, Axel Boersch-Supan, and Helen F. Ladd. 1988. *Property Taxes and House Values: The Theory and Estimation of Intrajurisdictional Property Tax Capitalization.* Cambridge, Mass.: Academic Press.

Yinger, John, and Helen F. Ladd. 1988. "The Determinants of State Assistance to Central Cities." Metropolitan Studies Program Occasional Paper No. 110. Syracuse, N.Y.: Syracuse University.

Yinger, John, and Carol Meyers. 1971. "If We Can't Tax the Capitol . . . : A Comparative Study of Revenues in the District of Columbia and Other Major Cities." Washington, D.C.: Washington Center for Metropolitan Studies.

Author Index

Subject Index